D1157097

FAMOUS POEMS

and the

LITTLE-KNOWN STORIES

BEHIND THEM

Revelations
of the lives and times
of those men and women
who had the gift
of turning their
deepest experiences
into
song

RALPH L. WOODS

FAMOUS POEMS
and the
LITTLE-KNOWN STORIES
BEHIND THEM

Hawthorn Books, Inc., *Publishers*
New York

First Edition, September, 1961
Third Printing, May, 1966

Acknowledgments

Grateful acknowledgment for permission to reprint material in this book is made to copyright owners as follows:

For Rupert Brooke's "The Soldier" and "The Dead" from *The Collected Poems of Rupert Brooke,* copyright 1915 by Dodd, Mead and Co., copyright 1943 by Edward Marsh, reprinted by permission of Dodd, Mead and Co., and McClelland and Stewart, Ltd.

For Walter De La Mare's prose passage from his essay on Christina Rossetti, by permission of Richard de la Mare, on behalf of the author's literary trustees.

For Robert Frost's "Bereft" from *West-Running Brook,* copyright 1928 by Holt, Rinehart and Winston, Inc., copyright 1956 by Robert Frost, reprinted by permission of Holt, Rinehart and Winston, Inc.

For Robert Graves's prose passage from *The Crowning Privilege,* copyright 1956, Doubleday and Co., Inc.

For Thomas Hardy's "The Going" from *Collected Poems,* copyright 1925 by The Macmillan Co. and used with their permission and The Trustees of the Hardy Estate, Macmillan and Co., Ltd., and The Macmillan Co. of Canada, Ltd.

For Rudyard Kipling's "If" from *Rewards and Fairies,* copyright 1910 by Rudyard Kipling, "Gunga Din" from *Departmental Ditties and Ballads and Barrack-Room Ballads,* by Rudyard Kipling, reprinted by permission of Mrs. George Bambridge, Doubleday and Co., Inc., A. P. Watt and Son, and The Macmillan Co. of Canada, Ltd.

For Vachel Lindsay's "The Congo" from *Collected Poems,* copyright 1914 by The Macmillan Co., renewed 1943 by Elizabeth C. Lindsay, used by permission of The Macmillan Co.

For Wilfred Owen's "Strange Meeting" from *The Poems of Wilfred Owen,* all rights reserved, reprinted by permission of New Directions, and Chatto and Windus, Ltd.

For John Cowper Powys's prose passage from *The Meaning of Culture,* copyright 1929 by W. W. Norton and Co.

For Edwin Arlington Robinson's "Mr. Flood's Party" from *Collected Poems,* copyright 1921 by E. A. Robinson, used by permission of The Macmillan Co.

For Alan Seeger's "I Have a Rendezvous With Death" from *Poems* by Alan Seeger, copyright 1916 by Charles Scribner's Sons, renewal copyright 1944 by Elsie Adams Seeger, reprinted with the permission of Charles Scribner's Sons.

For Karl Shapiro's "Elegy for a Dead Soldier" reprinted from *Poems 1940-1953,* by Karl Shapiro, copyright 1944 by Karl Shapiro, by permission of Random House, Inc.

For Dylan Thomas's "Do Not Go Gentle Into That Good Night" from *Collected Poems,* copyright 1939, 1942, 1946 by New Directions, copyright 1952, 1953, by Dylan Thomas, copyright 1957 by New Directions, reprinted by permission of New Directions, and J. M. Dent and Sons, Ltd.

For William Butler Yeats's "The Lake Isle of Innisfree" from *The Collected Poems of W. B. Yeats, Definitive Edition,* copyright 1906 by The Macmillan Co., renewed by William B. Yeats, used by permission of The Macmillan Co., Mrs. Yeats, A. P. Watt and Son, and The Macmillan Co. of Canada, Ltd.

OF POETS AND POEMS

Poetry takes its origin from emotion recollected in tranquillity. The emotion is contemplated till by a species of reaction the tranquillity disappears, and an emotion, kindred to that which was before the subject of contemplation, is gradually produced, and does itself actually exist in the mind.

WILLIAM WORDSWORTH

To explore the sources of poetic inspiration in any poet is to discover the governing power in that personality, the love that draws him as toward his own, or conversely, the hatred that fills him with zeal in the denunciation of all that is opposed to the thing beloved. Inspiration is like love rewarding desire. For whether a poet loves nature or a woman, sculpture or music, his spirit tends to be at one with the essence that he cares for; he takes upon his mind the stamp of the image of loveliness which he adores and gives back to it, when he tells of it in words, his own image and superscription.

MARGUERITE WILKINSON

The pathology of poetic composition is no secret. A poet finds himself caught in some baffling emotional problem, which is of such urgency that it sends him into a sort of trance. And in this trance his mind works with astonishing boldness and precision, on several imaginative levels at once. The poem is either a practical answer to his problem, or else it is a clear statement of it; and a problem clearly stated is half-way to solution.

ROBERT GRAVES

Wherever the wild-tossed branches of the tree of life creak in the wind, be it on lonely cattle drove or in lamplit street, the roaming falcon of poetry hovers, swoops and dips.

JOHN COWPER POWYS

One of the most absurd mistakes . . . concerning a poet is to regard his work as something entirely apart from his life. If that work is true to himself, it cannot but be the most uncompromising, essential, secret and infallible proof of his inmost spirit and his imagination. In that work he was alone—it is fruit of his solitude . . . It is a representation, vividly clear, of his reverie, experience and imagination.

WALTER DE LA MARE

FOREWORD

Some time ago I encountered the fascinating story behind William Wordsworth's famous poem "It is a Beauteous Evening, Calm and Free." I then re-read the sonnet with new insight and immediately realized *why* the poet was so serene.

It occurred to me that there must be many absorbing stories behind other famous poems: dramatic experiences, emotional conflicts and crises, and intellectual ferments in the lives of the poets which in turn became transmuted into golden lines that either dimly or distinctly reflect their origin. As George E. Woodberry said of poets: "They lived before they sang."

And if there are such stories behind famous poems, I assured myself, many other people would enjoy reading them in conjunction with the poems, rejoicing in the discovery that they led to a greater understanding and appreciation of the poems themselves.

This volume is the result of that happy initial thought and its pleasant pursuit through hundreds of books about and by the eighty-seven poets whose one hundred and fifty-one famous poems are here given with accounts of their origin in the lives and experiences of the poets.

This is not a snooping expedition or the revival of half-forgotten scandals, although some of the loveliest poems did flower from unsavory soil. In such instances I have neither whitewashed the poet nor painted him in more lurid colors than I found in the facts. Most of the poems, however, have quite respectable origins.

It should be recognized that every poet worthy of the name communicates experiences that have deeply moved him—moved him and his muse. Many of these are experiences with other people. Consequently, in going behind the often obscure or merely allusive façade of the poem to its origin and motivation one uncovers vital human details and circumstances that were necessarily dropped when the experience was distilled to its poetic essence.

Thus, the story behind a poem is as essentially a part of the poem's history as it is of the poet's history, and therefore a part of literary history. But equally important, the story deepens the understanding and increases the appreciation of those who read the poem that was written to be read.

Some readers may be disappointed to find a favorite poem and its accompanying story missing from this volume. I will perhaps often share their regret.

However, while many fine poems suggest or clearly indicate they stem from a memorable experience of the poet, nevertheless there is often no known or recorded event of the poet's life that can be linked to the poem.

In such instances I have refused to speculate. If I could not find substantial factual basis for the story behind a poem, then it has been ruled out no matter how appealing the poem itself. There are, in fact, a number of poets whose poems obviously and consistently voice profoundly stirring happenings in their lives, but which are not otherwise revealed either by the poet or his biographers. This is of course particularly true of contemporary poets. Time will often uncover the story—but by no means always. Some poets wanted no prying into their lives: William Wordsworth, Matthew Arnold, Walter De La Mare, Robert Bridges, and others. Some have been successful in frustrating inquiry; others have not.

It should moreover be noted that much great poetry is of such a nature that there is no tellable story behind it other than that the poet wrote it in a frenzy of inspiration, the source of which the poet himself does not know. There are other superb poems on subjects which have not the remotest relationship to the poet's life. These are poems without a history; there are no events or experiences to explain them.

I have not attempted technical analysis of any of the poems, or tried to define or explain the nature of either poetry or its inspiration. These are tasks beyond the scope of this volume and the talents of its author-editor. I will be content if readers find the stories accompanying each poem interesting in themselves and the poems better understood and enjoyed as a consequence.

I do not ever recall having had so interesting a period of research, or one so rewarding in reading riches served up by many learned chroniclers of the poets' lives. In fact, I can suggest no more pleasing excursion for a lover of a particular poet's work than to explore his life under the guidance of his best biographers. To that and other ends I have given in the back of the book a list "For Further Reading."

RALPH L. WOODS

CONTENTS

I
The Poems

Contents

Contents

II
The Songs

Part I

THE POEMS

MATTHEW ARNOLD (1822-1888)

Dover Beach

Matthew Arnold lived during a period of great conflict between science and religion, and between reason and imagination. He rejected the old creeds and urged the adoption of intuitively received or imaginatively grasped ethical truths distilled from traditional theology. He believed that poetry should be the chief medium for the expression of this new concept.

And yet, while pronouncing the doom of the old order, Arnold was by no means at peace with the modern scene:

> "This strange disease of modern life
> With its sick hurry, its divided aims" ("The Scholar Gipsy")

He was particularly disturbed by the English middle class, among whom he lived and worked, condemning their "defective type of religion, narrow range of intellect and knowledge, stinted sense of beauty and low type of manners." He yearned to liberate himself from this atmosphere and to gain a comprehensive vision of the whole of life.

Thus one finds Arnold often speaking in his verse of living in a world against which his nature rebels and condemning the ugliness and pettiness of life as he finds it. He longs for calm and insight that will bring him stability, and indicates that whatever the solution it must be a compromise.

Finally Arnold the intellectual, tormented by the problem of his own salvation, rejects a universe and a divinity responsive to human needs and finds in human love the only thing that makes modern life bearable. This is what the poet reveals in his "Dover Beach," which he said epitomizes "the main movement of my mind of the last quarter of a century."

> The sea is calm to-night.
> The tide is full, the moon lies fair
> Upon the straits;—on the French coast the light
> Gleams and is gone; the cliffs of England stand,
> Glimmering and vast, out in the tranquil bay.
> Come to the window, sweet is the night-air!
> Only, from the long line of spray
> Where the sea meets the moon-blanch'd sand,
> Listen! you hear the grating roar
> Of pebbles which the waves draw back, and fling,
> At their return, up the high strand,
> Begin, and cease, and then again begin,
> With tremulous cadence slow, and bring
> The eternal note of sadness in.

Sophocles long ago
Heard it on the Aegean, and it brought
Into his mind the turbid ebb and flow
Of human misery; we
Find also in the sound a thought,
Hearing it by this distant northern sea.

The sea of faith
Was once, too, at the full, and round earth's shore
Lay like the folds of a bright girdle furl'd.
But now I only hear
Its melancholy, long, withdrawing roar,
Retreating, to the breath
Of the night-wind, down the vast edges drear
And naked shingles of the world.

Ah, love, let us be true
To one another! for the world, which seems
To lie before us like a land of dreams,
So various, so beautiful, so new,
Hath really neither joy, nor love, nor light,
Nor certitude, nor peace, nor help for pain;
And we are here as on a darkling plain
Swept with confused alarms of struggle and flight,
Where ignorant armies clash by night.

EMILY BRONTË (1818-1848)

The Old Stoic
Last Lines

The village of Haworth, England, during the first half of the nineteenth century had not the least idea that in the gray parsonage on a rise at the edge of the moor lived one of the most remarkably gifted families: Reverend Patrick Brontë, his three daughters and one son.

Of these children, tall, dark-eyed and shy, Emily was the most brilliant, probing and courageous in a family that was as rich in these qualities as it was poor in robust health, social graces and daily contact with the world beyond their quiet but intellectually charged home.

Stripped of legendary accretions, Emily stands out a lonely but not unhappy or neurotic searcher of the human heart; a woman of iron will and rigid morality who passionately sought to penetrate the secret of spirit and the nature of good and evil. Music, painting, books, newspapers, magazines, solitary walks on the moor, housework and incessant study and writing filled the day for her and her sisters, Anne and Charlotte. They apparently felt no need or desire for active social life apart from one another.

Emily, Charlotte and Anne Brontë grew up familiar with death: their mother died when they were quite small, later followed in death by two sisters (Maria and Elizabeth) and their adored but irresponsible brother Branwell.

However the others may have acted, Emily is not known to have shed a tear on these or any other occasion, though her sympathies were quick and her loyalties deep. She simply never whimpered or indulged in self-pity. Once when she was bitten by a dog she quietly went to the kitchen, heated a bar of iron red-hot and applied it to the bite until she was confident the wound had been cauterized. Later when asked the reason for the bandage she said only that it was a dog bite.

It was this characteristic of silent courage, of self-mastery and of willing-ness to face reality, that marked her brief life and persuades people that "The Old Stoic" is her most self-revealing poem:

> Riches I hold in light esteem,
> And Love I laugh to scorn;
> And lust of fame was but a dream,
> That vanished with the morn:
>
> And if I pray, the only prayer
> That moves my lips for me
> Is, "Leave the heart that now I bear,
> And give me liberty!"
>
> Yes, as my swift days near their goal,
> 'Tis all that I implore;
> In life and death a chainless soul,
> With courage to endure.

In "The Old Stoic," written in 1841, Emily Brontë at the age of twenty-three was already thinking of death: "Yes, as my swift days near their goal." It was a subject she contemplated increasingly from that time on, though her health appeared good, she is not known to have had either happy or disas-trous love affairs, and life at the Haworth parsonage continued unruffled. Nevertheless, melancholy or sadness slowly seems to have come on her, as her poems revealed a growing awareness of individuality. Perhaps Emily's solitary musings on God, man, immortality and the destiny of the Brontës was exacting a penalty. Or, maybe the utter failure of a volume of poems by Emily and Charlotte—two copies sold, two brief magazine notices—made her indifferent to a future devoid of recognition.

Whatever the reason, in January, 1846, the brilliant young woman wrote her last poem—breathing defiance of death and voicing her courage and confidence in God and immortality. In December, 1848, her courage and confidence were unabated when she developed a bad cold and refused medicine, nursing or doctoring. In fact, on her last day she dressed and came downstairs to do her usual work. When she collapsed an hour or so later the valiant spirit had left her body before the doctor arrived. Her last poem, "Last Lines," is epitaph enough:

> No coward soul is mine,
>   No trembler in the world's storm-troubled sphere:
> I see Heaven's glories shine,
>   And faith shines equal, arming me from fear.
>
> O God within my breast,
>   Almighty, ever-present Deity!
> Life—that in me has rest,
>   As I—undying Life—have power in Thee.
>
> Vain are the thousand creeds
>   That move men's hearts: unutterably vain;
> Worthless as withered reeds,
>   Or idlest froth amid the boundless main,
>
> To waken doubt in one
>   Holding so fast by Thine infinity;
> So surely anchored on
>   The steadfast rock of immortality.
>
> With wide-embracing love
>   Thy Spirit animates eternal years,
> Pervades and broods above,
>   Changes, sustains, dissolves, creates, and rears.
>
> Though earth and man were gone,
>   And suns and universes ceased to be,
> And Thou were left alone,
>   Every existence would exist in Thee.
>
> There is not room for Death,
>   Nor atom that his might could render void:
> Thou—Thou art Being and Breath,
>   And what Thou art may never be destroyed.

RUPERT BROOKE (1887-1915)

The Soldier
The Dead

This "golden young Apollo" was the embodiment of the romantic conception of the poet: handsome almost to the point of being beautiful; personally magnetic, to cast a spell over those he met; mildly rebellious and unorthodox; restless, ardent and sensitive.

In the Spring of 1914, Brooke was returning home after travels through Canada, the United States and the South Seas. When his ship docked in England the young poet experienced an unexpected thrill over his native land and was so excited at seeing family, friends and familiar scenes that he hardly slept the first few days. After the fateful assassination at Sarajevo in late June, Brooke at first ignored its implications while he plunged into a round of banquets, parties, theaters and literary discussions. But when the possibility of war increased he wrote of his uneasiness and fright, adding "I'm anxious that England may act rightly. I can't bear it if she does wrong."

Six weeks after World War I began, the poet-aesthete enlisted and was in a training camp. He had rejected Winston Churchill's offer of a safe staff post (to keep him for poetry in the future). In early October, Brooke got a brief taste of war when his untrained outfit was rushed to the aid of besieged Antwerp. The city fell to the Germans. Brooke and his fellow soldiers were returned to England to complete their training.

It was in this training camp in Dorsetshire during the Autumn of 1914 that the dilettante poet become uncomplaining soldier began to think how futile and unproductive his life had been, how much he owed to his English heritage and what a privilege and honor it was to fight and, if need be, die for England. It was here in a crude hut near the seashore where he had spent carefree summers, that night after night when the other men—soldiers for whom he had developed deep respect as men and patriots—were asleep Brooke wrote the *Five Sonnets* (later titled *1914*) that made him world-famous. He called the sonnets his "five camp children"; the "children," a premonition told him, would soon be orphaned.

In February, 1915, Brooke and his outfit sailed to participate in the Dardanelles campaign. Aboard ship off Greece he wrote a farewell letter to a friend in London, expressing his expectation of death. Several weeks after his Sonnets were published in England, the twenty-eight-year-old poet died on April 14 of blood poisoning, and was buried at midnight in an olive grove on the island of Skyros.

If I should die, think only this of me:
That there's some corner of a foreign field
That is forever England. There shall be
In that rich earth a richer dust concealed;
A dust whom England bore, shaped, made aware,
Gave, once, her flowers to love, her ways to roam;
A body of England's, breathing English air,
Washed by the rivers, blest by the suns of home.
And think, this heart, all evil shed away,
A pulse in the eternal mind, no less
Gives somewhere back the thoughts by England given;
Her sights and sounds; dreams happy as her day;
And laughter, learnt of friends; and gentleness,
In hearts at peace, under an English heaven.

* * * * * * *

Blow out, you bugles, over the rich Dead!
There's none of these so lonely and poor of old,
But, dying, has made us rarer gifts than gold.
These laid the world away; poured out the red
Sweet wine of youth; gave up the years to be
Of work and joy, and that unhoped serene,
That men call age; and those who would have been,
Their sons, they gave, their immortality.
Blow, bugles, blow! They brought us, for our dearth,
Holiness, lacked so long, and Love, and Pain.
Honor has come back, as a king, to earth,
And paid his subjects with a royal wage;
And Nobleness walks in our ways again;
And we have come into our heritage.

ELIZABETH BARRETT BROWNING (1806-1861)

How Do I Love Thee?

Two months before their plans matured, Elizabeth Barrett and Robert
Browning were talking about the future. The lovers were anticipating their
life together at Pisa, Italy, where they expected to live after a secret marriage
and departure from England in order to avoid a scene with Elizabeth's insanely jealous and tyrannical father.

"You shall see some day at Pisa," said the shy, sickly poetess to her dashing
suitor, "what I will not show you now." When Robert pressed her she replied
with a touch of feminine mystery, "Does not Solomon say, 'There is a time

to read what is written'?" That was all she would say about her secret—forty-four sonnets she had been writing about the transformation Robert effected in her life, her initial doubts and fears and love's triumph over them.

But it was not until three years later, at Florence, in 1849, that Elizabeth one morning said to her husband, "Do you know I once wrote some poems about *you?*" And then she diffidently handed him a white notebook, saying, "There they are, if you care to see them."

Robert, touched and pleased, thought so highly of the sonnets that he urged they be published, but "under a veil." They chose the title "Sonnets From the Portuguese," because it would suggest a translation from the Portuguese. But they were really referring to "Catarina to Camoëns," a poem by Elizabeth immediately preceding the published sonnets. Catarina fell in love with the Portuguese poet Camoëns but died during his absence abroad. The poem greatly affected Browning and "in a loving fancy" associated Elizabeth with the Portuguese Catarina. Thus the Sonnets were "from the Portuguese" in a figurative sense. Because they are a clear and tasteful expression of a true and deep love, they have great appeal, as in this oft-quoted one:

> How do I love thee? Let me count the ways.
> I love thee to the depth and breadth and height
> My soul can reach, when feeling out of sight
> For the ends of Being and ideal Grace.
> I love thee to the level of every day's
> Most quiet need, by sun and candlelight.
> I love thee freely, as men strive for Right;
> I love thee purely, as they turn from Praise.
> I love thee with the passion put to use
> In my old griefs, and with my childhood's faith.
> I love thee with a love I seemed to lose
> With my lost saints,—I love thee with the breath,
> Smiles, tears, of all my life!—and, if God choose,
> I shall but love thee better after death.

ROBERT BROWNING (1812-1889)

The Lost Leader
Prospice

London's literary circle was quick to welcome twenty-three-year-old Robert Browning when his long poem "Paracelsus" was published at his father's expense in 1835. This psychological history of a man in quest of intellectual power, and the impotence of power without love, resulted in the darkly handsome and intense young poet meeting the leading literary figures of the day. Among these was William Wordsworth, to whom Browning and others looked up to as a leading spokesman for liberalism. The two poets subsequently met on several other occasions, but never became close friends.

In any event, the possibility of further friendship between them was foreclosed when Wordsworth, in 1842, accepted the poet laureateship with its annual pension of three hundred pounds. Browning joined others in regarding this as the climax of Wordsworth's "apostasy" when the people most needed defenders, reform, and eloquent poetic spokesmen. Moreover, Browning then realized Wordsworth's action was the final repudiation of his fiery youth and his enlistment in the ranks of the Tories.

In this aroused state of mind Browning wrote his blistering "The Lost Leader"—the "handful of silver" referring to the pension, and "the riband in his coat" meaning the laureateship. Wordsworth never indicated he noticed the poem.

Years later Browning insisted the stanzas were a piece of youthful impetuosity wherein he had used "the great and venerable personality of Wordsworth as a sort of painter's model," and confessed his "shame and contrition" for the attack. But he was in dead earnest when he wrote it, as indicated by his malicious ridicule of Wordsworth in court dress, in letters to Elizabeth Barrett.

> Just for a handful of silver he left us,
>   Just for a riband to stick in his coat—
> Found the one gift of which fortune bereft us,
>   Lost all the others she lets us devote;
> They, with the gold to give, doled him out silver,
>   So much was theirs who so little allowed:
> How all our copper has gone for his service!
>   Rags—were they purple, his heart had been proud!
> We that had loved him so, followed him, honoured him,
>   Lived in his mild and magnificent eye,
> Learned his great language, caught his clear accents,
>   Made him our pattern to live and to die!
> Shakespeare was of us, Milton was for us,
>   Burns, Shelley, were with us,—they watch from their graves!
> He alone breaks from the van and the freemen,
>   —He alone sinks to the rear and the slaves!
>
> We shall march prospering,—not through his presence;
>   Songs may inspirit us,—not from his lyre;

Deeds will be done,—while he boasts his quiescence,
  Still bidding crouch whom the rest bade aspire:
Blot out his name, then, record one lost soul more,
  One task more declined, one more footpath untrod,
One more devils'-triumph and sorrow for angels,
  One wrong more to man, one more insult to God!
Life's night begins: let him never come back to us!
  There would be doubt, hesitation and pain,
Forced praise on our part—the glimmer of twilight,
  Never glad confident morning again!
Best fight on well, for we taught him—strike gallantly,
  Menace our heart ere we master his own;
Then let him receive the new knowledge and wait us,
  Pardoned in heaven, the first by the throne!

Although Robert Browning's poetry is not ordinarily of a kind that lends itself easily to passionate love lyrics, nevertheless it would be strange to find them entirely lacking from his work when one considers his famous and enduring love for Elizabeth Barrett.

During the fifteen years of marriage they enjoyed he wrote two love poems embodying his love of the shy, semi-invalided poetess he married when she was forty and he thirty-four. One, "By The Fireside," was a long meditation of the peace and contentment of their life together; another, "One Word More," again tenderly celebrated the sweet and quiet joy of their married love.

Four months after Elizabeth died in his arms, at Rome in 1861, Robert Browning finally spoke out lyrically, revealing his continuing sorrow, his resolution to stand up to life, and ending with a passionate cry of confidence that death would return him to her. It was titled "Prospice," which means "Look Forward":

Fear death?—to feel the fog in my throat,
  The mist in my face,
When the snows begin, and the blasts denote
  I am nearing the place,
The power of the night, the press of the storm,
  The post of the foe;
Where he stands, the Arch Fear in a visible form,
  Yet the strong man must go:
For the journey is done and the summit attained,
  And the barriers fall,
Though a battle's to fight ere the guerdon be gained,
  The reward of it all.
I was ever a fighter, so—one fight more,

The best and the last!
I would hate that Death bandaged my eyes, and forebore,
  And bade me creep past.
No! let me taste the whole of it, fare like my peers
  The heroes of old,
Bear the brunt, in a minute pay glad life's arrears
  Of pain, darkness, and cold.
For sudden the worst turns the best to the brave,
  The black minute's at end,
And the elements' rage, the fiend-voices that rave,
  Shall dwindle, shall blend,
Shall change, shall become first a peace out of pain,
  Then a light, then thy breast,
O thou soul of my soul! I shall clasp thee again,
  And with God be the rest!

Browning died twenty-eight years after he wrote these lines. His poetic prayer was answered: he was conscious to the end and aware of its approach. The prophecy of the poem's opening line was fulfilled: he died of bronchitis.

WILLIAM CULLEN BRYANT (1794-1878)

Thanatopsis
To a Waterfowl
O, Fairest of the Rural Maids

During the Summer of 1811 seventeen-year-old Bryant happily roamed the fields and forests of his native Massachusetts studying nature; he read history and philosophy, toyed with the poetry he had been writing for several years, and otherwise amiably marked time until he should enter Yale in the Fall.

But things went wrong. Too few patients were paying the money due Dr. Peter Bryant, the youth's father. College was cancelled. Young Bryant thought the bottom had fallen out of his world; that his best years were now over. He went back to the October woods for comfort and nature's melancholy dress seemed to confirm his mother's Calvinist teaching of the vanity of human wishes, the transitory quality of all life, the constant presence of death in the midst of life; only the inanimate was permanent. They were the kind of thoughts a serious young man would be likely to harbor in the first shock of bitter disappointment.

But this youth returned to his home and put these solemn musings into heroic lines and deposited the completed poem in a drawer of his father's desk, without mentioning it to him. Several months later young Bryant began to study law in a law office, seven miles from his parents' home.

Six years later, Dr. Bryant, a lover of good literature, visited Boston and called on the editors of a new literary magazine, *The North American Review*. The editors urged the doctor to contribute to their periodical. The doctor wrote his son that the editors wanted something from his pen. But Bryant, by now practicing law in Bridgewater, Massachusetts, and enjoying much social life, was slow to reply.

Meanwhile, Dr. Bryant discovered the poem that years earlier had been put in his desk, read it with pride and astonishment, sent it to the magazine's editors, but refrained from mentioning it was written by a seventeen-year-old boy for fear they would not believe it. When the editors read "Thanatopsis" (which is Greek for "view of death"), they at first doubted it was an original American product. It was published in their *Review* September, 1817, and slowly became widely known and quoted:

> To him who in the love of Nature holds
> Communion with her visible forms, she speaks
> A various language; for his gayer hours
> She has a voice of gladness, and a smile
> And eloquence of beauty, and she glides
> Into his darker musings, with a mild
> And healing sympathy, that steals away
> Their sharpness, ere he is aware. When thoughts
> Of the last bitter hour come like a blight
> Over thy spirit, and sad images
> Of the stern agony, and shroud, and pall,
> And breathless darkness, and the narrow house,
> Make thee to shudder and grow sick at heart;—
> Go forth, under the open sky, and list
> To Nature's teachings, while from all around—
> Earth and her waters, and the depths of the air—
> Comes a still voice:—
>   Yet a few days, and thee
> The all-beholding sun shall see no more
> In all his course; nor yet in the cold ground,
> Where thy pale form was laid, with many tears,
> Nor in the embrace of ocean, shall exist
> Thy image. Earth, that nourished thee, shall claim
> Thy growth, to be resolved to earth again,
> And, lost each human trace, surrendering up
> Thine individual being, thou shalt go

To mix forever with the elements,
To be a brother to the insensible rock
And to the sluggish clod, which the rude swain
Turns with his share, and treads upon. The oak
Shall send his roots abroad, and pierce thy mould.

    Yet not to thine eternal resting-place
Shalt thou retire alone, nor couldst thou wish
Couch more magnificent. Thou shalt lie down
With patriarchs of the infant world—with kings,
The powerful of the earth—the wise, the good,
Fair forms, and hoary seers of ages past,
All in one mighty sepulchre. The hills
Rock-ribbed and ancient as the sun,—the vales
Stretching in pensive quietness between;
The venerable woods—rivers that move
In majesty, and the complaining brooks
That make the meadows green; and, poured round all,
Old Ocean's gray and melancholy waste,—
Are but the solemn decorations all
Of the great tomb of man. The golden sun,
The planets, all the infinite host of heaven,
Are shining on the sad abodes of death
Through the still lapse of ages. All that tread
The globe are but a handful to the tribes
That slumber in its bosom.—Take the wings
Of morning, pierce the Barcan wilderness,
Or lose thyself in the continuous woods
Where rolls the Oregon, and hears no sound,
Save his own dashings—yet the dead are there:
And millions in those solitudes, since first
The flight of years began, have laid them down
In their last sleep—the dead reign there alone.
So shalt thou rest, and what if thou withdraw
In silence from the living, and no friend
Take note of thy departure? All that breathe
Will share thy destiny. The gay will laugh
When thou art gone, the solemn brood of care
Plod on, and each one as before will chase
His favorite phantom; yet all these shall leave
Their mirth and their employments, and shall come
And make their bed with thee. As the long train
Of ages glides away, the sons of men—
The youth in life's fresh spring, and he who goes
In the full strength of years, matron and maid,

The speechless babe, and the gray-headed man—
Shall one by one be gathered to thy side,
By those, who in their turn shall follow them.

So live, that when thy summons comes to join
The innumerable caravan, which moves
To that mysterious realm, where each shall take
His chamber in the silent halls of death,
Thou go not, like the quarry-slave at night,
Scourged to his dungeon, but, sustained and soothed
By an unfaltering trust, approach thy grave
Like one who wraps the drapery of his couch
About him, and lies down to pleasant dreams.

After several years of legal studies, Bryant was admitted to the Massachusetts Bar and decided to open a law office at Plainfield, seven miles from
his home at Cummington. It was a December afternoon when he set out
on foot for Plainfield, but without the enthusiasm and thrill of combat of a
young man determined to conquer his world. The Yale disappointment still
vaguely rankled him. Poetic fame had proved a mirage and life had become
a complex of uncertainties. Country lawyers, he gloomily decided, were poor
and scorned as mediocrities. The law itself was a tiresome career. Surely
he would die unknown and unwept.

As Bryant slogged along the country road in this morose mood he noticed
off on the horizon a solitary bird—a waterfowl—bravely winging its way
south to join its companions in a warmer and happier clime. He began to
think how wonderful it was that God gave that lone bird the instinct and
will to fly hundreds of miles over strange and hazardous lands. And if Providence thus guides a bird to better things, surely a man will be equally
guided in his lonely journey through life. The poet in him was aroused.
When he reached Plainfield he had completed what has been called "one
of the finest short poems." It was called "To a Waterfowl":

Whither, midst falling dew,
While glow the heavens with the last steps of day,
Far, through their rosy depths, doest thou pursue
    Thy solitary way?

Vainly the fowler's eye
Might mark thy distant flight to do thee wrong,
As, darkly painted on the crimson sky,
    Thy figure floats along.

Seek'st thou the plashy brink
Of weedy lake, or marge of river wide,

Or where the rocking billows rise and sink
  On the chafed ocean-side?

There is a Power whose care
Teaches thy way along that pathless coast,—
The desert and illimitable air,—
  Lone wandering, but not lost.

All day thy wings have fanned
At that far height, the cold, thin atmosphere,
Yet stoop not, weary, to the welcome land,
  Though the dark night is near.

As soon that toil shall end;
Soon shalt thou find a summer home, and rest,
And scream among thy fellows; reeds shall bend,
  Soon, o'er thy sheltered nest.

Thou'rt gone, the abyss of heaven
Hath swallowed up thy form; yet, on my heart
Deeply hath sunk the lesson thou hast given,
  And shall not soon depart.

He who, from zone to zone,
Guides through the boundless sky thy certain flight,
In the long way that I must tread alone,
  Will lead my steps aright.

After a year of law practice at Plainfield, Bryant moved to Great Barring-
ton, Massachusetts, and there did well in his profession. Moreover, the
slender dandy with side-whiskers adorning his intelligent face, became socially popular in the town.

In the Spring of 1820 Bryant attended a church social and there met a
Mrs. Henderson and her sister, Frances Fairchild. Miss Fairchild was blond,
twenty-three, and far more poised than the young lawyer expected to find
in a visitor from the remote and wild Finger Lakes region of New York.
He was delighted to discover that this orphaned daughter of a farmer could
talk intelligently and with wit. He liked the way her gray eyes looked at
him. Bryant quickly and naturally fell in love with this dainty, dignified and
altogether lovely miss from the back country. The next year began the first
of forty-five happy married years with her.

But months before Bryant married he had to write a poem to his Frances
—a poem that Poe said was "the truest poem written by Bryant . . . . a
gem." He was referring to "O, Fairest of the Rural Maids":

O, fairest of the rural maids!
Thy birth was in the fairest shades;
Green boughs and glimpses of the sky
Were all that met thine infant eye.

Thy sports, thy wanderings when a child,
Were ever in the sylvan wild;
And all the beauty of the place
Is in thy heart and on thy face.

The twilight of the trees and rocks
Is in the light shade of thy locks;
Thy step is as the wind that weaves
Its playful way among the leaves.

Thine eyes are springs, in whose serene
And silent waters Heaven is seen;
Their lashes are the herbs that look
On their young figures in the brook.

The forest depths by foot impressed
Are not more sinless than thy breast:
The holy peace that fills the air
Of those calm solitudes, is there.

ROBERT BURNS (1759-1796)

Highland Mary
Of A' the Airts

Although the victim of malicious gossip and reckless myth-making, Robert Burns did do some hard drinking and had more than the customary quota of inamoratas—most of them freckled milkmaids and lasses who worked in the field and which his songs invested with irresistible charms.

But for all of his romancing and flirtations, Scotland's swaggering, sensitive, passionate and independent poetic genius sang most sweetly of an ideal love—his Highland Mary. For one so candid in admitting his conquests, troubles and shortcomings, Burns was singularly reticent about this "dear girl"—one Mary Campbell.

We do not know how the poet met Mary, who had been a maid-servant in the family of Gavin Hamilton, friends of Burns', and was a dairymaid at Coilsfield at the time of their betrothal. His proposal and her acceptance took place on Sunday, May 14, 1786, "in a sequestered spot on the banks of the Ayr," he said. The story is that they plighted their troth with each standing on either side of the stream, dipping their hands in the water, exchanging Bibles, and then parting. Mary returned to her parents at Argyle-shire to prepare for the nuptials. Five months later she died suddenly of a fever, at Greenock, while on her way to meet the poet.

Two years later Burns married Jean Armour. Then one year after the wedding he broke his silence about Mary with his beautiful "To Mary in Heaven." This was followed three years later, which was six years after the girl's death, by the poet's impassioned song to the great love of his checkered life, his Highland Mary. Burns' imagination may have beguiled his memory and conjured a love greater than he felt when Mary was alive. If so, poetry is the beneficiary.

Ye banks and braes, and streams around
　　The castle of Montgomery,
Green be your woods, and fair your flowers,
　　Your waters never drumlie!
There simmer first unfauld her robes
　　And there the langest tarry;
For there I took the last fareweel
　　O' my sweet Highland Mary.

How sweetly bloom'd the gay green birk,
　　How rich the hawthorn's blossom,
As underneath their fragrant shade
　　I clasp'd her to my bosom!
The golden hours, on angel wings,
　　Flew o'er me and my dearie;
For dear to me, as light and life,
　　Was my sweet Highland Mary.

Wi' monie a vow, and lock'd embrace,
　　Our parting was fu' tender;
And, pledging aft to meet again,
　　We tore oursels asunder;
But oh! fell death's untimely frost,
　　That nipt my flower sae early!
Now green's the sod, and cauld's the clay,
　　That wraps my Highland Mary!

O pale, pale now, those rosy lips,
　　I aft hae kiss'd sae fondly!

And closed for aye the sparkling glance
   That dwelt on me sae kindly!
And mold'ring now in silent dust,
   That heart that lo'ed me dearly!
But still within my bosom's core
   Shall live my Highland Mary.

Burns other great love was Jean Armour, whom he married after an erratic and tempestuous courtship during which she gave birth to two sets of twins and was cast from her home by her father. There is no doubt the poet truly loved heroic and long-suffering Jean, even though his muse responded with more passion to the vision of Mary wrought by time and imagination. Perhaps Jean was too close to him, and their financial and other difficulties too numerous and severe to inspire song.

But about the time of their marriage Burns did write a lovely if relatively casual tribute to Jean. Incidentally, it is comforting to know that after the poet died at the age of thirty-seven, the people of Scotland subscribed to a fund that permitted the widow of their idol to raise her children without hardship and to end her days without distress.

Of a' the airts the wind can blaw,
   I dearly like the west,
For there the bonnie lassie lives,
   The lassie I lo'e best.
There wild woods grow, and rivers row,
   And monie a hill between,
But day and night my fancy's flight
   Is ever wi' my Jean.

I see her in the dewy flowers—
   I see her sweet and fair.
I hear her in the tunefu' birds—
   I hear her charm the air:
There's not a bonnie flower that springs
   By fountain, shaw, or green,
There's not a bonnie bird that sings,
   But minds me o' my Jean.

JOHN BURROUGHS (1837-1921)

Waiting

Rarely has an obscure, struggling man of twenty-five written a poem which accurately expressed the inner convictions by which he would live the rest of his long and famous life.

But John Burroughs, the naturalist, did precisely that one evening during the Civil War when he was a rural school teacher in Ulster County, N. Y. After eight years of teaching, and now married, he had started to study medicine in his spare time at the office of the local doctor, in the hope of escaping the poverty of a teacher rather than because of any marked interest in medicine. He had earlier wanted to join the Union Army but was dissuaded from this by his wife and parents.

It was the gloomiest period of Burroughs' life, and years before he turned to Nature for a career. Blindly groping for a way out of his miserable circumstances, he pushed aside the textbook on anatomy he was studying, and wrote "Waiting." It came easily to him, as did other poems in those days, all but three of which he destroyed. Although published in the Knickerbocker Magazine, the poem attracted no attention until many years later when the author was achieving fame as a naturalist.

The gentle authority on birds and animals later said the poem was "more felt and spontaneous than anything else I ever put into verse. Because it voiced a real feeling it touched others." It was, he added, a "watered down" expression of the religious beliefs his parents had inculcated in him. But it has strengthened, comforted and calmed uncounted anxious men and women.

Serene I fold my hands and wait,
Nor care for wind, or tide, or sea;
I rave no more 'gainst Time or Fate,
For, lo! my own shall come to me.

I stay my haste, I make delays,
For what avails this eager pace?
I stand amid the eternal ways,
And what is mine shall know my face.

Asleep, awake, by night or day,
The friends I seek are seeking me;
No wind can drive my bark astray,
Nor change the tide of destiny.

What matter if I stand alone?
I wait with joy the coming years;

My heart shall reap where it has sown,
And garner up its fruits of tears.

The waters know their own and draw
The brook that springs in yonder height;
So flows the good with equal law
Unto the soul of pure delights.

The stars come nightly to the sky;
The tidal wave unto the sea;
Nor time, nor space, nor deep, nor high,
Can keep my own away from me.

GEORGE GORDON, LORD BYRON (1788-1824)

When We Two Parted
"I Speak Not, I Trace Not, I Breathe Not Thy Name"
Fare Thee Well
So We'll Go No More A'Roving
Maid of Athens

Although much of Byron's poetry stems from his hectic and scandalous life, paradoxically the verse itself gives scant hint of that side of the author. The fact that the poems are superior to the conduct of their author suggests that Byron's muse is the voice of his better self. Surely a wholly cruel and insensitive man could not have written lyrics so lovely.

Admittedly Byron was arrogantly selfish and impulsively generous, aware of his rank and quick to abuse its privileges. He bore the marks of his dissolute, unstable and spendthrift ancestry, and of a mother who alternated between tantrums and penitential calms. Given the restless age in which he lived, it is not surprising that the brilliant, undisciplined and strikingly handsome poet with a clubfoot had numerous amours, some of the backstairs kind.

When Byron's old friend James Wedderburn Webster married Lady Frances Annesley the twenty-three-year-old poet, already a practiced seducer, wrote that the bride "is very pretty," observed that already she treated her husband with "conjugal contempt," and darkly hinted that the husband would be betrayed within three years. Two years later Byron accepted an invitation to visit the Webster home. From there he wrote that Lady Frances "inevitably expects to be attacked and seems prepared for a brilliant defense," and expressed annoyance at his host's suspicions and jealousies. But on this visit the poet admitted he "behaved very well."

However, several days after his departure Byron was writing Lady Melbourne that he had been seeing Lady Frances and that she was no longer indifferent: "I have made love, and it is returned." Then Webster and his wife visited Byron at his Newstead Abbey and it was there, on a later occasion, Byron reported, that the twenty-year-old wife surrendered and offered herself to the poet. "I spared her," wrote Byron. "Poor thing—she is either the most *artful* or *artless* of her age I ever encountered." Although Lady Frances continued for some time to write Byron, he lost interest.

Several years later, when Lady Frances was publicly and scandalously linked with the Duke of Wellington, Byron recalled his former emotions in the tender yet cynical "When We Two Parted":

When we two parted
　　In silence and tears,
Half broken-hearted
　　To sever for years,
Pale grew thy cheek and cold,
　　Colder thy kiss;
Truly that hour foretold
　　Sorrow to this.

The dew of the morning
　　Sunk chill on my brow—
It felt like the warning
　　Of what I feel now.
Thy vows are all broken,
　　And light is thy fame:
I hear thy name spoken,
　　And share in its shame.

They name thee before me,
　　A knell to mine ear;
A shudder comes o'er me—
　　Why wert thou so dear?
They know not I knew thee,
　　Who knew thee too well:—
Long, long shall I rue thee,
　　Too deeply to tell.

In secret we met—
　　In silence I grieve,
That thy heart could forget,

Thy spirit deceive.
If I should meet thee
After long years,
How should I greet thee?
With silence and tears.

When Byron's relatively tame affair with Lady Frances was terminated
he turned with renewed interest to the blackest of his intrigues: his fatal
love for his voluptuous, silly and unresisting half-sister, Mrs. Augusta Leigh,
wife of an improvident and wandering gambler. He began to see more and
more of Augusta, both at her home outside London and for weeks at a time
in London. She fascinated the poet, returned his love and strove only to
give him pleasure. Morality apparently never occurred to her, though she
demurred when Byron planned to take her to the Continent with him.

Byron, on the other hand, did have periods of remorse concerning "that
perverse passion" which was "my deepest after all." But repeatedly he defended this "most unselfish person in the world," insisting it was "my own
folly and her weakness . . . her only error has been my fault entirely."

When Thomas Moore returned to London in the Spring of 1814 he saw
much of Byron, and found confirmation of hints his friend had given in letters that a secret love affair was preying on his mind. When Moore asked
the poet for some words to a song, Byron, with Augusta dominating his
thoughts, wrote the impassioned "I speak not, I trace not" etc.

Not long after Byron wrote this poem about Augusta, the two illicit lovers
agreed that the only solution was for the poet to marry. But he never forgot
Augusta, wrote other stanzas on her, regularly and sometimes ardently corresponded with her when he left England, and in his deathbed delirium kept
talking incoherently about her.

I speak not, I trace not, I breathe not thy name;
There is grief in the sound, there is guilt in the fame;
But the tear which now burns on my cheek may impart
The deep thoughts that dwell in that silence of heart.
Too brief for our passion, too long for our peace,
Were those hours—can their joy or their bitterness cease?
We repent, we abjure, we will break from our chain,—
We will part, we will fly to—unite it again!
Oh! thine be the gladness, and mine be the guilt!
Forgive me, adored one!—forsake if thou wilt;
But the heart which is thine shall expire undebased,
And *man* shall not break it—whatever *thou* may'st.
And stern to the haughty, but humble to thee,
This soul in its bitterest blackness shall be;

And our days seem as swift, and our moments more sweet,
With thee by my side, than with worlds at our feet.
One sigh of thy sorrow, one look of thy love,
Shall turn me or fix, shall reward or reprove.
And the heartless may wonder at all I resign—
Thy lips shall reply, not to them, but to mine.

The most disastrous and ill-advised of Byron's misadventures was his marriage at the age of twenty-seven to Annabelle Milbanke, a rigidly proper young lady he had met in London society. She was charmed by the handsome sinner and confident of her power to extinguish the roué in him. Byron was induced to marry as a means of reformation, particularly to break the spell of his long and incestuous relations with Augusta Leigh, his half-sister. Annabelle was then unaware of the illicit affair.

Byron's letters to Annabelle admitted his weakness and expressed the hope she would mend his habits and character. To others the poet said that if his bride did not "govern" him the marriage would fail. If he did not intend to reform himself, he was apparently willing to be reformed by the skill and force of a wife. Annabelle was not equal to the task, if indeed any woman could have been.

From the beginning it became evident the marriage was fore-doomed to failure. On their honeymoon Byron told Annabelle of his detestation of her mother, complained of her family's meager marriage settlement, frightened her with his unpredictable moods and nightmares, disturbed her by reading lines from a letter Augusta had written him. Prim and didactic, Annabelle was not the person to cope with so outrageous a personality, however much she loved him. Nevertheless, they had periods of happiness and got along reasonably well together in the beginning.

The marriage moved into troubled waters when the couple went to London to live, first stopping for an ominous visit at Augusta's home. The two women were mutually cordial, but every evening of their visit Byron insisted upon remaining up with Augusta and would insult Annabelle into retiring to her room if she lingered. Perhaps the seed of suspicion was first planted then.

By the time they had leased and settled in the Duchess of Devonshire's elaborate house in Piccadilly Terrace, Annabelle was three months pregnant and Byron was back in the swing of London life with friends that made his wife uneasy. Then this charming young woman did a thing that is inexplicable in one so well endowed with a superior mind: she invited Augusta Leigh to visit them. "You are a fool," the poet told her, "for letting her come to the house." Years later Annabelle referred to the playfulness and familiarity she witnessed between her husband and Augusta, and said "There were moments when I could have plunged a dagger into her heart."

With creditors pressing Byron, a bailiff even sleeping in the Piccadilly Terrace home, the poet frequently getting drunk and abusive, once visiting for six days at Augusta's home, the collapse of the marriage became increasingly evident. "It is my destiny to ruin all I come near," the poet said to his wife in one of his calmer moods. But more and more he excoriated her and her family, made desperate threats, drunkenly and obscenely boasted of his affairs with actresses, and even threatened to bring a mistress into the home during Annabelle's impending confinement. Although Byron had moments of tenderness and kindness, they became increasingly brief and less frequent. If he wasn't unbalanced he might just as well have been. In any case, Annabelle began to fear that her husband was deranged.

The denouement came shortly after Annabelle gave birth to a girl, an event that seemed only to increase the father's rage. Lady Byron and her newly-born infant left the Byron household for her parents' home on January 15, 1816, if not at the poet's insistence then certainly with no objection from him. In fact, Byron suggested and encouraged her to leave, apparently was non-committal about seeing her again, and avoided being present when she departed.

Lady Byron's tenderness toward this exasperating man is illustrated by two affectionate notes she wrote Byron while en route to her parents' home. But from then on the lawyers took charge and she was forbidden to see or write her husband.

When Byron learned that his wife was planning a legal separation he wrote her several gentle and conciliatory letters suggesting she return, but received in reply only a terse note that "authorized friends" could best settle matters. Lady Byron evidently told her lawyers of her strong suspicions of incest but wanted to avoid a court trial. By this time London society seethed with rumors about Byron and Augusta, a situation the poet appeared to treat with indifference. Even when he and his half-sister were pointedly avoided and snubbed at London social affairs he ignored the insults. Finally the separation agreement and settlement was privately negotiated and signed, on March 17th.

Shortly thereafter Byron's over-wrought condition abated when his creditors seized for auction the contents of the Byron household in Piccadilly Terrace. He fell into a melancholy calm, pacing the rooms and thinking of tender hours with Annabelle and of times they had given each other mutual peace and contentment. He sat down and in his grief the poetry flowed out of him in the famous "Fare Thee Well." He sent the poem to Lady Byron with a note saying "I send you the first thing I have ever attempted to compose upon you." She never acknowledged it. Six weeks later Byron left England for Italy, writing Annabelle "Wherever I may go—and I am

going far—you and I can never meet in this world—nor in the next." But
no doubt Lady Byron must have occasionally over the years read the only
poetry written to her by the fascinating scoundrel she so foolishly married:

> Fare thee well! and if forever,
> Still forever, *fare thee well:*
> Even though unforgiving, never
>   'Gainst thee shall my heart rebel.
> Would that breast were bared before thee
>   Where thy head so oft hath lain,
> While that placid sleep came o'er thee
>   Which thou ne'er canst know again:
> Would that breast, by thee glanced over,
>   Every inmost thought could show!
> Then thou wouldst at last discover
>   'Twas not well to spurn it so.
> Though the world for this commend thee—
>   Though it smile upon the blow,
> Even its praises must offend thee,
>   Founded on another's woe:
> Though my many faults defaced me,
>   Could no other arm be found,
> Than the one which once embraced me,
>   To inflict a cureless wound?
> Yet, oh yet, thyself deceive not;
>   Love may sink by low decay,
> But by sudden wrench, believe not
>   Hearts can thus be torn away:
> Still thine own its life retaineth—
>   Still must mine, though bleeding, beat;
> And the undying thought which paineth
>   Is—that we no more may meet.
> These are words of deeper sorrow
>   Than the wail above the dead;
> Both shall live—but every morrow
>   Wake us from a widowed bed.
> And when thou wouldst solace gather,
>   When our child's first accents flow
> Wilt thou teach her to say "Father!"
>   Though his care she must forego?
> When her little hands shall press thee,
>   When her lip to thine is press'd,
> Think of him whose prayer shall bless thee,
>   Think of him thy love *had* blessed!
> Should her lineaments resemble

Those thou never more mayst see,
   Then thy heart will softly tremble
With a pulse yet true to me.
All my faults perchance thou knowest,
   All my madness none can know;
All my hopes—where'er thou goest,
   Wither, yet with *thee* they go.
Every feeling hath been shaken;
   Pride—which not a world could bow,
Bows to thee—by thee forsaken.
   Even my soul forsakes me now.
But 'tis done—all words are idle—
   Words from me are vainer still;
But the thoughts we cannot bridle
   Force their way without the will.
Fare thee well! thus disunited,
   Torn from every nearer tie,—
Sear'd in heart, and lone, and blighted,
   More than this I scarce can die.

A few months after leaving England, Byron was living in the home of a "merchant of Venice," Signor Segati, and writing friends about the merchant's wife, twenty-two-year-old Marianna: "in her appearance altogether like an antelope . . . large, black, Oriental eyes . . . features are regular . . . skin clear and soft . . . her hair is of the dark gloss, her figure is light and pretty, and she is a famous songstress." He confessed he was in "fathomless love" with his landlord's wife: "Our little arrangement is completed; the usual oaths having been taken, and everything fulfilled according to the understood relations of such liaisons. . . . We are one of the happiest unlawful couples on this side of the Alps."

In February, 1817, Venice had its annual Carnival. Every night Byron and Marianna joined the revels and wandered the streets until dawn. But this dissipation left the twenty-nine-year-old poet physically exhausted and mentally unhappy with his aimless life. Satiated and coming down with fever—perhaps malaria—Byron addressed to Marianna one of his loveliest lyrics: "So We'll Go No More A'Roving":

So we'll go no more a roving
   So late into the night,
Though the heart be still as loving,
   And the moon be still as bright.

For the sword outwears its sheath,
   And the soul wears out the breast,

> And the heart must pause to breathe,
>   And love itself have rest.
>
> Though the night was made for loving,
>   And the day returns too soon,
> Yet we'll go no more a roving
>   By the light of the moon.

But go a roving Byron eventually did. Marianna was jealous, had too many tantrums and was taking the affairs much too seriously. Possibly Byron also feared he was too much charmed by her. Besides, the wife of a Venetian baker—"fit to breed gladiators from"—was taking a strong hold on the poet. So he left Marianna and to go on to "a world of other harlotry" as he put it.

On Christmas Day, 1819, Byron arrived in Athens and immediately took an apartment in a double house owned by widowed Mrs. Tarsia Macri, who lived in it with her daughters Marianna, Katinka and Theresa, all under fifteen.

The poet found life there increasingly pleasant and was delighted by the youthful freshness and innocence of the "three graces"—the Macri sisters. Finally, his interest became greatest in dark-eyed, pale Theresa, the youngest. But he did not spoil the propriety and pleasantness of his relationships with the Macri family by succumbing to his demons. Besides, as soon as his business affairs in England were settled he planned to go to Constantinople, thence to Persia and India.

On March 4th the English sloop-of-war *Pylades* stopped at Piraeus and offered Byron passage to Smyrna if he was prepared to leave the next day. Byron agreed, though he had grown fond of Athens and of the Macris, particularly of thirteen-year-old Theresa. That evening he wrote his famous "Maid of Athens," a romantic idealization of Theresa's beauty and no doubt an expression of the desires he had managed to keep under control:

> Maid of Athens, ere we part,
> Give, oh give me back my heart!
> Or, since that has left my breast,
> Keep it now, and take the rest!
> Hear my vow, before I go,
> Ζωή μου, σᾶς ἀγαπῶ.*
>
> By those tresses unconfined,
> Woo'd by each Aegean wind;

---

* "My life, I love you."

By those lids whose jetty fringe
Kiss thy soft cheeks' blooming tinge;
By those wild eyes like the roe,
Ζωή μου, σᾶς ἀγαπῶ.

By that lip I long to taste;
By that zone-encircled waist;
By all the token-flowers that tell
What words can never speak so well;
By love's alternate joy and woe,
Ζωή μου, σᾶς ἀγαπῶ.

Maid of Athens! I am gone:
Think of me, sweet! when alone.
Thought I fly to Istambol,
Athens holds my heart and soul:
Can I cease to love thee? No!
Ζωή μου, σᾶς ἀγαπῶ.

Several months later Byron was back in the Macri home in Athens. But before long his relations with the mother became strained when Mrs. Macri insisted upon a large sum of money before she would release Theresa to him either in marriage or otherwise. "I have better amusements," wrote Byron.

His "amusements," however, were ended within a few years. He died in Greece in 1834, at the age of thirty-six.

THOMAS CAMPBELL (1777-1844)

The Soldier's Dream

Three years after graduating from the University of Glasgow, Thomas Campbell suddenly found himself famous upon publication of his long poem "The Pleasures of Hope." He promptly gave up tutoring and thoughts of a medical career, in favor of a literary pilgrimage to Germany on the modest sum he received from the poem's sale. Campbell left for Hamburg on June 1, 1800. It was the likable young Scotsman's first absence from his native land.

After a brief stay at Hamburg the poet proceeded to Ratisbon in Bavaria, apparently undaunted by the fact that he would be traveling in troubled regions. In fact, he was stirred by his encounters with various military units preparing for battle. One of his letters tells how he watched 5,000 Austrian troops, moving toward the point of an expected French attack, turn off the road and encamp "in a wide plain at one extremity of the valley." He spoke of the "picturesque groups, sleeping on the bare ground, with their horses tied to trees whilst the sound of the Austrian trumpets died faintly away among the echoes of the hills."

This encampment scene was the germ of a famous poem. But the poet had first to witness actual warfare before he would have the perspective to view the soldier's pause for sleep with sympathetic understanding.

A day or so later he was both a fascinated and horrified spectator of the French-Austrian battle for Ratisbon, and strove to erase the memory of it from his mind.

However disturbing the war scenes may have been, they did enable Campbell to envision the dream of a soldier sleeping on the field between battles. He had seen the soldiers sleeping before the conflict, watched the bloody clash at arms, and again seen the exhausted men reach for rest before the sickening contest was resumed. He was confident he knew what would be in the mind and heart of the simple sleeping soldier:

> Our bugles sang truce—for the night-cloud had lowered,
>   And the sentinel stars set their watch in the sky;
> And thousands had sunk on the ground overpowered,
>   The weary to sleep, and the wounded to die.
>
> When reposing that night on my pallet of straw,
>   By the wolf-scaring faggot that guarded the slain,
> At the dead of the night a sweet vision I saw,
>   And thrice ere the morning I dreamt it again.
>
> Methought from the battle-field's dreadful array,
>   Far, far I had roamed on a desolate track:
> 'Twas autumn,—and sunshine arose on the way
>   To the home of my fathers, that welcomed me back.
>
> I flew to the pleasant fields, traversed so oft
>   In life's morning march, when my bosom was young;
> I heard my own mountain-goats bleating aloft,
>   And knew the sweet strain that the corn-reapers sung.
>
> Then pledged we the wine-cup, and fondly I swore
>   From my home and my weeping friends never to part;
> My little ones kissed me a thousand times o'er,
>   And my wife sobbed aloud in her fulness of heart.

"Stay, stay with us,—rest, thou art weary and worn!"
    And fain was their war-broken soldier to stay;
But sorrow returned with the dawning of morn,
    And the voice in my dreaming ear melted away.

HENRY CAREY (1663-1743)

Sally in Our Alley

It would seem improbable that a man who titled a play *Chrononho-tonthologos* could also write so charming a lyric as "Sally in Our Alley." But that is what this most popular poet, lyricist, composer and playwright of eighteenth-century London did.

It came about this way: Carey noticed a shoemaker's apprentice and his sweetheart setting off in London for a holiday, and was so struck by the sweet simplicity of their courtship that he decided to follow them at a discreet distance and observe where they went and what they did.

If not to Carey's astonishment, then to ours, he trailed them to Bedlam, the famous—or infamous—London insane asylum that tourists of a crueler day visited to be amused by the antics of the inmates. After Bedlam the couple went to "puppet shows, the flying chairs and all the elegancies of Moorfields." Carey then followed them to the "Farthing Pye-House." Surely he must have been amazed when he watched the apprentice and his love eat "buns, cheesecakes, gammon of bacon, stuffed beef, and bottled ale." Carey decided that he should celebrate in a poem the "beauty of a chaste and disinterested passion, even in the lowest class of human life." "Sally in Our Alley" was at first ridiculed, but eventually polite society applauded it into a popularity that still lingers today.

Of all that girls that are so smart
    There's none like pretty Sally;
She is the darling of my heart,
    And she lives in our alley.
There is no lady in the land
    Is half so sweet as Sally;
She is the darling of my heart,
    And she lives in our alley.

Her father he makes cabbage-nets,
    And through the streets does cry 'em;
Her mother she sells laces long

To such as please to buy 'em;
But sure such folks could ne'er beget
    So sweet a girl as Sally!
She is the darling of my heart,
    And she lives in our alley.

When she is by I leave my work,
    I love her so sincerely;
My master comes like any Turk,
    And bangs me most severely.
But let him bang his bellyful,
    I'll bear it all for Sally;
For she's the darling of my heart,
    And she lives in our alley.

Of all the days that's in the week
    I dearly love but one day,
And that's the day that comes betwixt
    The Saturday and Monday;
For then I'm drest in all my best
    To walk abroad with Sally;
She is the darling of my heart,
    And she lives in our alley.

My master carries me to church,
    And often am I blamèd
Because I leave him in the lurch
    As soon as text is namèd:
I leave the church in sermon-time,
    And slink away to Sally;
She is the darling of my heart,
    And she lives in our alley.

When Christmas comes about again,
    O, then I shall have money!
I'll hoard it up, and box it all,
    And give it to my honey;
I would it were ten thousand pound!
    I'd give it all to Sally;
She is the darling of my heart,
    And she lives in our alley.

My master and the neighbors all
    Make game of me and Sally,
And, but for her. I'd better be

> A slave, and row a galley;
> But when my seven long years are out,
> O, then I'll marry Sally!
> O, then we'll wed, and then we'll bed,—
> But not in our alley!

LEWIS CARROLL (CHARLES LUTWIDGE DODGSON) (1832-1898)

Father William

People are often surprised when they learn that the superb nonsense of *Alice's Adventures in Wonderland* was written by an old-maidish Oxford don who was a professional mathematician and logician, an Anglican Churchman, and a shy, eccentric bachelor.

Many who have read *Alice* just for the sheer fun in it are even more surprised when probing critics assure them that Carroll's graceful fancies and extravagant drolleries are often intended to deflate Victorian pretenses and pomposities.

This is not to say that the Reverend Charles Lutwidge Dodgson stepped into the character of Lewis Carroll simply because he desired to mock and shatter imbecilities that irritated him. The man had an instinct for the fanciful and a mind that could not resist performing difficult mental acrobatics. But he was also a scholar of high principles and rigid integrity. Consequently he used the occasion of his nonsense-writing as a lance with which to impale evils and stupidities that were susceptible to his method.

Carroll's "Father William" is an entertaining example of both his genius for nonsense and his distaste of bad poetry, cheap morality, superficial theology and pious posing. It is a parody of Robert Southey's homily in heavy-footed verse: "The Old Man's Comforts and How He Gained Them." Carroll wrote other parodies, but this is probably his best, perhaps because Southey's extreme egotism, fawning of the rich and powerful and preposterous moral strutting made an excellent target. Incidentally, no personal malice was involved. Carroll was eleven when Southey died.

However, Carroll was no iconoclast. He was sincerely and deeply religious, with a marked aversion to indelicacies and irreverences. Moreover, he dreaded religious argument, and was unfailingly tolerant of other people's rights to their own beliefs. He remained loyal to the faith which his clergyman father had inculcated in him.

But Carroll's integrity of mind made it impossible for him to ignore smug formalism, copybook morality and pompous hypocrisy. Consequently when Southey—among others—expected his dreadful effusion to be taken seriously, it was too much for Carroll. He apparently felt obliged to demolish it with his acute ridicule. He did this, as John Ciardi recently pointed out, "by pretending to preserve the heavily moral tone and by pretending to take seriously the pat moral subject while rearranging the details of the subject into an obvious absurdity."

So that the reader may best appreciate Carroll's skill, the first eight lines of Southey's verse is shown immediately below, followed by Carroll's delicious parody:

> You are old, Father William, the young man cried,
> The few locks which are left you are gray;
> You are hale, Father William, a hearty old man;
> Now tell me the reason, I pray.
>
> In the days of my youth, Father William replied,
> I remembered that youth would fly fast,
> And abused not my health and my vigor at first,
> That I never might need them at last.

                    *   *   *   *

> "You are old, Father William," the young man said,
>   "And your hair has become very white;
> And yet you incessantly stand on your head—
>   Do you think, at your age, it is right?"
>
> "In my youth," Father William replied to his son,
>   "I feared it might injure the brain;
> But now that I'm perfectly sure I have none,
>   Why, I do it again and again."
>
> "You are old," said the youth, "as I mentioned before,
>   And have grown most uncommonly fat;
> Yet you turned a back-somersault in at the door—
>   Pray, what is the reason of that?"
>
> "In my youth," said the sage, as he shook his gray locks,
>   "I kept all my limbs very supple
> By the use of this ointment—one shilling the box—
>   Allow me to sell you a couple?"
>
> "You are old," said the youth, "and your jaws are too weak
>   For anything tougher than suet;

Yet you finished the goose, with the bones and the beak—
  Pray, how did you manage to do it?"

"In my youth," said his father, "I took to the law,
  And argued each case with my wife;
And the muscular strength which it gave to my jaw,
  Has lasted the rest of my life."

"You are old," said the youth, "one would hardly suppose
  That your eye was as steady as ever;
Yet you balanced an eel on the end of your nose—
  What made you so awfully clever?"

"I have answered three questions, and that is enough,"
  Said his father; "Don't give yourself airs!
Do you think I can listen all day to such stuff?
  Be off, or I'll kick you downstairs."

JOHN CLARE (1793-1864)

Secret Love

From 1837 to 1864 the Northampton [England] General Lunatic Asylum harbored a shy and forgotten little man who in 1820 had been hailed by literary London as the remarkable Peasant-Poet of Northamptonshire—John Clare. But even during those years of oblivion the gentle man, when not suffering protracted spells of melancholia and confusion, wrote an unending stream of lucid and often beautiful poems—poems that years after his death would again draw attention to the man and his work.

Clare was a genuine peasant of his time and place. His father was a day-laborer who could read a little; his mother was illiterate; he had eight years of school with frequent interruptions for work in the fields, and then himself became a day-laborer, apprentice gardener and a lime-burner.

But from about his fourteenth year poetry began to claim the attention and add to the happiness of the lonely boy. Clare wrote and secreted poems, many of them about the natural life he loved and so carefully observed.

During his childhood Clare met Mary Joyce, a blue-eyed farmer's daughter who became the ideal and the romantic vision of his life. They were schoolmates when he was ten. Years later he recalled: "I was a lover very early in life. . . . If I could but gaze on her face or fancy a smile on her countenance, it was sufficient. . . . We played with each other, but named nothing of love. . . . Yet young as my heart was, it would turn chill when I touched her hand. . . . I cannot forget her little playful fairy form and witching smile tender as a bird's."

When Clare left school to work as a laborer on farms he seldom saw Mary. But when he was sixteen their friendship was renewed and quickly became an idyllic love. However, within a year they parted. Clare implied that Mary decided the difference between their respective stations in life was too great; a factor not easily dismissed in those class-conscious days. They met briefly once again a few years later. It was their last meeting, although they continued to live within a few miles of one another.

Clare had other romances, subsequently married and fathered a large family, but it was still Mary under that and other names he most frequently celebrated in his love-poems.

When Clare's first volume of poems was published they were praised by English critics, a trust fund was raised to relieve the poet's poverty and he met many of the literary greats of the day. During the following seventeen years his fame declined and his poems were no longer sought by the public. Vague illnesses, headaches, severe depression and confusion made it necessary for him to be committed to a mental institution. There he spent the rest of his life as the mildest and oftenest the sanest of patients.

And during these bleak years Clare continued to think of Mary Joyce, and to address poems to her. He realized he could never have her (in fact, she died unmarried while Clare was in the asylum). His love for her then became secret—a secret joy in finding her everywhere and in all things beautiful and wonderful. After Clare's death of a stroke this tender jewel was found among his poems—one of the loveliest of his lines to the spirit of his love for Mary:

> I hid my love when young till I
> Couldn't bear the buzzing of a fly;
> I hid my love to my despite
> Till I could nor bear to look at light:
> I dare not gaze upon her face
> But left her memory in each place;
> Where'er I saw a wild flower lie
> I kissed and bade my love goodbye.
>
> I met her in the greenest dells,
> Where dewdrops pearl the wood bluebells;
> The lost breeze kissed her bright blue eye,
> The bee kissed and went singing by,
> A sunbeam found a passage there,

A gold chain round her neck so fair;
As secret as the wild bee's song
She lay there all the summer long.

I hid my love in field and town
Till e'en the breeze would knock me down;
The bees seemed singing ballads o'er,
The fly's bass turned a lion's roar;
And even the silence found a tongue,
To haunt me all the summer long;
The riddle nature could not prove
Was nothing else but secret love.

ARTHUR HUGH CLOUGH (1819-1861)

Say Not, the Struggle Naught Availeth
There is No God

Nietzsche said one must have chaos within to give birth to a dancing star. Although Clough's best-known lyrics are hardly "dancing stars," nevertheless the spiritual agitation he experienced during his entire life after entering college did result in several famous poems.

The poet's spiritual difficulties stem in the first instance from his earliest years when he lived with his English parents who resided at Charleston, South Carolina. His very religious mother, in her determination that he should be a conscientious and idealistic boy, greatly over-emphasized the necessity for him to adhere to Duty. Moreover, she discouraged the growing child from making friends in the United States.

The stern precepts of his influential mother remained with him and in fact were reinforced when Clough was returned to England and entered Rugby. At this famous private school the serious youth came under the care of Thomas Arnold, the school's headmaster and father of Matthew Arnold, the poet. Clough was specially favored by Arnold, a strict disciplinarian who dwelt everlastingly on the student's responsibility to exemplify rigid standards of conduct and morality and continually stressed the sinfulness of human nature. Arnold was almost fierce in his resolution to mold his students to his particular concept of Christianity, which he viewed primarily as a medium for the dissemination of morality with the support of the state.

Gentle, sensitive Clough's already overdeveloped conscience was soon weighed down by Arnold's muscular demands.

As a consequence of his pre-occupation with the Rugby brand of religion and morality, Clough encountered deep difficulties when he entered Oxford at a time that university was seething with religious controversy. Clough interested himself in the Oxford religious upheaval, brooded about self-control and self-discipline, lived ascetically, until gradually grave doubts began to torment him. Finally his skepticism become so strong in 1848 that he could no longer subscribe to the Church of England's Thirty-nine Articles as required by Oxford and he therefore resigned his fellowship at the University.

Departure from Oxford was a wrench for Clough, who liked the University and loved to teach. Moreover, he was buffeted by his spiritual storm and strife. His skepticism, fear and doubts warred continually with the strict precepts of his childhood and years at Rugby.

It was shortly after he left Oxford that Clough wrote "Say Not, The Struggle Naught Availeth," his eloquent defiance of the doubt and pessimism that pursued him:

> Say not, the struggle naught availeth,
>   The labour and the wounds are vain,
> The enemy faints not, nor faileth,
>   And as things have been they remain.
>
> If hopes were dupes, fears may be liars;
>   It may be, in yon smoke concealed,
> Your comrades chase e'en now the fliers,
>   And, but for you, possess the field.
>
> For while the tired waves, vainly breaking,
>   Seem here no painful inch to gain,
> Far back, through creeks and inlets making,
>   Comes silent, flooding in, the main.
>
> And not by eastern windows only,
>   When daylight comes, comes in the light;
> In front, the sun climbs slow, how slowly,
>   But westward, look, the land is bright.

And in the same year that the above was written Clough wrote "Dipsychus," somewhat of a spiritual autobiography in which are the following familiar lines, perhaps as much of an affirmation as the poor troubled poet could make:

"There is no God," the wicked saith,
  "And truly it's a blessing,
For what He might have done with us
  It's better only guessing."

"There is no God," a youngster thinks,
  "Or really, if there may be,
He surely did not mean a man
  Always to be a baby."

"There is no God, or if there is,"
  The tradesman thinks, "'twere funny
If He should think it ill in me
  To make a little money."

"Whether there be," the rich man says,
  "It matters very little,
For I and mine, thank somebody,
  Are not in want of victual."

Some others, also, to themselves,
  Who scarce so much as doubt it,
Think there is none, when they are well
  And do not think about it.

But country folks who live beneath
  The shadow of the steeple;
The parson and the parson's wife,
  And mostly married people;

Youths green and happy in first love,
  So thankful for illusion;
And men caught out in what the world
  Calls guilt, in first confusion;

And almost everyone when age,
  Disease, or sorrow strike him,
Inclines to think there is a God,
  Or something very like Him.

SAMUEL TAYLOR COLERIDGE (1772-1834)

The Rime of the Ancient Mariner
Kubla Khan

Late one autumn afternoon in 1797 William Wordsworth and Samuel Taylor Coleridge set out from Alfoxden, the Wordsworth home in England's Lake Country, on a walking trip to Linton and the Valley of Stones near it. Since their united funds were sparse, they agreed to defray the tour's expenses by jointly writing a poem.

As they strode along the Quantock Hills toward Wachet, Coleridge suggested their poem be based on a theme that had been in mind for some time: a friend's dream of a skeleton ship with skeleton figures aboard it.

Wordsworth, acknowledging that "much the greatest part of the story was Mr. Coleridge's invention," recorded in his *Memoirs* that as they continued their walk he suggested that the Old Navigator should commit some crime which would bring upon him a spectral persecution and cause him to wander the earth. He then mentioned he had been reading Shelvocke's *Voyages* in which are described encounters with albatrosses while rounding Cape Horn. "Suppose," added Wordsworth, "you represent him as having killed one of these birds on entering the South Sea, and that the tutelary spirits of these regions take upon themselves to avenge the crime?" Wordsworth further suggested that Coleridge have the ship manned by the reanimated dead men, but he made no other contributions to the scheme of the poem.

That same evening the two poets began their collaboration, but Wordsworth soon realized their styles were so different that "it would have been presumptuous in me to do anything but separate from an undertaking upon which I could only have been a clog."

He had fanned the flame and furnished valuable links to the narrative. Coleridge caught fire: his magnificent imagination took dormant memories of his vast reading and transmuted them into poetic gold.

For example, as John Livingston Lowes demonstrates in his fascinating *The Road to Xanadu* (1927), Coleridge was steeped in the literature and lore of Oriental mysticism and the esoteric elements of Judaism and Christianity; he was fascinated by strange phantasms, interested in ancient cults, and had written about "The Wandering of Cain" and knew well the legend of The Wandering Jew, both of which find their echo in "The Ancient Mariner."

Moreover, there are indications in Coleridge's *Notebooks* that he was familiar with an account by Paulinus, a fourth century bishop of Nola, of a mariner's miraculous homeward voyage, striking similarities to which are found in Coleridge's masterpiece.

It would be false, however, to suppose that Coleridge's ballad is not an imaginative work. For all the jumble of sources, suggestions and impressions that crowded the poet's mind, he still had to bring order out of chaos by choosing the alternatives offered by numerous disparate elements, and then merge and blend them into a narrative design clothed in beautiful language.

Four months and ten days after his fateful afternoon walk with Wordsworth, Coleridge arrived in Alfoxden and read his completed poem.

An ancient Mariner
meeteth three Gallants
bidden to a wedding-
feast, and detaineth one.

It is an ancient Mariner,
And he stoppeth one of three.
"By thy long grey beard and glittering eye,
Now wherefore stopp'st thou me?

The Bridegroom's doors are opened wide,
And I am next of kin;
The guests are met, the feast is set:
May'st hear the merry din."

He holds with his skinny hand,
"There was a ship," quoth he.
"Hold off! unhand me, grey-beard loon!"
Eftsoons his hand dropt he.

The Wedding-Guest is
spell-bound by the eye
of the old seafaring man,
and constrained to hear
his tale.

He holds him with his glittering eye—
The Wedding-Guest stood still,
And listen like a three years' child:
The Mariner hath his will.

The Wedding-Guest sat on a stone:
He cannot chose but hear;
And thus spake on that ancient man,
The bright-eyed Mariner.

The Mariner tells how
the ship sailed southward
with a good wind and
fair weather, till it
reached the Line.

"The ship was cheered, the harbour cleared,
Merrily did we drop
Below the kirk, below the hill,
Below the lighthouse top.

"The Sun came up upon the left,
Out of the sea came he!

And he shone bright, and on the right
Went down into the sea.

"Higher and higher every day,
Till over the mast at noon—"
The Wedding Guest here beat his breast,
For he heard the loud bassoon.

*The Wedding-Guest
heareth the bridal
music; but the Mariner
continueth his tale.*

The bride hath paced into the hall,
Red as a rose is she;
Nodding their heads before her goes
The merry minstrelsy.

The Wedding-Guest he beat his breast,
Yet he cannot choose but hear;
And thus spake on that ancient man,
The bright-eyed Mariner.

*The ship drawn by a
storm toward the
south pole.*

"And now the storm blast came, and he
Was tyrannous and strong:
He struck with his o'er taking wings,
And chased us south along.

"With sloping mast and dipping prow,
As who pursued with yell and blow
Still treads the shadow of his foe,
And forward bends his head,
The ship drove fast, loud roared the blast,
And southward ay we fled.

*The land of ice, and of
fearful sounds, where no
living thing was to be
seen.*

"And now there came both mist and snow,
And it grew wondrous cold:
And ice, mast-high, came floating by,
As green as emerald.

"And through the drifts the snowy clifts
Did send a dismal sheen:
Nor shapes of men nor beasts we ken—
The ice was all between.

"The ice was here, the ice was there,
The ice was all around:
It cracked and growled, and roared and howled,
Likes noises in a swound!

Till a great sea-bird called the Albatross, came through the snow-fog, and was received with great joy and hospitality.

"At length did cross an Albatross:
Through the fog it came;
As if it had been a Christian soul,
We hailed it in God's name.

"It ate the food it ne'er had eat,
And round and round it flew.
The ice did split with a thunder-fit;
The helmsman steered us through!

And lo! the Albatross proveth a bird of good omen, and followeth the ship as it returned northward through the fog and floating ice.

"And a good south wind sprung up behind;
The Albatross did follow,
And every day, for food or play,
Came to the mariner's hollo!

"In mist or cloud, on mast or shroud,
It perched for vespers nine;
While all the night, through fog-smoke white,
Glimmered the white moonshine."

The ancient Mariner inhospitably killeth the pious bird of good omen.

"God save thee, ancient Mariner!
From the fiends, that plague thee thus!—
Why look'st thou so?"—"With my cross-bow
I shot the Albatross."

PART THE SECOND

"The Sun now rose upon the right:
Out of the sea came he,
Still hid in mist, and on the left
Went down into the sea.

"And the good south wind still blew behind,
But no sweet bird did follow,
Nor any day for food or play
Came to the mariners' hollo!

His shipmates cry out against the ancient Mariner for killing the bird of good luck.

"And I had done a hellish thing,
And it would work 'em woe:
For all averred, I had killed the bird
That made the breeze to blow.
Ah wretch! said they, the bird to slay,
That made the breeze to blow!

But when the fog cleared off, they justify the same and thus make themselves accomplices in the crime.

"Nor dim nor red, like God's own head,
The glorious Sun uprist:
Then all averred, I had killed the bird
That brought the fog and mist.
'Twas right, said they, such birds to slay,
That bring the fog and mist.

The fair breeze continues; the ship enters the Pacific Ocean, and sails northward, even till it reaches the Line.

"The fair breeze blew, the white foam flew,
The furrow followed free;
We were the first that ever burst
Into that silent sea.

The ship hath been suddenly becalmed.

"Down drop the breeze, the sails dropt down,
'Twas sad as sad could be;
And we did speak only to break
The silence of the sea!

"All in a hot and copper sky,
The bloody Sun, at noon,
Right up above the mast did stand,
No bigger than the Moon.

"Day after day, day after day,
We stuck, nor breath nor motion;
As idle as a painted ship
Upon a painted ocean.

And the Albatross begins to be avenged.

"Water, water, everywhere,
And all the boards did shrink;
Water, water, everywhere,
Nor any drop to drink.

"The very deep did rot: O Christ!
That ever this should be!
Yea, slimy things did crawl with legs
Upon the slimy sea.

"About, about, in reel and rout
The death-fires danced at night;
The water, like a witch's oils,
Burnt green, and blue and white.

A Spirit had followed them; one of the invisible inhabitants of this planet, neither departed souls nor angels; concerning whom the learned Jew, Josephus and the Platonic Constantinopolitan, Michael Psellus, may be consulted. They are very numerous, and there is no climate or element without one or more.

"And some in dreams assuréd were
Of the Spirit that plagued us so;
Nine fathom deep he had followed us
From the land of mist and snow.

The shipmates, in their sore distress, would fain throw the whole guilt on the ancient Mariner; in sign whereof they hang the dead sea-bird round his neck.

"And every tongue, through utter drought,
Was withered at the root;
We could not speak, no more than if
We had been choked with soot.

"Ah! well a day! what evil looks
Had I from old and young!
Instead of the cross, the Albatross
About my neck was hung.

PART THE THIRD

"There passed a weary time. Each throat
Was parched, and glazed each eye.
A weary time! a weary time!
How glazed each weary eye,
When looking westward, I beheld
A something in the sky.

The ancient Mariner beholdeth a sign in the element afar off.

"At first it seemed a little speck,
And then it seemed a mist;
It moved and moved, and took at last
A certain shape, I wist.

"A speck, a mist, a shape, I wist!
And still it neared and neared:
As if it dodged a water-sprite,
It plunged and tacked and veered.

At its nearer approach it seemeth him to be a ship; and at a dear ransom he freeth his speech from the bonds of thirst.

"With throats unslaked, with black lips baked,
We could not laugh nor wail;
Through utter drought all dumb we stood!
I bit my arm, I sucked the blood,
And cried, "A sail! a sail!

A flash of joy.

"With throats unslaked, with black lips baked,
Agape they heard me call:
Gramercy! they for joy did grin,

And all at once their breath drew in,
As they were drinking all.

And horror follows.
For can it be a ship
that comes forward
without wind or tide?

" 'See! see!' (I cried) 'she tacks no more!
Hither to work us weal;
Without a breeze, without a tide,
She steadies with upright keel'

"The western wave was all a-flame.
The day was well-nigh done!
Almost upon the western wave
Rested the broad bright Sun;
When that strange shape drove suddenly
Betwixt us and the Sun.

It seemeth him but the
skeleton of a ship.

"And straight the Sun was flecked with bars,
(Heaven's Mother send us grace!)
As if through a dungeon-grate he peered
With broad and burning face.

"Alas! (thought I, and my heart beat loud)
How fast she nears and nears!
Are those her sails that glance in the Sun,
Like restless gossameres?

And its ribs are seen as
bars on the face of the
setting Sun.
The Spectre-Woman and
her Death-mate, and no
other on board the
skeleton ship.
Like vessel, like crew!

"Are those her ribs through which the Sun
Did peer, as through a grate?
And is that Woman all her crew?
Is that a DEATH? and are there two?
Is DEATH that woman's mate?

"Her lips were red, her looks were free,
Her locks were yellow as gold:
Her skin was as white as leprosy,
The Nightmare Life-in-Death was she,
Who thicks man's blood with cold.

Death and Life-in-Death
have diced for the ship's
crew, and she (the latter)
winneth the ancient
Mariner.

"The naked hulk alongside came,
And the twain was casting dice;
'The game is done! I've won, I've won!'
Quoth she, and whistles thrice.

No twilight within the
courts of the sun.

"The Sun's rim dips; the stars rush out:
At one stride comes the dark;
With far-heard whisper, o'er the sea,
Off shot the spectre-bark.

"We listened and looked sideways up!
Fear at my heart, as at a cup,
My life-blood seemed to sip!

*At the rising of
the Moon.*

The stars were dim, and thick the night,
The steersman's face by his lamp gleamed white;
From the sails the dew did drip—
Till clomb above the eastern bar
The hornèd Moon, with one bright star
Within the nether tip.

One after another,

"One after one, by the star-dogged Moon,
Too quick for groan or sigh,
Each turned his face with a ghastly pang,
And cursed me with his eye.

*His shipmates drop
down dead.*

"Four times fifty living men,
(And I heard nor sigh nor groan)
With heavy thump, a lifeless lump,
They dropped down one by one.

*But Life-in-Death
begins her work on the
ancient Mariner.*

"The souls did from their bodies fly,—
They fled to bliss or woe!
And every soul, it passed me by,
Like the whizz of my cross-bow!"

PART THE FOURTH

*The Wedding-Guest
feareth that a Spirit
is talking to him;*

"I fear thee, ancient Mariner!
I fear thy skinny hand!
And thou art long, and lank, and brown,
As is the ribbed sea-sand.

"I fear thee and thy glittering eye,
And thy skinny hand, so brown."—

*But the ancient Mariner
assureth him of his
bodily life, and pro-
ceedeth to relate his
horrible penance.*

"Fear not, fear not, thou Wedding-Guest!
This body dropt not down.

"Alone, alone, all, all alone,
Alone on a wide wide sea!
And never a saint took pity on
My soul in agony.

*He despiseth the
creatures of the calm.*

"The many men, so beautiful!
And they all dead did lie:
And a thousand thousand slimy things
Lived on; and so did I.

And envieth that they should live, and so many lie dead.

"I looked upon the rotting sea,
And drew my eyes away;
I looked upon the rotting deck,
And there the dead men lay.

"I looked to heaven, and tried to pray;
But or ever a prayer had gusht,
A wicked whisper came, and made
My heart as dry as dust.

"I closed my lids, and kept them close,
And the balls like pulses beat;
For the sky and the sea, and the sea and the sky
Lay like a load on my weary eye,
And the dead were at my feet.

But the curse liveth for him in the eye of the dead men.

"The cold sweat melted from their limbs,
Nor rot nor reek did they:
The look with which they looked on me
Had never passed away.

"An orphan's curse would drag to hell
A spirit from on high;
But oh! more horrible than that
Is the curse in a dead man's eye!
Seven days, seven nights, I saw that curse,
And yet I could not die!

In his loneliness and fixedness he yearneth towards the journeying Moon and the stars that still sojourn, yet still move onward; and every-where the blue sky belongs to them, and is their appointed rest, and their native country and their own natural homes, which they enter unannounced, as lords that are certainly expected and yet there is a silent joy at their arrival.
By the light of the Moon he beholdeth God's creatures of the great calm.

"The moving Moon went up the sky,
And nowhere did abide:
Softly she was going up,
And a star or two beside—

"Her beams bemocked the sultry main,
Like April hoar-frost spread;
But where the ship's huge shadow lay,
The charmèd water burnt always
A still and awful red.

"Beyond the shadow of the ship,
I watched the water-snakes:
They moved in tracks of shining white,
And when they reared, the elfish light
Fell off in hoary flakes.

"Within the shadow of the ship
I watched their rich attire:
Blue, glossy green, and velvet black,
They coiled and swam; and every track
Was a flash of golden fire.

Their beauty and
their happiness.

He blesseth them
in his heart.

"O happy living things! no tongue
Their beauty might declare:
A spring of love gushed from my heart,
And I blessed them unaware:
Sure my kind saint took pity on me,
And I blessed them unaware.

The spell begins
to break.

"The selfsame moment I could pray;
And from my neck so free
The Albatross fell off, and sank
Like lead into the sea."

PART THE FIFTH

"Oh sleep! it is a gentle thing,
Beloved from pole to pole!
To Mary Queen the praise be given!
She sent the gentle sleep from Heaven,
That slid into my soul.

By grace of the holy
Mother, the ancient
Mariner is refreshed
with rain.

"The silly buckets on the deck,
That had so long remained,
I dreamt that they were filled with dew;
And when I awoke, it rained.

"My lips were wet, my throat was cold,
My garments all were dank;
Sure I had drunken in my dreams,
And still my body drank.

"I moved, and could not feel my limbs:
I was so light—almost
I thought that I had died in sleep,
And was a blessed ghost.

He heareth sounds and
seeth strange sights and
commotions in the sky
and the element.

"And soon I heard a roaring wind:
It did not come anear;
But with its sound it shook the sails,
That were so thin and sere.

"The upper air burst into life!
And a hundred fire-flags sheen,
To and fro they were hurried about!
And to and fro, and in and out,
The wan stars danced between.

"And the coming wind did roar more loud,
And the sails did sigh like sedge;
And the rain poured down from one black cloud;
The Moon was at its edge.

"The thick black cloud was cleft, and still
The Moon was at its side:
Like waters shot from some high crag,
The lightning fell with never a jag,
A river steep and wide.

The bodies of the ship's crew are inspired, and the ship moves on;

"The loud wind never reached the ship,
Yet now the ship moved on!
Beneath the lightning and the Moon
The dead men gave a groan.

"They groaned, they stirred, they all uprose,
Nor spake, nor moved their eyes;
It had been strange, even in a dream,
To have seen those dead men rise.

"The helmsman steered, the ship moved on;
Yet never a breeze upblew;
The mariners all 'gan work the ropes,
Where they were wont to do;
They raised their limbs like lifeless tools—
We were a ghastly crew.

But not by the souls of the men, nor by daemons of earth or middle air, but by a blessed troop of angelic spirits, sent down by the invocation of the guardian saint.

"The body of my brother's son
Stood by me, knee to knee:
The body and I pulled at one rope,
But he said nought to me."

"I fear thee, ancient Mariner!"
"Be calm, thou Wedding-Guest!
'Twas not those souls that fled in pain,
Which to their corses came again,
But a troop of spirits blest:

"For when it dawned—they dropped their arms,
And clustered round the mast;
Sweet sounds rose slowly through their mouths,
And from their bodies passed.

"Around, around, flew each sweet sound,
Then darted to the Sun;
Slowly the sounds came back again,
Now mixed, now one by one.

"Sometimes a-dropping from the sky
I heard the sky-lark sing;
Sometimes all little birds that are,
How they seemed to fill the sea and air
With their sweet jargoning!

"And now 'twas like all instruments,
Now like a lonely flute;
And now it is an angel's song,
That makes the heavens be mute.

"It ceased; yet still the sails made on
A pleasant noise till noon,
A noise like of a hidden brook
In the leafy month of June,
That to the sleeping woods all night
Singeth a quiet tune.

"Till noon we quietly sailed on,
Yet never a breeze did breathe:
Slowly and smoothly went the ship,
Moved onward from beneath.

*The lonesome Spirit
from the south-pole
carries on the ship as
far as the Line, in
obedience to the angelic
troop, but still requireth
vengeance.*

"Under the keel nine fathom deep,
From the land of mist and snow,
The spirit slid: and it was he
That made the ship to go.
The sails at noon left off their tune,
And the ship stood still also.

The Sun, right up above the mast,
Had fixed her to the ocean:
But in a minute she 'gan stir,
With a short uneasy motion—
Backwards and forwards half her length
With a short uneasy motion.

Then like a pawing horse let go,
She made a sudden bound:
It flung the blood into my head,
And I fell down in a swound.

"How long in that same fit I lay,
I have not to declare;
But ere my living life returned,
I heard and in my soul discerned
Two voices in the air.

" 'Is it he?' quoth one, 'Is this the man?
By him who died on cross,
With his cruel bow he laid full low
The harmless Albatross.

" 'The spirit who bideth by himself
In the land of mist and snow,
He loved the bird that loved the man
Who shot him with his bow.'

"The other was a softer voice,
As soft as honeydew:
Quoth he: 'The man hath penance done,
And penance more will do.'

PART THE SIXTH

First Voice
" 'But tell me, tell me! speak again,
Thy soft response renewing—
What makes that ship drive on so fast?
What is the ocean doing?'

Second Voice
" 'Still as a slave before his lord,
The ocean hath no blast;
His great bright eye most silently
Up to the Moon is cast—

" 'If he may know which way to go;
For she guides him smooth or grim.
See, brother, see! how graciously
She looketh down on him.'

*The Mariner hath been
cast into a trance; for the
angelic power causeth
the vessel to drive northward faster than human
life could endure.*

First Voice

" 'But why drives on that ship so fast,
Without or wave or wind?'

Second Voice

" 'The air is cut away before,
And closes from behind.

" 'Fly, brother, fly! more high, more high!
Or we shall be belated:
For slow and slow that ship will go,
When the Mariner's trance is abated.'

*The supernatural motion
is retarded, the Mariner
awakes, and his penance
begins anew.*

"I woke and we were sailing on
As in a gentle weather:
'Twas night, calm night, the moon was high;
The dead men stood together.

"All stood together on the deck,
For a charnel-dungeon fitter:
All fixed on me their stony eyes,
That in the Moon did glitter.

"The pang, the curse, with which they died,
Had never passed away:
I could not draw my eyes from theirs,
Nor turn them up to pray.

*The curse is finally
expiated.*

"And now this spell was snapt: once more
I viewed the ocean green,
And looked far forth, yet little saw
Of what had else been seen—

"Like one, that on a lonesome road
Doth walk in fear and dread,
And having once turned round walks on,
And turns no more his head;
Because he knows, a frightful fiend
Doth close behind him tread.

"But soon there breathed a wind on me,
Nor sound nor motion made:
Its path was not upon the sea,
In ripple or in shade.

"It raised my hair, it fanned my cheek
Like a meadow-gale of spring—
It mingled strangely with my fears,
Yet it felt like a welcoming.

"Swiftly, swiftly flew the ship,
Yet she sailed softly too:
Sweetly, sweetly blew the breeze—
On me alone it blew.

And the ancient Mariner beholdeth his native country.

"Oh! dream of joy! is this indeed
The light-house top I see?
Is this the hill? is this the kirk?
Is this mine own countree?

"We drifted o'er the harbour-bar,
And I with sobs did pray—
O let me be awake, my God!
Or let me sleep alway.

"The harbour-bay was clear as glass,
So smoothly it was strewn!
And on the bay the moonlight lay,
And the shadow of the Moon.

"The rock shone bright, the kirk no less,
That stands above the rock:
The moonlight-steeped in silentness
The steady weathercock.

The Angelic spirits leave the dead bodies,

"And the bay was white with silent light
Till rising from the same,
Full many shapes, that shadows were,
In crimson colours came.

And appear in their own forms of light.

"A little distance from the prow
Those crimson shadows were:
I turned my eyes upon the deck—
Oh, Christ! what saw I there!

"Each corse lay flat, lifeless and flat,
And, by the holy rood!
A man all light, a seraph-man,
On every corse there stood.

"This seraph-band, each waved his hand:
It was a heavenly sight!
They stood as signals to the land,
Each one a lovely light:

"This seraph-band, each waved his hand,
No voice did they impart—
No voice; but oh! the silence sank
Like music on my heart.

"But soon I heard the dash of oars,
I heard the Pilot's cheer;
My head was turned perforce away,
And I saw a boat appear.

"The Pilot and the Pilot's boy,
I heard them coming fast:
Dear Lord in Heaven! it was a joy
The dead men could not blast.

"I saw a third—I heard his voice:
It is the Hermit good!
He singeth loud his godly hymns
That he makes in the wood.
He'll shrive my soul, he'll wash away
The Albatross's blood.

PART THE SEVENTH

The Hermit of the Wood,

"This Hermit good lives in that wood
Which slopes down to the sea.
How loudly his sweet voice he rears!
He loves to talk with marineres
That come from a far countree.

"He kneels at morn, and noon, and eve—
He hath a cushion plump:
It is the moss that wholly hides
The rotted old oak-stump.

"The skiff-boat neared: I heard them talk,
'Why this is strange, I trow!
Where are those lights so many and fair,
That signal made but now?'

*Approacheth the ship
with wonder.*
" 'Strange, by my faith!' the Hermit said—
'And they answered not our cheer!
The planks look warped! and see those sails,
How thin they are and sere!
I never saw aught like to them,
Unless perchance it were

" 'Brown skeletons of leaves that lag
My forest-brook along;
When the ivy-tod is heavy with snow,
And the owlet whoops to the wolf below,
That eats the she-wolf's young.'

" 'Dear Lord! it hath a fiendish look'—
(The Pilot made reply)
'I am a-feared'—'push-on, push-on!'
Said the Hermit cheerily.

"The boat came closer to the ship,
But I nor spake nor stirred;
The boat came close beneath the ship,
And straight a sound was heard.

*The ship suddenly
sinketh.*
"Under the water it rumbled on,
Still louder and more dread:
It reached the ship, it split the bay;
The ship went down like lead.

*The ancient Mariner is
saved in the Pilot's boat.*
"Stunned by that loud and dreadful sound,
Which sky and ocean smote,
Like one that hath been seven days drowned
My body lay afloat;
But swift as dreams, myself I found
Within the Pilot's boat.

"Upon the whirl, where sank the ship,
The boat spun round and round;
And all was still, save that the hill
Was telling of the sound.

"I moved my lips—the Pilot shrieked
And fell down in a fit;
The holy Hermit raised his eyes,
And prayed where he did sit.

"I took the oars: the Pilot's boy,
Who now doth crazy go,
Laughed loud and long, and all the while
His eyes went to and fro.
'Ha! ha!' quoth he, 'full plain I see,
The Devil know how to row.'

"And now, all in my own countree,
I stood on the firm land!
The Hermit stepped forth from the boat,
And scarcely he could stand.

*The ancient Mariner
earnestly entreateth the
Hermit to shrive him;
and the penance of life
falls on him.*

" 'O shrive me! shrive me, holy man!'
The Hermit crossed his brow.
'Say quick,' quoth he, 'I bid thee say—
What manner of man art thou?'

"Forthwith this frame of mine was wrenched
With a woeful agony,
Which forced me to begin my tale;
And then it left me free.

*And ever and anon
throughout his future life
an agony constraineth
him to travel from land
to land,*

"Since then, at an uncertain hour,
That agony returns:
And till my ghastly tale is told,
This heart within me burns.

"I pass, like night, from land to land;
I have strange power of speech;
That moment that his face I see,
I know the man that must hear me:
To him my tale I teach.

"What loud uproar burst from that door!
The wedding guests are there:
But in the garden-bower the bride
And bride-maids singing are:
And hark the little vesper bell,
Which biddeth me to prayer!

"O Wedding-Guest! this soul hath been
Alone on a wide wide sea:
So lonely 'twas, that God Himself
Scarce seemed there to be.

"O sweeter than the marriage feast,
'Tis sweeter far to me,
To walk together to the kirk
With a goodly company!—

"To walk together to the kirk,
And all together pray,
While each to his great Father bends,
Old men, and babes, and loving friends,
And youths and maidens gay!

And to teach, by his own
example, love and rever-
ence to all things that
God made and loveth.

"Farewell, farewell! but this I tell
To thee, thou Wedding-Guest!
He prayed well, who loveth well
Both man and bird and beast.

"He prayeth best, who loveth best
All things both great and small;
For the dear God who loveth us,
He made and loveth all."

The Mariner, whose eye is bright,
Whose beard with age is hoar,
Is gone: and now the Wedding-Guest
Turned from the bridegroom's door.

He went like one that hath been stunned,
And is of sense forlorn:
A sadder and a wiser man,
He rose the morrow morn.

Several months after Coleridge had launched his Ancient Mariner on his peregrinations, he was plunged into the depths of misery by a variety of circumstances. He was frightened by the burden of a second child Mrs. Coleridge had given birth to; his finances were in a customarily precarious state; a friend, Charles Lloyd, had written in Coleridge's home a novel, *Edmund Oliver,* which revealed confessions the poet had confided to him in friendship and then went on to imply that the poet was a drunk, a drug addict, and hinted at un-named "vices."

Wordsworth and his sister Dorothy joined Coleridge when he set out to confront Lloyd at Cross. Finding Lloyd had left for Birmingham, the three walked to Cheddar, thence to the valley of the Wye and the Thelwall farm, where they remained as guests for several days. Despondency there got a firmer grip on the brilliant neurotic and one day he wandered off by himself, convinced his reputation was gone, feeling ill and with real or imagined pains that he persuaded himself demanded relief. With a book and a bottle of opium derivative Coleridge went to a deserted farmhouse between Porlock and Linton and for several days invited escape from his torment.

On one of these days Coleridge gave himself a dose of opium and sat down to read his copy of *Purchas His Pilgrimage.* Just before the drug put him to sleep the poet read: "In Xandu did Cublain Can build a stateley Palace, encompassing sixteene miles of plaine ground with a wall, wherein are fertile Meddowes, pleasant springs, delightful Streames, and all sorts of beasts of chace and game, and in the middest thereof a sumptuous house of pleasure . . ." For three hours Coleridge dreamily wandered through an enchanting land, experiencing sights, sounds and fragrances denied one in waking hours. The real world was forgotten; the past had never happened, the future not thought of. As the opium wore off Coleridge awoke with a distinct recollection of his vision and instantly wrote down the lines of "Kubla Khan." When he had written the line "And drunk the milk of Paradise" a creditor entered the house and insisted that the poet accompany him to Porlock. Coleridge returned to the farmhouse an hour or so later but could not add another line—the magic of his vision was gone.

This "archangel a little damaged," in Lamb's phrase, returned to his wife and children, but his creative powers quickly waned and his irresponsibility and procrastination made it difficult for him to cope with the world of reality.

> In Xanadu did Kubla Khan
> A stately pleasure-dome decree:
> Where Alph, the sacred river, ran
> Through caverns measureless to man
> Down to a sunless sea.
> So twice five miles of fertile ground
> With walls and towers were girdled round:
> And there were gardens bright with sinuous rills,
> Where blossomed many an incense-bearing tree;
> And here were forests ancient as the hills,
> Enfolding sunny spots of greenery.
>
> But O! that deep romantic chasm which slanted
> Down the green hill athwart a cedarn cover!
> A savage place! as holy and enchanted
> As e'er beneath a waning moon was haunted
> By woman wailing for her demon-lover!
> And from this chasm, with ceaseless turmoil seething,
> As if this Earth in fast thick pants were breathing,
> A mighty fountain momently was forced,

Amid whose swift half-intermitted burst
Huge fragments vaulted like rebounding hail,
Or chaffy grain beneath the thresher's flail:

And 'mid these dancing rocks at once and ever
It flung up momently the sacred river.
Five miles meandering with a mazy motion
Through wood and dale the sacred river ran,
Then reached the caverns measureless to man,
And sank in tumult to a lifeless ocean:
And 'mid this tumult Kubla heard from far
Ancestral voices prophesying war!

  The shadow of the dome of pleasure
  Floated midway on the waves;
  Where was heard the mingled measure
  From the fountain and the caves.
It was a miracle of rare device,
A sunny pleasure-dome with caves of ice!

  A damsel with a dulcimer
  In a vision once I saw:
  It was an Abyssinian maid,
  And on her dulcimer she played,
  Singing of Mount Abora.
  Could I revive within me
  Her symphony and song,
  To such a deep delight 'twould win me
That with music loud and long,
I would build that dome in air,
That sunny dome! those caves of ice!
And all who heard should see them there,
And all should cry, Beware! Beware!
His flashing eyes, his floating hair!
Weave a circle round him thrice,
And close your eyes with holy dread,
For he on honey-dew hath fed,
And drunk the milk of Paradise.

ABRAHAM COWLEY (1618-1667)

The Wish

In his essay "Of Myself," Cowley relates that as far back in his life as he could remember, he always yearned for solitude away from the haunts of man. In fact, when he was thirteen he wrote the familiar ode which begins:

> "This only grant me, that my means may lie
> Too low for envy, for contempt too high."

However, it was years before Cowley achieved the sought-for isolation—and then with surprising results. He was destined first to become deeply involved in the political strife of his day.

Soon after entering Cambridge he was ejected for his royalist sympathies. He then entered Oxford, where the royalists were headquartered. When Queen Henrietta Maria left England for France, Cowley joined her there and remained twelve years, engaging in political intrigues and missions in behalf of King Charles. Six years after Charles was beheaded, and when the Puritan regime began to totter, Cowley ventured back to England only to be arrested as a spy and released on bail. Following Cromwell's death Cowley returned to France, remaining there until the Restoration came several years later.

Once more back in England at the age of forty, with the bright literary promise of his youth practically extinguished, Cowley was confident that the Restoration would reward his loyalty with political preferment. But doubts concerning him were raised in some antagonistic quarters. His wishes were ignored.

Cowley explains that never during these years of great activity "contrary to the original design of my life" and "daily sights of greatness" did it "bewitch or entice me when I saw it was adulterate." His position was not unlike that of many a person today who becomes enmeshed in a system, organization or pattern of life and finds it difficult to break away from it. Thus Cowley's "The Wish"—written at this time—expresses the sentiments of many people today who would like to flee "The crowd, the buzz, and murmurings/Of this great hive, the city."

And, no doubt, some of us would react as Cowley did when he had his wish. The melancholy poet was granted a lease on some lands belonging to the Queen and each year given a respectable retirement fund. Here he had his fields, gardens, plants and a pleasant house. But the phantom he had pursued turned on him when he embraced it. He had the place of his dreams and didn't like it, or the people. Seven years later he died, after sleeping in the fields through which he had walked one night while drunk.

> Well, then, I now do plainly see
> This busy world and I shall ne'er agree;
> The very honey of all earthly joy
>   Does of all meats the soonest cloy.
>   And they, methinks, deserve my pity,
> Who fit it can endure the stings,
> The crowd, and buzz, and murmurings
>   Of this great hive, the city.
>
> Ah! yet I ere descend to th' grave,
> May I a small house and large garden have,
> And a few friends, and many books, both true,
>   Both wise, and both delightful too!
>   And since love ne'er will from me flee,
> A mistress moderately fair,
> And good as guardian angels are,
>   Only beloved, and loving me!
>
> O fountains! when in you shall I
> Myself eased of unpeaceful thoughts, espy?
> O fields! O woods! when, when shall I be made
>   The happy tenant of your shade?
>   Here's the spring-head of Pleasure's flood,
> Where all the riches lie, that she
> Has coined and stamped for good.
>
> Pride and ambition here
> Only in far-fetched metaphors appear;
> Here nought but winds can hurtful murmurs scatter,
>   And nought but Echo flatter.
>   The gods, when they descend hither
> From heaven, did always choose their way;
> And therefore we may boldly say,
>   That 'tis the way to thither.
>
> How happy here should I,
> And one dear She live, and embracing die!
> She who is all the world, and can exclude
>   In deserts solitude.
>   I should have then this only fear,
> Lest men, when they my pleasures see,
> Should hither throng to live like me,
>   And so make a city here.

WILLIAM COWPER (1731-1800)

Light Shining Out of Darkness
To Mary Unwin

The casual reader of Cowper's poetry, and of his delightful letters, is given little or no indication that his adult life was blighted by long spells of extreme melancholia and morbid despair. And yet the recurring mental breakdowns at least indirectly resulted in several of his finest poems.

Whatever the cause of his mental difficulties (some say cruel fagging at school, others blame it on his Calvinism), at the age of thirty-five gentle, shy Cowper had apparently reached the end of his road: early disappointed in love, a failure in the practice of law, spared from the success of several attempts at suicide only by his blundering; without funds, forgotten by the few friends he had, unknown as a poet. His situation was so desperate that relatives settled an allowance upon him.

Then occurred the providential turning point in the life of this frightened man. In Huntingdon he met the Reverend Morley Unwin and soon became a boarder in the Unwin home. When Mr. Unwin died some months later, Cowper continued on as a boarder and moved with the family to Olney. This was his refuge from the world, where he participated fully in the family life and became an expert gardener, florist, and raiser of domestic animals.

But however congenial this life was for Cowper, he did not free himself of the mental seizures. In fact, all during 1773 he was in a deep melancholia, cared for by Reverend John Newton and Mrs. Unwin, and by them prevented from the suicide the tormented poet thought God desired of him.

It was before and after this dreadful attack that Cowper contributed to a book of hymns, the "Olney Hymns," that Newton was preparing for publication. And it was during one of his calm and hopeful phases that Cowper looked unafraid into the darkness and with the eyes of faith saw "Light Shining Out of Darkness":

> God moves in a mysterious way
> His wonders to perform;
> He plants his footsteps in the sea,
> And rides upon the storm.
>
> Deep in unfathomable mines
> Of never-failing skill,
> He treasures up his bright designs,
> And works his sovereign will.

Ye fearful saints, fresh courage take,
The clouds ye so much dread
Are big with mercy, and shall break
In blessings on your head.

Judge not the Lord by feeble sense,
But trust him for his grace;
Behind a frowning providence
He hides a smiling face.

His purposes will ripen fast,
Unfolding every hour;
The bud may have a bitter taste,
But sweet will be the flower.

Blind unbelief is sure to err,
And scan his work in vain:
God is His own interpreter,
And He will make it plain.

From his earliest days in the Unwin home Cowper was attracted to Mrs. Mary Unwin, a prim but cheerful Puritan lady of strong religious convictions. She and Cowper lived in affectionate but chaste companionship, and they would probably have married but for a dream Cowper had wherein he became convinced he was sentenced to damnation.

Over the years Mary Unwin gave the poet love and care he could not have received anywhere else. Fascinating and charming as Cowper often was, he was also a heavy burden to Mrs. Unwin because of his neurotic introspection and self-pity, and his protracted spells of morbidity. Nevertheless here he lived as congenially as could be expected, thanks to Mary Unwin's compassionate care and understanding.

Eventually Cowper had the opportunity to render somewhat similar attention to Mrs. Unwin, and to his credit he did not shrink from tasks difficult to one of his nature. In late 1787 Mary Unwin was badly burned; several months later she fell and was crippled for months, and then she suffered a series of strokes, each more damaging than its predecessor. During the seven years of Mrs. Unwin's repeated illnesses and almost steady decline, Cowper fought off despair, nursed her tenderly and two years before her death in 1795 wrote his poignant "To Mary Unwin"—a beautiful payment of his debt of gratitude. After her death Cowper never mentioned her name, spent his remaining five years of life listlessly and in 1800 was buried next to his Mary.

The twentieth year is well-nigh past
Since first our sky was overcast;
Ah would that this might be the last!
    My Mary!

Thy spirits have a fainter flow,
I see thee daily weaker grow—
'Twas my distress that brought thee low,
    My Mary!

Thy needles, once a shining store,
For my sake restless heretofore,
Now rust disused, and shine no more;
    My Mary!

For though thou gladly wouldst fulfil
The same kind office for me still,
Thy sight now seconds not thy will,
    My Mary!

But well thou play'dst the housewife's part,
And all thy threads with magic art
Have wound themselves about this heart,
    My Mary!

Thy indistinct expressions seem
Like language utter'd in a dream;
Yet me they charm, whate'er the theme,
    My Mary!

Thy silver locks, once auburn bright,
Are still more lovely in my sight,
Than golden beams of orient light,
    My Mary!

For could I view nor them nor thee,
What sight worth seeing could I see?
The sun would rise in vain for me,
    My Mary!

Partakers of thy sad decline,
Thy hands their little force resign;
Yet, gently pressed, press gently mine,
    My Mary!

Such feebleness of limbs thou prov'st,
That now at every step thou mov'st
Upheld by two; yet still thou lov'st,
    My Mary!

And still to love, thou pressed with ill,
In wintry age to feel no chill,
With me is to be lovely still,
    My Mary!

But ah! by constant heed I know
How oft the sadness that I show
Transforms thy smiles to looks of woe,
    My Mary!

And should my future lot be cast
With much resemblance of the past,
Thy worn-out heart will break at last—
    My Mary!

EMILY DICKINSON (1830-1886)

A Selection of Ten Love-Poems

Any reasonably curious reader of the poems of Emily Dickinson will inevitably wonder about this most elusive woman and the full meaning of her many cryptic allusions. Not that her poems lack essential clarity, but simply that her playful reticence tempts inquiry and invites speculation.

This is particularly true of the hundreds of love-poems the secluded spinster wrote and secreted in the Dickinson family home in Amherst, Massachusetts, which were found and published after her death. Her biographers (the best of whom is George F. Whicher) have attempted to discover the story behind these love-poems; none have been able to do more than conjecture from fragmentary evidence.

It is highly improbable that so many impassioned utterances would come wholly from her rich imagination, especially since the poems contain a number of references to specific incidents that are paralleled by known happenings in the life of this intensely individual and uncompromising artist.

When the legends about Emily Dickinson are put aside, there still remain enough facts to form the framework of a love story that the poems themselves enrich.

It is known, for instance, that following her year at Mount Holyoke Seminary she had at least a deeply satisfying intellectual companionship with B. F. Newton, employed in her father's law office; "I have found a beautiful new friend," she wrote in 1848. After two years Newton returned to his home in Worcester, but corresponded with Emily until his unexpected death. Nine years later Emily said in a letter: "I had a friend who taught me Immortality, but venturing too near, himself, he never returned." And again, "I was old enough to admire the strength, the grace, of an intellect far surpassing my own . . . When he went from us, it was as an older brother, loved very much, indeed." If Newton did not stir Emily romantically, he was certainly a great influence in her life and his death left her lonely and depressed.

As the heart-ache from Newton's death eased, it was replaced by a different and more lasting feeling. In 1854 Emily, who was twenty-three, was on a rare trip away from Amherst, with her family. In Philadelphia she met Reverend Charles Wadsworth, a happily married, forty-year-old minister of great force and dedication. In later years Emily referred to him as "the atom I preferred to all the lists of clay," her "dearest earthly friend," and the "fugitive whom to know was life."

Although she cherished this man above all others, there is not even a hint that he returned her love or that there was any romantic alliance between them. He was firm and intensely moral, of great eloquence, dignity and compassion.

When Emily returned to Amherst they corresponded; frequently, she intimated. In 1860 Mr. Wadsworth called on her at Amherst when he was visiting friends in a nearby town. He *may* have visited her on one or more other occasions. Two years later he accepted a pastorate in California. Emily's letters and poems of this period indicate she was desperately staving off some kind of crisis, and apparently Mr. Wadsworth was involved in it, whether he knew it or not.

In any event, during the twenty years that passed before Emily saw Mr. Wadsworth again, she put her heart's troubles and messages into her poetry, while more and more withdrawing from the world until she became a legendary recluse. During these years she corresponded with this "fathomless" man whom she adored.

Then suddenly, in 1880, Mr. Wadsworth visited her one summer evening in Amherst. Apparently it was her last meeting with the "dim companion" whom she knew only "in vision and veto," the yearning for whom she once called "the old nail in my breast." Wadsworth died two years later; Emily lingered for four more years. But her love lives on in her poems, as illustrated by the following ones:

Of all the souls that stand create
I have elected one.
When sense from spirit flies away
And subterfuge is done;

When that which is and that which was
Apart, intrinsic, stand,
And this brief tragedy of flesh
Is shifted like a sand:

When figures show their royal front
And mists are carved away,—
Behold the atom I preferred
To all the lists of clay!

*   *   *   *

I gave myself to him,
And took himself for pay.
The solemn contract of a life
Was ratified this way.

The wealth might disappoint,
Myself a poorer prove
Than this great purchaser suspect,
The daily own of Love

Depreciate the vision;
But, till the merchant buy,
Still fable, in the isles of spice,
The subtle cargoes lie.

At least 't is a mutual risk,—
Some found it mutual gain;
Sweet debt of Life,—each night to owe,
Insolvent, every noon.

*   *   *   *

Mine by the right of the white election!
Mine by the royal seal!
Mine by the sign in the scarlet prison
Bars cannot conceal!

Mine, here in vision and in veto!
Mine, by the grave's repeal

Titled, confirmed,—delirious charter!
Mine, while the ages steal!

* * * *

You left me, sweet, two legacies,—
A legacy of love
A Heavenly Father would content,
Had He the offer of;

You left me boundaries of pain
Capacious as the sea,
Between eternity and time,
Your consciousness and me.

* * * *

Elysium is as far as to
The very nearest room,
If in that room a friend await
Felicity or doom.

What fortitude the soul contains,
That it can so endure
The accent of a coming foot,
The opening of a door!

* * * *

If you were coming in the fall,
I'd brush the summer by
With half a smile and half a spurn,
As housewives do a fly.

If I could see you in a year,
I'd wind the months in balls,
And put them each in separate drawers,
Until their time befalls.

If only centuries delayed,
I'd count them on my hand,
Subtracting till my fingers dropped
Into Van Diemen's land.

If certain, when this life was out,
That yours and mine should be,
I'd toss it yonder like a rind,
And taste eternity.

But now, all ignorant of the length
Of time's uncertain wing,
It goad me, like the goblin bee,
That will not state its sting.

* * * *

Wild night! Wild nights!
Were I with thee,
Wild nights should be
Our luxury!

Futile the winds
To a heart in port,—
Done with the compass,
Done with the chart.

Rowing in Eden!
Ah! the sea!
Might I but moor
To-night in thee!

* * * *

I cannot live with you,
It would be life,
And life is over there
Behind the shelf.

The sexton keeps the keys to,
Putting up
Our life, his porcelain,
Like a cup

Discarded of the houswife,
Quaint or broken;
A newer Sèvres pleases,
Old ones crack.

I could not die with you,
For one must wait
To shut the other's gaze down,—
You could not.

And I, could I stand by
And see you freeze,

Without my right of frost,
Death's privilege?

Nor could I rise with you,
Because your face
Would out Jesus',
That new grace

Glow plain and foreign
On my homesick eye,
Except that you, than he
Shone closer by.

They'd judge us—how?
For you served Heaven, you know,
Or sought to;
I could not,
Because you saturated sight,
And I had no more eyes
For sordid excellence
As Paradise.

And were you lost, I would be,
Though my name
Rang loudest
On the heavenly fame.

And were you saved,
And I condemned to be
Where you were not,
That self were hell to me.

So we must keep apart,
You there, I here,
With just the door ajar
That oceans are,
And prayer,
And that pale sustenance,
Despair!

* * * *

There came a day at summer's full
Entirely for me;
I thought that such were for the saints,
Where revelations be.

The sun, as common, went abroad,
The flowers, accustomed, blew,
As if no soul the solstice passed
That maketh all things new.

The time was scarce profaned by speech;
The symbol of a word
Was needless, as at sacrament
The wardrobe of our Lord.

Each was to each the sealed church,
Permitted to commune this time,
Lest we too awkward show
At supper of the Lamb.

The hours slid fast, as hours will,
Clutched tight by greedy hands;
So faces on two decks look back,
Bound to opposing lands.

And so, when all the time had failed,
Without external sound,
Each bound the other crucifix,
We gave no other bond.

Sufficient troth that we shall rise—
Deposed, at length, the grave—
To that new marriage, justified
Through Calvaries of Love!

* * * *

That I did always love,
I bring thee proof:
That till I loved
I did not love enough.

That I shall love alway,
I offer thee
That love is life,
And life hath immortality.

This, dost thou doubt, sweet?
Then have I
Nothing to show
But Calvary.

JOHN DONNE (1573-1631)

"Sweetest Love, I Do Not Go"
A Valediction Forbidding Mourning

John Donne was extremely reticent about his personal life, but his poetry reveals significant phases of his spiritual and emotional life because of the essential veracity of his writing.

The "Divine Poems," for example, written immediately after Donne completed his studies at Oxford, reveal his Catholic heritage and his sincere attachment to that Church.

Then suddenly there is a reaction from the asceticism to which he had been bred. While the breach between Catholicism and Anglicanism widened, Donne embarked upon a career of travel and sensualism. There was little the brilliant young scholar did not experience during this phase of arrogant skepticism. It culminated when he fell in love with a woman married to a wealthy man who was deformed and incapacitated. She offered little or no resistance to the headstrong youth, who apparently did not hesitate to violate the husband's hospitality by conducting an on-the-premises liaison with the unfaithful wife. During this affair the future Dean of St. Paul's wrote some of the most sensual poetry in the English language, including the famous "Love's War." But after a year or so the affair's termination was recorded in a series of poems: "The Curse," "The Message," "The Will," and finally "The Apparition."

Donne then entered upon a more tender, truer and deeper love affair. He had become secretary to Lord Ellesmere, and in his home met sixteen-year-old Anne More, Lady Ellesmere's niece and the daughter of Sir George More. Since Donne worked in the Ellesmere home and Anne visited there for protracted periods, they had ample opportunities to conduct a clandestine love affair.

After two years of furtive love-making, Donne and Anne married secretly in late 1602, in violation of canon and civil law which required the consent of the bride's father. When Sir George learned of the marriage he was so furious he confined Anne to her parents' home, prevailed upon Lord Ellesmere to discharge Donne, and then had the poet imprisoned.

Donne effected his release from prison after a short time and rejoined Anne after the gentle girl refused to be dissuaded by her father's efforts to blacken Donne's reputation. Sir George soon relented and gave the couple his blessing—but nothing else. During the fifteen years of married life Donne and his Anne's love for each other remained true and strong.

This is beautifully revealed by two of Donne's finest poems, written in

1612, when he was in his fortieth year. He was planning to make a trip to France. Anne, in the late stages of one of her frequent pregnancies, asked her husband to forego the trip, explaining that she had a premonition harm would come to him. Donne first acceded to her wishes but at the urging of friends changed his mind and decided to go. Anne then relented, but with misgivings. When Donne was in France he had a vision of Anne with a dead baby in her arms—which later proved accurate in that while her husband was away Anne was delivered of a child born dead. However, before Donne left for France he wrote to Anne the two following poems, the latter of which, "A Valediction Forbidding Mourning," has been hailed as his finest.

Donne's enduring love for his wife is suggested by his desolation when she died in 1617, worn out from the birth of twelve children in fifteen years, seven of which survived her. Donne promised his older children that he would not marry again—a promise he kept.

> Sweetest love, I do not go
>   For weariness of thee,
> Nor in hope the world can show
>   A fitter Love for me:
>   But since that I
> Must die at last, 'tis best
> To use myself in jest
>   Thus by feigned deaths to die.
>
> Yesternight the sun went hence
>   And yet is here to-day;
> He hath no desire nor sense,
>   Nor half so short a way.
>   Then fear not me,
> But believe that I shall make
> Speedier journeys, since I take
>   More wings and spurs than he.
>
> Oh, how feeble is man's power,
>   That, if good fortune fall,
> Cannot add another hour,
>   Nor a lost hour recall!
>   But come bad chance,
> And we join it to our strength,
> And we teach it art and length,
>   Itself o'er us to advance.
>
> When thou sigh'st, thou sigh'st not wind,
>   But sigh'st my soul away;

When thou weep'st, unkindly kind,
  My life's blood doth decay.
    It cannot be
That thou lov'st me as thou say'st,
If in thine my life thou waste;
  Thou art the best of me.

Let not thy divining heart
  Forethink me any ill;
Destiny may take thy part,
  And may thy fears fulfill:
    But think that we
Are but turned aside to sleep:
They who one another keep
  Alive, ne'er parted be.

* * * * *

As virtuous men pass mildly away,
  And whisper to their souls to go,
Whilst some of their sad friends do say,
  "The breath goes now," and some say "No";

So let us melt and make no noise,
  No tear-floods nor sigh-tempests move;
'Twere profanation of our joys
  To tell the laity our love.

Moving of th' earth brings harms and fears;
  Men reckon what it did and meant;
But trepidation of the spheres,
  Though greater far, is innocent.

Dull sublunary lovers' love
  (Whose soul is sense) cannot admit
Absence, because it doth remove
  Those things which elemented it.

But we by a love so much refined
  That ourselves know not what it is,
Inter-assurèd of the mind,
  Careless eyes, lips, and hands to miss.

Our two souls, therefore, which are one,
  Though I must go, endure not yet

A breach, but an expansion,
　　Like gold to airy thinness beat.

If they be two, they are two so
　　As stiff twin compasses are two;
Thy soul, the fixt foot, makes no show
　　To move, but both do if the other do.

And though it in the center sit,
　　Yet when the other far doth roam,
It leans and harkens after it,
　　And grows erect as that comes home.

Such wilt thou be to me, who must
　　Like th' other foot, obliquely run;
Thy firmness makes my circle just,
　　And makes me end, where I begun.

ERNEST DOWSON (1867-1900)

Non Sum Qualis Eram Bonae Sub Rego Cynarae

Who was "Cynara?" Many have wondered; no one can be positive. But there are abundant clues in Dowson's life; the life of a man far more dissolute and weak-willed than the beautiful lyric suggests.

The poet's childhood and youth foreshadowed the man he would become. His parents were prosperous and cultured but with a predisposition to tuberculosis that made them preoccupied with their health, and gave the home a weary, morbid atmosphere. The child's training suffered as a consequence. He had no religious teaching, there were gaps in his education because he accompanied his parents on their frequent trips in search of health, he rarely mingled with other children, and nothing was done to bolster the child's own frailty.

Dowson entered Oxford at nineteen, pale, shy, five feet seven inches, weighing one hundred and twenty pounds, devoid of competitive instinct and interested only in literature. His university years were morose and embittered, relieved by experiments with various narcotics and considerable drinking.

After Oxford, Dowson worked as a bookkeeper in his father's London business, and spent the nights in continual drinking and carousing. One day in

1891 he went into a cheap but respectable restaurant known as Poland, in the Soho section. While there he was immediately attracted to the freshness and innocence of the proprietor's twelve-year-old daughter, Adelaide Faltinowicz. The poet was delighted by the artless charm and grace of the dark-haired girl who wore her youthful beauty without affectation. He began to go nightly to the restaurant to see Adelaide. Her parents were friendly but never encouraged Dowson's interest in their carefully protected daughter.

Before long Dowson, who associated with libertines and patronized prostitutes, became interested in the unspoiled twelve-year-old girl; or perhaps more accurately, he was charmed by the loveliness and sweet innocence the child embodied.

One evening in 1891 Dowson stopped, as was his habit, at a bar named The Cock, before going to Poland for supper. Here he often sat in a corner and wrote poems. On this particular evening he wrote his famous "Cynara" poem, which on publication was highly praised by literary London. Dowson himself believed it was his best work.

But who was Cynara? Many have stated without qualification that it was Adelaide. And it may well be that she was the one whom Dowson had in mind, especially since the fact she was twelve or thirteen and he twenty-four would not likely occur to him as an impediment to an idealized love. On the other hand, it was *after* the poem was written that the poet's love for her became serious.

A more likely solution is suggested by Dowson's most recent biographer, Mark Longaker. He observed that "Cynara" might well have been a composite of Dowson's tenuous ideals—his art, the Catholicism he adopted but seldom practiced, his quest of beauty, his paradoxical devotion to innocence, and Adelaide—to all of them he had been unfaithful by his habitually heavy drinking and sordid affairs with bar maids, models, chorus girls and streetwalkers.

In any case, Dowson continued to love Adelaide the rest of his brief life, even when she married a waiter. After a brief flurry of success, the poet contracted tuberculosis, his parents committed suicide, and he became a slovenly sot who lived in the lowest dives of Limehouse. He collapsed and died at the age of thirty-two.

Dowson's delicate poetry, giving no hint of his real life, must have been the pathetic man's only escape from a world with which he could not cope. And surely Adelaide deeply influenced that poetry, the best of which was written after he met her.

> Last night, ah, yesternight, betwixt her lips and mine
> There fell thy shadow, Cynara! thy breath was shed
> Upon my soul between the kisses and the wine;

And I was desolate and sick of an old passion,
    Yea, I was desolate and bowed my head:
I have been faithful to thee, Cynara! in my fashion.

All night upon mine heart I felt her warm heart beat,
Night-long within mine arms in love and sleep she lay;
Surely the kisses of her bought red mouth were sweet;
But I was desolate and sick of an old passion,
    When I awoke and found the dawn was grey:
I have been faithful to thee, Cynara! in my fashion.

I have forgot much, Cynara! gone with the wind,
Flung roses, roses riotously with the throng,
Dancing, to put thy pale, lost lilies out of mind;
But I was desolate and sick of an old passion,
    Yea, all the time, because the dance was long:
I have been faithful to thee, Cynara! in my fashion.

I cried for madder music and for stronger wine;
But when the feast is finished and the lamps expire,
Then falls thy shadow, Cynara! the night is thine;
And I am desolate and sick of an old passion,
    Yea, hungry for the lips of my desire:
I have been faithful to thee, Cynara! in my fashion.

MICHAEL DRAYTON (1563-1631)

Since There's No Help
So Well I Love Thee

Toward the close of his life Michael Drayton, a somewhat lonely bachelor of quiet and frugal habits, said in a letter to a friend: "When I love I love for years." And his lifetime friendship with Anne Goodere proves he spoke the truth.

He met Anne when he lived as a page at Polesworth Hall near Athertone, England, the home of her father, Sir Henry Goodere. Here Drayton got a good home and training, and in later years, paid grateful tribute to Sir Henry's memory as "the first cherisher of my muse" and to "the happy and generous family of the Gooderes."

Anne was Sir Henry's youngest daughter and reported as beautiful and "of a gallant structure of body." She and Drayton grew up together. But the poet said he did not "lose his wit" on her account until he was twenty-eight. It was probably then that he began to write the sonnets later published as "Ideas's Mirror"; "Idea" being Anne Goodere.

Even after Anne married Sir Henry Rainsford, in 1596, Drayton continued to sing her praises in gallant terms. But, too, Anne's husband became Drayton's good friend and welcomed the poet every summer to Clifford Hall, their country home. Gradually the alchemy of time appeared to change Drayton's passion into a deep friendship, one that remained so after the death of Anne's husband in 1622.

And yet, it is not difficult to suppose that in these later years Drayton still subscribed to the sentiments of the last two lines of his most famous sonnet to Anne:

> Since there's no help, come, let us kiss and part,—
> Nay I have done, you get no more of me;
> And I am glad, yea glad with all my heart,
> That thus so cleanly I myself can free;
> Shake hands for ever, cancel all our vows,
> And when we meet at any time again,
> Be it not seen in either of our brows
> That we one jot of former love retain.
> Now at the last gasp of Love's latest breath,
> When his pulse failing, Passion speechless lies,
> When Faith is kneeling by his bed of death,
> And Innocence is closing up his eyes,—
>> Now if thou would'st, when all have given him over,
>> From death to life thou migh'st him yet recover!

In fact, the night before he died at sixty-eight, the tired old man still loved Anne and addressed to her these final exquisite lines of adoration:

> So well I love thee, as without thee I
> Love Nothing; if I might Choose, I'd rather die
> Than be one day debarred thy company.
>
> Since Beasts, and plants do grow, and live and move,
> Beasts are those men, that such a life approve:
> He only Lives, that Deadly is in Love.
>
> The Corn that in the ground is sown first dies
> And of one seed do many Ears arise:
> Love, this world's Corn, by dying Multiplies.
>
> The seeds of Love first by thy eyes were thrown
> Into a ground untilled, a heart unknown
> To bear such fruit, till by thy hands t'was sown.

Look as your Looking glass by Chance may fall
Divide and break in many pieces small
And yet show forth, the self same face in all;

Proportions, Features, Graces just the same,
And in the smallest piece as well the name
Of Fairest one deserves, as in the richest frame.

So all my Thoughts are pieces but of you
Which put together make a glass so true
As I therein no other's face but yours can View.

RALPH WALDO EMERSON (1803-1882)

Good-Bye
The Concord Hymn

It is hardly surprising that America's most eloquent spokesman for self-reliant individualism should have, at the age of twenty, bid so emphatic a farewell to the town and urban turmoil as in his "Good-Bye."

It is even more understandable when we recall the nature and circumstances of the poet. Emerson was an unhappy youth after his graduation from Harvard. His health was not good; he fretted for fear his abilities were unequal to his ambitions; he disliked the teaching he was engaged in at a girls' school in Boston run by his brother; he was undecided about pursuing the ministerial career his mother so fervently desired; he could not reconcile his ideals and his belief that nature reveals spirit, with life in the Boston he was born and raised in. At this time he wrote: "The dreams of my childhood are all fading away and giving place to some very sober and very very disgusting views of a quiet mediocrity of talents and conditions." In brief, Emerson was a delicate, sensitive, idealistic and extremely thoughtful young man who had not yet found himself and yearned for solitude to discover what he believed and should do with his life.

When Emerson's mother moved from Boston to a farmhouse in the rough and wooded countryside of Roxbury, Massachusetts, four miles from Boston, the delighted teacher-scholar-philosopher-poet wrote his farewell to the urban masses, noise, materialism and vulgarity.

In later years Emerson learned to retain his independence in the midst of crowds. And in his old age his dislike of this poem "Good-Bye" was so intense he would not permit its inclusion in his *Selected Poems*. But posterity has not shared his distaste of it.

> Good-bye, proud world! I'm going home:
> Thou art not my friend, and I'm not thine.
> Long through thy weary crowds I roam;
> A river-ark on the ocean brine,
> Long I've been tossed like the driven foam;
> But now, proud world! I'm going home.
>
> Good-bye to Flattery's fawning face;
> To Grandeur with his wise grimace;
> To upstart Wealth's averted eye;
> To supple Office, low and high;
> To crowded halls, to court and street;
> To frozen hearts and hasting feet;
> To those who go, and those who come;
> Good-bye, proud world! I'm going home.
>
> I am going to my own hearth-stone,
> Bosomed in yon green hills alone,—
> A secret nook in a pleasant land,
> Whose groves the frolic fairies planned;
> Where arches green, the livelong day,
> Echo the blackbird's roundelay,
> And vulgar feet have never trod
> A spot that is sacred to thought and God.
>
> O, when I am safe in my sylvan home,
> I tread on the pride of Greece and Rome;
> And when I am stretched beneath the pines,
> Where the evening star so holy shines,
> I laugh at the lore and the pride of man,
> At the sophist schools and the learned clan;
> For what are they all, in their high conceit,
> When man in the bush with God may meet?

Sixty years after the American colonists fought the British redcoats at Concord Bridge, Emerson's grandfather, Reverend Ezra Ripley, offered the town of Concord a piece of land on condition it should be fenced with heavy stone and a monument commemorating the battle be erected by July 4, 1837.

It was natural that Concord officials should turn to Emerson for appropriate stanzas that could be sung to the familiar music of *One Hundred* at the monument's dedication. It was fitting not only because Emerson was the town's leading intellect, but also because two hundred years earlier one of the poet's ancestors was one of the town's founders, and since that time the community's pulpit had been occupied by a succession of Emerson forebears. Moreover, Emerson had played his part in American history. When he was nine years old he and other children were dismissed from school to help in the building of earthen breastworks for that city's defense in the War of 1812.

However, the discriminating among the many gathered at the elaborate exercises the afternoon of July 4, 1837, may well have been surprised when Dr. Ripley stepped forward and read, before the choir (which included Henry David Thoreau) sang, the glowing lines written for the occasion by the coldly intellectual Emerson, who that day was visiting in Plymouth, Massachusetts.

Here was emotion the common man could understand and subscribe to; here was poetry one would hardly expect from an introspective thinker whose verse was highly intellectualized and often lacked metrical appeal.

There is a not unusual irony in the fact that these few quickly dashed-off lines immediately became popular and eventually a part of the American tradition, whereas Emerson's many more carefully thought and wrought poems never achieved popularity.

A pleasant sequel to *The Concord Hymn* is that Concord celebrated the centennial of the famous skirmish by commissioning Daniel Chester French to sculpture a statue, "The Minute Man," with lines from Emerson's poem engraved on the base.

By the rude bridge that arched the flood,
    Their flag to April's breeze unfurled,
Here once the embattled farmers stood,
    And fired the shot heard round the world.

The foe long since in silence slept;
    Alike the conqueror silent sleeps;
And Time the ruined bridge has swept
    Down the dark stream which seaward creeps.

On this green bank, by this soft stream,
    We set today a votive stone;
That memory may their deed redeem,
    When, like our sires, our sons are gone.

Spirit, that made those heroes dare
    To die, and leave their children free,
Bid Time and Nature gently spare
    The shaft we raise to them and thee.

EDWARD FITZGERALD (1809-1883)

Rubáiyát of Omar Khayyám

If Edward Fitzgerald had not met Edward Byles Cowell, a noted Oriental scholar, he would have remained an unremembered English gentleman of comfortable means and eccentric habits who spent his life writing occasional poems, studying languages, reading classics and translating various rather obscure works for the pleasure it gave him.

But Cowell's influence led to Fitzgerald's fame when he encouraged the "silent Vesuvius" to learn Persian, which in 1853 he began to do indifferently but with quickened interest when he encountered Firdusi's *Gulisan* and turned to translating Sádi and Jámi. He was soon deeply immersed in Oriental literature.

In July, 1856, Cowell made and gave to Fitzgerald a transcript of a rare Persian manuscript he found in the Bodleian Library, London. It was the rubáiyát, or quatrains, of Omar Khayyám, an eleventh-century poet of Nai-shápúr, virtually unknown in the West but in his own day and land famous as a philosopher, astronomer, and denounced as a free thinker.

Fitzgerald liked these "curious Infidel and Epicurean Testratichs." He found in Omar a temperament akin to his own: a lover of beauty, a senti-mental recollection of past glories and delights, and a sad recognition that all pleasures quickly end. Fitzgerald agreed with Omar that man's spirit finally becomes trapped and nothing can be done about it.

The melancholy, fastidious scholar wandered leisurely through an entire year, brooding and dabbling with his Omar manuscript. He wrote that "Omar breathes a sort of consolation to me. Poor Fellow; I think of him, and Oliver Basselin, and Anacreon; lighter Shadows among the Shades, perhaps, over which Lucretius presides so grimly."

Then Fitzgerald earnestly began to mine this ore, turning it into the gold of stately rhythmic musings, touching it with cynical smiles and gentle pathos, yet making it lucid and epigrammatic. Unwittingly and with no thought of fame, the retiring scholar who delighted in unknown little books had encountered one that was perfectly fitted to his temperament, and to which he could bring imaginative editing and his superb skill in preserving the thought and spirit while both simplifying and embellishing. Fitzgerald never lost his fondness for Omar, whom he affectionately called "the old Sinner." After the quatrains' first publication he fussed over them for years, constantly retouching and altering.

Stranger than the conjunction of manuscript and translator, was the fate of the 250 pamphlet-volumes of the *Rubáiyát* Fitzgerald had printed at his own expense, and which a London bookseller offered at one shilling each in 1859. Not a copy was sold, not one review or notice of it appeared. When the bookseller cut the price to one penny, an unknown passer-by bought a few copies and gave them to friends. Rossetti and Swinburne were among the recipients and they promptly bought copies and the poems became popular among a select group that had no idea who had done the translating. Nine years later Charles Eliot Norton, while visiting London, was handed a copy of the *Rubáiyát* and gave the volume its first public recognition with an enthusiastic notice in the *North American Review*. The book quickly became popular in the United States, and two years later began to receive notice in England, especially when Fitzgerald's role became known.

Fitzgerald's first version contains 101 quatrains. Here are the best-known and more popular of the quatrains.

> Wake! For the Sun who scattered into flight
> The Stars before him from the Field of Night,
>   Drives Night along with them from Heaven, and strikes
> The Sultán's Turret with a Shaft of Light.

> Before the phantom of False morning died,
> Methought a Voice within the Tavern cried,
>   "When all the Temple is prepared within,
> Why nods the drowsy Worshiper outside?"

                         .   .   .   .

> Come, fill the Cup, and in the fire of Spring
> Your Winter-garment of Repentance fling:
>   The Bird of Time has but a little way
> To flutter—and the Bird is on the Wing.

> Whether at Naishápúr or Babylon,
> Whether the Cup with sweet or bitter run,
>   The Wine of Life keeps oozing drop by drop,
> The Leaves of Life keep falling one by one.

                         .   .   .   .

II

> A Book of Verses underneath the Bough,
> A Jug of Wine, a Loaf of Bread—and Thou
>   Beside me singing in the Wilderness—
> Oh, Wilderness were Paradise enow!

Some for the Glories of this World; and some
Sigh for the Prophet's Paradise to come;
   Ah, take the Cash, and let the Credit go,
Nor heed the rumble of a Distant Drum!

Look to the blowing Rose about us—"Lo,
Laughing," she says, "into the world I blow,
   At once the silken tassel of my Purse
Tear, and its Treasures on the Garden throw."

And those who husbanded the Golden grain,
And those who flung it to the winds like Rain,
   Alike to no such aureate Earth are turned
As, buried once, Men want dug up again.

The Worldly Hope men set their Hearts upon
Turns Ashes—or its prospers; and anon,
   Like Snow upon the Desert's dusty Face,
Lighting a little hour or two—was gone.

III

Think, in this battered caravanserai
Whose Portals are alternate Night and Day,
   How Sultán after Sultán with his Pomp
Abode his destined Hour, and went his way.

They say the Lion and the Lizard keep
The Courts where Jamshyd gloried and drank deep:
   And Bahrám, that great Hunter—the Wild Ass
Stamps o'er his Head, but cannot break his Sleep.

I sometimes think that never blows so red
The Rose as where some buried Caesar bled;
   That every Hyacinth the Garden wears
Dropped in her Lap from some once lovely Head.

And this reviving Herb whose tender Green
Fledges the River-Lip on which we lean—
   Ah, lean upon it lightly! for who knows
From what once lovely Lip it springs unseen!

IV

Ah, my Beloved, fill the Cup that clears
To-day of past Regret and future Fears:

To-morrow!—Why, To-morrow I may be
Myself with Yesterday's Seven Thousand Years.

For some we loved, the loveliest and the best
That from his Vintage rolling Time hath pressed,
    Have drunk their Cup a Round or two before,
And one by one crept silently to rest.

And we that now make merry in the Room
They left, and Summer dresses in new bloom,
    Ourselves must we beneath the Couch of Earth
Descend—ourselves to make a Couch—for whom?

Ah, make the most of what we yet may spend,
Before we too into the Dust descend;
    Dust into Dust, and under Dust, to lie,
Sans Wine, sans Song, sans Singer, and—sans End!

.   .   .   .   .   .

V

Why, all the Saints and Sages who discussed
Of the two Worlds so wisely—they are thrust
    Like foolish Prophets forth; their Words to Scorn
Are scattered, and their Mouths are stopped with Dust.

.   .   .   .   .   .

With them the seed of Wisdom did I sow,
And with mine own hand wrought to make it grow;
    And this was all the Harvest that I reaped—
"I came like Water, and like Wind I go."

Into this Universe, and *Why* not Knowing
Nor *Whence*, like Water willy-nilly flowing;
    And out of it, as Wind along the Waste,
I know not *Whither*, willy-nilly blowing.

What, without asking, hither hurried *Whence?*
And, without asking, *Whither* hurried hence!
    Oh, many a Cup of this forbidden Wine
Must drown the memory of that insolence!

.   .   .   .   .   .

VI

A Hair perhaps divides the False and True;
Yes; and a single Alif were the clue—
   Could you but find it—to the Treasure-house,
And peradventure to the Master too:

Whose secret Presence, through Creation's veins
Running Quicksilver-like eludes your pains;
   Taking all shapes from Máh to Máhi; and
They change and perish all—but He remains;

A moment guessed—then back behind the Fold
Immersed of Darkness round the Drama Rolled
   Which, for the Pastime of Eternity,
He doth Himself contrive, enact, behold.

    .   .   .   .   .

VII

I sent my Soul through the Invisible
Some letter of that After-life to spell:
   And by and by my Soul returned to me,
And answered, "I Myself am Heaven and Hell."

    .   .   .   .   .

The Ball no question makes of Ayes and Noes,
But Here or There, as strikes the Player, goes;
   And He that tossed you down into the Field,
He knows about it all—He knows—HE knows!

The Moving Finger writes; and, having writ,
Moves on: nor all your Piety nor Wit
   Shall lure it back to cancel half a Line
Nor all your Tears wash out a Word of it.

    .   .   .   .   .

VIII

What! out of senseless Nothing to provoke
A conscious Something to resent the yoke
   Of unpermitted Pleasure, under pain
Of Everlasting Penalties, if broke!

    .   .   .   .   .

O Thou, who didst with pitfall and with gin
Beset the Road I was to wander in,
   Thou wilt not with Predestined Evil round
Enmesh, and then impute my Fall to Sin!

Oh Thou, who Man of Baser Earth didst make,
And ev'n with Paradise devise the Snake:
   For all the Sin wherewith the Face of Man
Is blackened—Man's forgiveness give—and take!

    .   .   .   .   .   .

IX

Ah, with the Grape my fading Life provide,
And wash the Body whence the Life has died,
   And lay me, shrouded in the living Leaf,
By some not unfrequented Garden-side.

That even my buried Ashes such a snare
Of Vintage shall fling up into the Air
   As not a True-Believer passing by
But shall be overtaken unaware.

    .   .   .   .   .   .

X

Yet Ah, that Spring should vanish with the Rose!
That Youth's sweet-scented manuscript should close!
   That Nightingale that in the branches sang,
Ah whence, and whither flown again, who knows!

Would but the Desert of the Fountain yield
One glimpse—if dimly, yet indeed, revealed,
   To which the fainting Traveller might spring,
As springs the trampled herbage of the field!

Would but some winged Angel ere too late
Arrest the yet unfolded Roll of Fate,
   And make the stern Recorder otherwise
Enregister, or quite obliterate!

Ah Love! could you and I with Him conspire
To grasp this sorry Scheme of Things entire,
   Would not we shatter it to bits—and then
Remould it nearer to the Heart's desire!

    .   .   .   .   .   .

XI

Yon rising Moon that looks for us again—
How oft hereafter will she wax and wane;
   How oft hereafter rising look for us
Through this same Garden—and for *one* in vain!

And when like her, oh Sákí, you shall pass
Among the Guests Star-scattered on the Grass,
   And in your joyous errand reach the spot
Where I made One—turn down an empty Glass!

ROBERT FROST (1875-   )

Bereft

The one quality in Robert Frost that runs like a golden thread through his poetry is *integrity*. Not blind stubbornness or intransigeance, but sturdy, quiet conviction; an affirmative conviction that man is equal to life's tests and to his own high hopes. The poet may, on occasion, banter and spoof a bit, but he does not waver or equivocate when sternly challenged. Beneath the surface calm and careful understatement there is an unyielding frame-work of life-hardened steel.

It is not surprising that so integral a part of the man was manifested and voiced early in his life. As a boy of eleven Frost knew tragedy, when he was stricken by the death of his adventurous and improvident father in Cali-fornia and when his mother and her two children had to cross the continent with the body for burial in the father's native New England. He knew deprivation when his mother supported herself and children by teaching in a rural school for nine dollars a week. He knew the nature and costs of independence when his mother moved herself and children to modest quarters rather than put up with the complaints and reproaches of "purse-proud" in-laws who were motivated by little more than duty.

But of greatest importance, the young man was gradually beginning to know himself—a discovery made in anguish and brief despair, but one that gave him resolution and the world a great poet.

When he completed High School in Lawrence, Massachusetts, Robert Frost was a confused youth. He had no determination for either a practical or an artistic world. He had written a few poems but had no faith in his ability to make this a career. When his paternal grandfather decided he should enter Dartmouth College he went, but with doubts as to its value to him, and asking himself who he was, what he wanted to be and do, and what all this life was about?

Apparently Frost did not find the answers to his troubled questions at Dartmouth. Teachers made no impression on the dreamy youth who walked the countryside alone by day and by night, who rebelled at routine and after several months left the college without notice to its dean.

This precipitate action earned young Frost the scorn and condemnation of all the New England relatives, but not of his courageous mother. Who was he, the relatives asked, to spurn the education offered by his grandfather—that severe and powerful giant of the family? What muddleheaded ideas possessed this indecisive nitwit?

If Frost had answers he did not give them. He knew only that Dartmouth was doing him no good, and that he was unable to conform to the ideas of his elders. He realized he was confronting forces that seemed designed to defeat his resolution to be independent. Nevertheless the eighteen-year-old youth determined that neither individuals nor society would bend him to their will nor press him into a conventional pattern.

It was obviously the crisis of his life; a dark and lonely ordeal between himself and his God—a trial from which he would emerge to begin to become the man he is.

Some years later Robert Frost recalled this crucial struggle against fate and darkness in his poem "Bereft":

> Where had I heard this wind before
> Change like this to a deeper roar?
> What would it take my standing there for,
> Holding open a restive door,
> Looking down hill to a frothy shore?
> Summer was past and day was past.
> Sombre clouds in the west were massed.
> Out in the porch's sagging floor,
> Leaves got up in a coil and hissed,
> Blindly struck at my knee and missed.
> Something sinister in the tone
> Told me my secret must be known:
> Word I was in the house alone
> Somehow must have gotten abroad,
> Word I was in my life alone,
> Word I had no one left but God.

THOMAS GRAY (1716-1771)

Elegy Written in a Country Churchyard

Thomas Gray's whole life, metaphorically, was a slow meditative walk toward the obscure churchyard he made famous, and in which he lies buried. Few poems so accurately, yet unwittingly, reveal their author as does this magnificent *Elegy*.

Gray was a sensitive, precocious child (the only one of twelve to survive infancy) whose frailty and timidity turned him to books as companions. When at nine he was sent to Eton he began the only period of his life when his mind was untroubled. They were nine years of sunshine. At Cambridge University he avoided social life in favor of long solitary walks and the composing of poetry, writing his only close friend that "low spirits are my true and faithful companions."

This lifeless routine was interrupted by the death of his ne'er-do-well father, whom he feared, and of an aunt who left him a small estate.

When his widowed mother went to Stokes Poges to live with her sisters, Gray spent most of his long vacations in this secluded village of widely dispersed groups of homes in the Buckinghamshire countryside. About a mile from the Gray home was a sixteenth-century church, originally intended for the devotion of the inmates of a nearby poorhouse and their burial beneath the elms and yews in the churchyard.

This was the serene place where the morose and lonely young poet spent every Spring and Summer; taking his musing walks through fields and paths, observing the tiny community's life, watching the gradual ripening of the fruits of the soil, and thinking of the obscure men who labored in the fields until laid at rest in the churchyard.

Year after year Gray walked and watched and grew in sympathy and understanding of the toil, sorrows and life of these simple people, who seemed not to be troubled by the inexorable demands and brevity of life, or the oblivion awaiting them at its end. The genius of the poet saw the profound and universal application of these rural meditations and, in the words of Samuel Johnson, left us a poem "with sentiments to which every heart returns an echo."

It is believed the *Elegy* was begun following the death of Richard West, the poet's dear friend. Gray was then twenty-six. Its first publication, years later without Gray's permission, distressed the poet. But it was an immediate success and by the time of his death at fifty-six it was world-famous. The three final stanzas are Gray's own eloquent epitaph:

The curfew tolls the knell of parting day,
　　The lowing herd winds slowly o'er the lea,
The plowman homeward plows his weary way,
　　And leaves the world to darkness and to me.

Now fades the glimmering landscape on the sight,
　　And all the air a solemn stillness holds,
Save where the beetle wheels his droning flight,
　　And drowsy tinklings lull the distant folds:

Save from that yonder ivy-mantled tower
　　The moping owl does to the moon complain
Of such as, wandering near her secret bower,
　　Molest her ancient solitary reign.

Beneath these rugged elms, that yew-tree's shade,
　　Where heaves the turf in many a mouldering heap,
Each in his narrow cell for ever laid,
　　The rude forefathers of the hamlet sleep.

The breezy call of incense-breathing morn,
　　The swallow tittering from the straw-built shed,
The cock's shrill clarion, or the echoing horn,
　　No more shall rouse them from their lowly bed.

For them no more the blazing hearth shall burn,
　　Or busy housewife ply her evening care:
No children run to lisp their sire's return,
　　Or climb his knees the envied kiss to share.

Oft did the harvest to their sickle yield,
　　Their furrow oft the stubborn glebe has broke:
How jocund did they drive their team afield!
　　How bowed the woods beneath their sturdy stroke!

Let not Ambition mock their useful toil,
　　Their homely joys, and destiny obscure;
Nor Grandeur hear with a disdainful smile
　　The short and simple annals of the poor.

The boast of heraldry, the pomp of power,
　　And all that beauty, all that wealth e'er gave,
Await alike the inevitable hour:
　　The paths of glory lead but to the grave.

Nor you, ye proud, impute to these the fault
    If Memory o'er their tomb no trophies raise,
Where through the long-drawn aisle and fretted vault
    The pealing anthem swells the note of praise.

Can storied urn or animated bust
    Back to its mansion call the fleeting breath?
Can Honour's voice provoke the silent dust,
    Or Flattery soothe the dull cold ear of death?

Perhaps in this neglected spot is laid
    Some heart once pregnant with celestial fire;
Hands, that the rod of empire might have swayed,
    Or waked to ecstasy the living lyre.

But Knowledge to their eyes her ample page
    Rich with the spoils of time did ne'er unroll;
Chill Penury repressed their noble rage,
    And froze the genial current of the soul.

Full many a gem of purest ray serene
    The dark unfathomed caves of ocean bear:
Full many a flower is born to blush unseen,
    And waste its sweetness on the desert air.

Some village Hampden that, with dauntless breast,
    The little tyrant of his fields withstood,
Some mute inglorious Milton here may rest,
    Some Cromwell guiltless of his country's blood.

The applause of listening senates to command,
    The threats of pain and ruin to despise,
To scatter plenty o'er a smiling land,
    And read their history in a nation's eyes,

Their lot forbade: nor circumscribed alone
    Their growing virtues, but their crimes confined;
Forbade to wade through slaughter to a throne,
    And shut the gates of mercy on mankind;

The struggling pangs of conscious truth to hide,
    To quench the blushes of ingenuous shame,
Or heap the shrine of Luxury and Pride
    With incense kindled at the Muse's flame.

Far from the madding crowd's ignoble strife,
   Their sober wishes never learned to stray;
Along the cool, sequestered vale of life
   They kept the noiseless tenor of their way.

Yet even these bones from insult to protect
   Some frail memorial still erected nigh,
With uncouth rhymes and shapeless sculpture decked,
   Implore the passing tribute of a sigh.

Their names, their years, spelt by the unlettered Muse,
   The place of fame and elegy supply:
And many a holy text around she strews,
   That teach the rustic moralist to die.

For who, to dumb Forgetfulness a prey,
   This pleasing anxious being e'er resigned,
Left the warm precincts of the cheerful day,
   Nor cast one longing lingering look behind?

On some fond breast the parting soul relies,
   Some pious drops the closing eye requires;
E'en from the tomb the voice of Nature cries,
   E'en in our ashes live their wonted fires.

For thee, who, mindful of the unhonoured dead,
   Dost in these lines their artless tale relate;
If chance, by lonely contemplation led,
   Some kindred spirit shall inquire thy fate,—

Haply some hoary-headed swain may say,
   "Oft have we seen him at the peep of dawn
Brushing with hasty steps the dews away
   To meet the sun upon the upland lawn.

"There at the foot of yonder nodding beech
   That wreathes its old fantastic roots so high,
His listless length at noontide would he stretch,
   And pore upon the brook that babbles by.

"Hard by yon wood, now smiling as in scorn,
   Muttering his wayward fancies he would rove,
Now drooping, woeful-wan, like one forlorn,
   Or crazed with care, or crossed in hopeless love.

"One morn, I missed him on the 'customed hill,
  Along the heath, and near his favourite tree;
Another came; nor yet beside the rill,
  Nor up the lawn, nor at the wood was he:

"The next, with dirges due in sad array,
  Slow through the church-way path we saw him borne,
Approach and read (for thou canst read) the lay
  Graved on the stone beneath yon aged thorn"?

THE EPITAPH

Here rests his head upon the lap of Earth
  A Youth, to Fortune and to Fame unknown.
Fair Science frowned not on his humble birth,
  And Melancholy marked him for her own.

Large was his bounty, and his soul sincere,
  Heaven did a recompense as largely send:
He gave to Misery (all he had) a tear,
  He gained from Heaven ('twas all he wished) a friend.

No farther seek his merits to disclose,
  Or draw his frailties from their dread abode,
(There they alike in trembling hope repose,)
  The bosom of his Father and his God.

FITZ-GREENE HALLECK (1790-1867)

Joseph Rodman Drake

Fitz-Greene Halleck, a shy, serious young clerk who wrote verse, was on an excursion boat in New York Harbor one September afternoon in 1813, when he met a handsome young physician named Joseph Rodman Drake. A brief shower caused Halleck to muse on the delights of another world and observe it would be heaven for him if he could "lounge on a rainbow and read Tom Campbell." This comment appealed to Drake, who also wrote poetry. This was the beginning of a friendship as famous in American literature as it was enduring in fact.

Poetry was the great common bond between the studious bookkeeper from Connecticut and the handsome young New York doctor. Each man had great faith in the other's poetic ability and this mutual admiration and encouragement led to their eventual collaboration on a series of satirical sketches of prominent personalities, that caught the nation's fancy. Drake, moreover, urged Halleck to abandon business and devote himself wholly to poetry, which Halleck did later as his confidence increased and his personality expanded under the stimulus of their friendship.

By 1820 Halleck had become very much a man of the world, socially adept and a popular satirist. But Drake had gone South in the hope of conquering the first stages of tuberculosis. He was worse when he returned to New York in the Spring of that year. After months of devoted care by Halleck, the widely popular doctor died the following September, at the age of twenty-five.

On the way home from Drake's funeral Halleck said to a friend, "There will be less sunshine for me hereafter, now that Joe's gone." And when he got home Halleck wrote his magnificent tribute to the friend he had first met eight years earlier. Halleck never intended the poem for publication. But friends of both men saw it and sent it to a literary magazine. Halleck never moved entirely beyond the shadow of his friend's death; the sadness lingered with him through life. As late as 1841 he told in verse of his happy days with Drake. But never again did he approach the lines of his first tribute— lines engraved on a bronze tablet and placed at Drake's grave in 1915 by the Bronx Society of Arts and Sciences:

> Green be the turf above thee,
>   Friend of my better days!
> None knew thee but to love thee,
>   Nor named thee but to praise.
>
> Tears fell, when thou wert dying,
>   From eyes unused to weep,
> And long, where thou art lying,
>   Will tears the cold turf steep.
>
> When hearts, whose truth was proven,
>   Like thine, are laid in earth,
> There should a wreath be woven
>   To tell the world their worth;
>
> And I, who woke each morrow
>   To clasp thy hand in mine,
> Who shared the joy and sorrow,
>   Whose weal and woe were thine,
>
> It should be mine to braid it
>   Around thy faded brow,

> But I've in vain essayed it,
> And feel I cannot now.
>
> While memory bids me weep thee,
> Nor thoughts nor words are free,
> The grief is fixed too deeply
> That mourns a man like thee.

THOMAS HARDY (1840-1928)

The Going

In his eighty-fifth year Thomas Hardy said that he had never been an "ardent" man—never ardent about anything.

This self-appraisal is supported by his novels, many of his poems, and by what is known of his first marriage of thirty-eight years duration. The grave, kindly little man was as cynical about love as he was about the universe and life in general. His writings dealt frequently with the impermanence of love—its erosion by the tyranny of Time and the persistent malignity of chance. Seductive women, said Hardy, are the manifestation of an objective force for the preservation of the species—a force indifferent to man's torment and to his ultimate disillusionment in the integrity of pledges of eternal fidelity.

Nevertheless, at the time this point of view was finding increasing expression in his writing, Hardy himself fell in love with a high-spirited young woman. Four years later they were married. She was thirty-three, he thirty-four.

When Hardy's novels brought him fame this marriage became the subject of tea-table chit-chat, barbed observations in print, and even outright statements that it was a dreary failure.

As is so often the case in matters of this kind, the truth is apparently mid-way. The marriage was discussed because of Hardy's fame and his novels attacking marriage, instead of its being essentially different from many other marriages.

Emma Lavinia Gifford was a strong-willed woman, outspokenly proud that her father was a solicitor, her uncle a canon of Worcester Cathedral and archdeacon of London, and her brother-in-law a rector. She was religiously orthodox, socially ambitious, intellectually narrow, and erroneously believed herself to be a writer of superior poetry and fiction.

Hardy was sensitive of his humbler origin, iconoclastic, unimpressed and bored by empty-headed social lights, and had a realistic outlook that bombarded optimism and sweetness.

Naturally these two people had clashes, and with a woman such as Mrs. Hardy some of them inevitably became known. For example, she once said in the presence of others: "Try to remember, Thomas Hardy, you married a lady." On a number of occasions she indicated to visitors that she helped Hardy write his books, extensively revised them and was in fact as competent a writer as her husband but that he would not allow her work to be published. Several times she protested her husband had become vain because of the flattery of women in London. She threw aside the manuscript of *Jude the Obscure,* characterizing it as vile and tried to get a friend of Hardy's to induce the author to burn the manuscript.

Unquestionably Hardy must have had many distressing periods during his married life. But he never revealed them, had no extra-marital affairs, gave no indication he desired to dissolve his marriage, and was a considerate husband and always anxious to have his wife accompany him on his travels. Obviously it was not a rapturous marriage; they grew apart and some of Hardy's poems suggest there was a "division" between them. Yet there must have been some bond of loyalty and dormant love since there was no break between them.

When Mrs. Hardy died suddenly in 1912 her husband was immediately stricken with sorrow. Within three weeks he said: "In spite of the differences between us, which it would be affectation to deny, and certain painful delusions she suffered from at times, my life is intensely sad to me now without her."

Nor was that the end of it. More and more the cynical poet and novelist who was never "ardent," went back over his early years with Emma "when our day was fair." He made a pilgrimage to the little town in Wales where he first met her; he visited the first home they shared, and became immersed in a sentimental reconstruction of their life together.

But even more important, Hardy wrote a series of poems titled "Poems 1912-1913," wherein he reminisces of their days of contented love, sings the praises of his dead wife, and reveals his great sorrow that he knows there is no hope of reunion after death. These poems are Hardy's finest lyrics—deeply felt, wistful, yet emotionally restrained. The closest any of them come to an overflow of emotion is "The Going":

> Why did you give no hint that night
> That quickly after the morrow's dawn,
> And calmly, as if indifferent quite,
> You would close your term here, up and be gone

Where I could not follow
With wings of swallow
To gain one glimpse of you ever anon!

Never to bid good-bye,
Or lip me the softest call,
Or utter a wish for a word, while I
Saw morning harden upon the wall,
Unmoved, unknowing
That your great going
Had place that moment, and altered all.

Why do you make me leave the house
And think for a breath it is you I see
At the end of the alley of bending boughs
Where so often at dusk you used to be;
Till in darkening dankness
The yawning blankness
Of the perspective sickens me!

You were she who abode
By those red-veined rocks far West,
You were the swan-necked one who rode
Among the beetling Beeny Crest,
And, reining nigh me,
Would muse and eye me,
While Life unrolled us its very best.

Why, then, latterly did we not speak,
Did we not think of those days long dead,
And ere your vanishing strive to seek
That time's renewal? We might have said,
"In this bright spring weather
We'll visit together
Those places that once we visited."

Well, well! All's past amend,
Unchangeable. It must go.
I seem but a dead man held on end
To sink down soon . . . O you could not know
That such swift fleeing
No soul foreseeing—
Not even I—would undo me so!

FELICIA DOROTHEA HEMANS (1793-1835)

The Landing of the Pilgrim Fathers

In the town of Rhyllon in Wales a greengrocer wrapped some purchases and delivered them to Mrs. Felicia Dorothea Hemans. As Mrs. Hemans casually unwrapped the package she noticed with surprise that the wrapping was a Boston newspaper, published in far away United States, a country she knew little about.

The novelist and poet smoothed the tattered pages and began to read with quickening interest. When she turned to an account of the 1824 celebration of Forefathers' Day she was fascinated. She had not previously read of the Forefathers, knew very little about the Pilgrims and had never before heard of the Plymouth colony. Everything she read about them in that newspaper fired her imagination. She immediately sat down and began to write the ode that dramatically drew attention to the Pilgrims, and is her own chief claim to remembrance.

Naturally, the poem is purely imaginative in many of its details since the poet knew no more about the Pilgrims than she learned that day in 1825 from the old paper.

The story is told that one of the New England Channings called on Mrs. Hemans at her home, and after congratulating her on the poem pompously proceeded to point out her factual errors: the Pilgrims first landed at Cape Cod, not Plymouth; the *Mayflower* was not a "bark" but a full-rigged ship; the coast of Plymouth is not "stern and rock-bound," and so on. Poor Mrs. Hemans burst into tears and fled her tormentor.

She need not have been so upset. She had captured the spirit of the Pilgrims, put it down in stirring fashion, and gave the Pilgrims a fame they might not otherwise have achieved.

> The breaking waves dashed high
> On a stern and rock-bound coast;
> And the woods against a stormy sky,
> Their giant branches tossed;
> And the heavy night hung dark
> The hills and water o'er—
> When a band of exiles moored their bark
> On a wild New England shore.
>
> Not as the conqueror comes,
> They, the true-hearted, came;—
> Not with the roll of stirring drums,

And the trumpets that sing of fame;—
Not as the flying come,
In silence and in fear;
They shook the depth of the desert's gloom
With their hymns of lofty cheer.

Amidst the storm they sang,
And the stars heard, and the sea!
And the sounding aisles of the dim woods rang
To the anthem of the free;
The ocean eagle soared
From his nest by the white wave's foam,
And the rocking pines of the forest roared:—
This was their welcome home!

There were men with hoary hair
Amidst that pilgrim band;
Why had they come to wither there,
Away from their childhood's land?
There was woman's fearless eye,
Lit by her deep love's truth;
There was manhood's brow serenely high,
And the fiery heart of youth.

What sought they thus afar?
Bright jewels of the mine?
The wealth of seas? the spoils of war?
They sought a faith's pure shrine!
Ay, call it holy ground,
The soil where first they trod!
They left unstained what there they found
Freedom to worship God!

WILLIAM ERNEST HENLEY (1849-1903)

Invictus

Life had never been gentle or lenient to big, roaring and zestful William Ernest Henley, a mostly self-taught poet and editor who became stoical when he failed to relate his increasing problems and difficulties to a power beyond himself.

But the bitterest blow came when he was twenty-five. One foot was amputated to check tuberculosis of the bone, and the other foot was treated and eventually saved at Edinburgh Infirmary by the great Joseph Lister, pioneer of asepsis and surgeon. Between periodical scraping of the bone of the remaining leg by Lister, Henley lay on his hospital cot month after agonizing month and became filled with wonder at the famous doctor's dedication to the relief of human suffering. Gradually the belligerent poet recognized there was nobility and grandeur to be found in individual human beings.

It was on one of those days in 1875 that the pain-racked, poor and lonely poet looked squarely at the face of the doom he believed impending, and wrote sixteen celebrated lines—his shield against the pain, sorrows and disappointments life would continue to deal him. Lister had given Henley a vision—or enriched one he already had—that each man must fight his own battle for victory over weakness and reverses, accepting defeat when necessary, but never quitting the contest.

As the "Chained Titan" hobbled through life on his wooden leg and crutch, he suffered a long series of adversities but remained true to the famous lines inscribed on the banner he held aloft—lines that have been a spur and a support to wavering hearts made tremulous by pain and defeat.

> Out of the night that covers me,
> Black as the Pit from pole to pole,
> I thank whatever gods may be
> For my unconquerable soul.
>
> In the fell clutch of circumstance
> I have not winced nor cried aloud.
> Under the bludgeoning of chance
> My head is bloody, but unbowed.
>
> Beyond this place of wrath and tears
> Looms but the horror of the shade,
> And yet the menace of the years
> Finds, and shall find me, unafraid.
>
> It matters not how strait the gate,
> How charged with punishments the scroll,
> I am the master of my fate;
> I am the captain of my soul.

GEORGE HERBERT (1593-1632)

The Collar

George Herbert said he had "a longing desire to haste forward." His life shows he longed to "haste forward" in the service of God. To that end he originally planned to take holy orders, but after becoming a major fellow of Trinity College at Cambridge University he decided he could serve God equally well in the world by working for peace when seventeenth-century Europe was in the throes of the Thirty-Year War.

After making this decision the earnest young aristocrat accepted the position of Public Orator at Cambridge and set his sights on becoming Secretary of State during the reign of peace-loving King James, who was stoutly opposing the many Englishmen who wanted to war against Catholic Spain.

However, scholarly Herbert eventually discovered that it was no simple matter for a public office to be "joined with heaven." When he failed to secure the post of Secretary of State, he was elected to a Parliament that forced the King to war with Spain. When James died in 1625 he was succeeded by his son Charles, who promptly began feuding with Parliament.

Herbert had enough. His dreams of peace and that one could serve God in a Government post had become nightmares. Moreover, he could not decide now what he should do in fulfillment of his purpose to dedicate his life to the service of God. Few of those who knew this cheerful and likeable gentleman had any idea that he was a lonely pilgrim who had drifted off his chosen path and was, in spite of frail health and personal sorrows, trying to find the road toward his life-long goal. Eventually he married happily, became a much-loved country clergyman and died peacefully with faith in God, at the age of forty.

After Herbert's death it was found that he had written a group of poems that revealed the anguish of his heart—his spiritual desolation and longing to be useful. During this period of personal chaos he found refuge in poetry and brought to it order, control and truth that was born of his own experience of inner turmoil and frustration. This is most beautifully expressed in "The Collar":

> I struck the board and cried, No more;
>   I will abroad.
> What, shall I ever sigh and pine?
> My lines and life are free, free as the road,
> Loose as the wind, as large as store.
>   Shall I be still in suit?
> Have I no harvest but a thorn

To let me blood, and not restore
What I have lost with cordial fruit?
  Sure there was wine
Before my sighs did dry it; there was corn
Before my tears did drown it.
Is the year only lost to me?
Have I no bays to crown it?
No flowers, no garlands gay? All blasted?
  All wasted?
Not so, my heart; but there is fruit,
  And thou hast hands.

Recover all thy sigh-blown age
On double pleasurer: leave thy cold dispute
Of what is fit and not; forsake thy cage,
  Thy ropes of sands
Which petty thoughts have made, and made to thee
Good cable, to enforce and draw,
  And be thy law,
While thou dost wink and would'st not see.
  Away: take heed,
  I will abroad.
Call in thy death's-head there: tie up thy fears.
  He that forbears
  To suit and serve his need
  Deserves his load.
But as I raved and grew more fierce and wild
  At every word,
Methought I heard one calling "Child!"
And I replied "My Lord."

ROBERT HERRICK (1591-1674)

Whenas in Silks My Julia Goes
The Night-Piece, to Julia

Herrick lived at a time when the writing of graceful love lyrics to real
or imagined mistresses was the fashion, and it delighted him to conform to
the custom. But it has never been determined whether there was a real
Julia to whom the easy-going, pleasure-loving clergyman directly addressed
some fifty-two poems.

Some of Herrick's editors flatly assert Julia was a conventional fiction; others merely discuss the pros and cons; still others state definitely that Julia stood for a real but unrequited love.

Not much is known about Herrick apart from what he chose to reveal about himself in his poetry. After six years as an apprentice goldsmith in London and seven years at Cambridge University, he lived a gay and bibulous life as a law student in London, then took holy orders and was given a rural parish in Devonshire.

That Herrick was a hard-drinking cleric, kept a pet pig which drank beer out of a tankard, was burly of body and gross of face, and waxed poetic about a woman's thigh or petticoat tells us *something* about the jovial vicar, but proves nothing about his Julia.

It is by no means difficult to believe there was a real Julia, whatever her real name. Herrick wrote poems about other women, but those to Julia have a devotion, a richness of incident and a reflection of emotional experiences not found in his other poems. Their total effect is that of a good-natured Christian with a pagan tinge, writing from an overflowing heart, about a fickle and coquettish Julia, who enchanted him but did not desolate him by her rejection. As Robert Lynd said: "The songs of Julia . . . are songs of experience." And more recently Marchette Chute pointed out that the Julia poems have a tone similar to that of Herrick's poems to "demonstrably real women."

Although Herrick could be amusing about Julia, such as:

> "Fain would I kiss my Julia's dainty leg,
> Which is as white and hairless as an egg."

and objective, as when he wrote:

> "Black and rolling is her eye,
> Double-chinn'd and forehead high."

he could also be charming:

> Whenas in silks my Julia goes,
> Then, then, me thinks, how sweetly flows
> That liquefaction of her clothes.
>
> Next, when I cast mine eyes and see
> That brave vibration each way free,
> O how that glittering taketh me!

And Herrick could rise to glorious heights, as in the famous Night-Piece to Julia:

Her eyes the glow-worm lend thee,
The shooting stars attend thee;
    And the elves also,
    Whose little eyes glow
Like the sparks of fire, befriend thee.

No Will-o'-th'-Wisp mislight thee,
Nor snake or slow-worm bite thee;
    But on, on thy way,
    Not making a stay,
Since ghost there's none to affright thee.

Let not the dark thee cumber;
What though the moon does slumber?
    The stars of the night
    Will lend thee their light
Like tapers clear, without number.

Then, Julia, let me woo thee,
Thus, thus to come unto me;
    And when I shall meet
    Thy silvery feet,
My soul I'll pour into thee.

The kindly old poet died in his eighty-third year, with people still wondering if what he said of poets applies also to him:

Wantons we are; and though our words be such,
Our Lives do differ from our Lines by much."

OLIVER WENDELL HOLMES (1809-1894)

Old Ironsides

A young man, born and raised in a distinguished Boston family, with ancestors who participated in the American Revolution, would almost inevitably be a patriot. But Oliver Wendell Holmes no doubt developed a special pride in the U. S. Navy through his older sister's husband, Dr. Usher Parsons, who served as a Navy surgeon under Commodore Perry at the Battle of Lake Erie, during the War of 1812. Surely the thirteen-year-old boy thrilled to hear Parsons' eyewitness account of such stirring events as Captain Lawrence's dying request "Don't give up the ship."

All this bore poetic fruit when Holmes, at twenty-one, was a law student at Harvard, which profession he soon abandoned for medicine. On September 14, 1830, he read in the *Boston Advertiser* that the Secretary of Navy had recommended the frigate *Constitution* be disposed of. Holmes bristled with indignation at the thought of the gallant conqueror of the *Guerrière* and seven other British ships in the War of 1812 being junked by an unfeeling Government. He knew that public clamor in England had saved Lord Nelson's *Victory* from a similar fate.

That evening young Holmes wrote his fervent protest "Old Ironsides," which appeared in the *Boston Advertiser* on September 16, 1830, and spread like a prairie-fire across the nation. It crystallized public opinion for the famous vessel's preservation. Thanks to the poet and his poem, the *Constitution* today may be visited by the public at the U. S. Naval Shipyard in Boston.

Ay, tear her battered ensign down!
Long has it waved on high,
And many an eye has danced to see
That banner in the sky;
Beneath it rung the battle shout,
And burst the cannon's roar;—
The meteor of the ocean air
Shall sweep the clouds no more!

Her deck, once red with heroes' blood,
Where knelt the vanquished foe,
When winds were hurrying o'er the flood,
And waves were white below,
No more shall feel the victor's tread,
Or know the conquered knee;—
The harpies of the shore shall pluck
The eagle of the sea!

Oh, better that her shattered hulk
Should sink beneath the wave;
Her thunders shook the mighty deep,
And there should be her grave;
Nail to the mast her holy flag,
Set every threadbare sail,
And give her to the god of storms,
The lightning and the gale!

THOMAS HOOD (1799-1845)

The Song of the Shirt

Although Thomas Hood made his living as a humorist, he is remembered today for several poems which plead for justice and charity toward the exploited and unfortunate.

Hood spoke from a heart instinctively sympathetic to the needs and trials of the masses who struggled in the murky environs of London during the middle of the last century. Even his facetious sketches of the city's poor and unknown were informed with kindly understanding. Hood wrote of the homeless and poor with authority not only because as a London journalist he knew them, but also because from the age of thirteen until his death at forty-six he lived a hand-to-mouth existence, aggravated by tuberculosis that gradually conquered and killed him. He was a poet of the heart because his own was often heavy, though usually masked by the role of jester that enabled him to provide for his devoted wife Jane and their two children.

Late in 1844, when Hood was waging the last and losing battle of his lifetime against tuberculosis, he read in the press about a woman arrested in London for pawning articles that belonged to her employer. The woman made trousers for sevenpence a pair, earning at the most seven shillings per week. Her employer testified this was "a good living for a woman who had herself and two infant children to support."

Hood, touched by the poor woman's plight and stung by the employer's hypocrisy and greed, that evening wrote his searing "The Song of the Shirt." It was immediately published and swept through England like a crusade, being recited in churches, put to music and sung in the streets.

> With fingers weary and worn,
>   With eyelids heavy and red,
> A woman sat, in unwomanly rags,
>   Plying her needle and thread,—
>   Stitch—stitch—stitch!
> In poverty, hunger, and dirt;
>   And still with a voice of dolorous pitch
> She sang the "Song of the Shirt!"
>
> "Work—work—work
>   While the cock is crowing aloof!
> And work—work—work
>   Till the stars shine through the roof!

It's oh! to be a slave
  Along with the barbarous Turk,
Where woman has never a soul to save,
  If this is Christian work!

"Work—work—work
  Till the brain begins to swim!
Work—work—work
  Till the eyes are heavy and dim!
Seam, and gusset, and band,
  Band and gusset, and seam—
Till over the buttons I fall asleep,
  And sew them on in a dream!

"O men with sisters dear!
  O men with mothers and wives!
It is not linen you're wearing out,
  But human creatures' lives!
    Stitch—stitch—stitch,
In poverty, hunger, and dirt,—
Sewing at once, with a double thread,
  A shroud as well as a shirt!

"But why do I talk of death,—
  That phantom of grisly bone?
I hardly fear his terrible shape,
  It seems so like my own,—
  Because of the fasts I keep;
O God! that bread should be so dear,
  And flesh and blood so cheap!

"Work—work—work!
  My labour never flags;
And what are its wages? A bed of straw,
  A crust of bread—and rags.
That shattered roof—and this naked floor—
  A table—a broken chair—
And a wall so blank my shadow I thank
  For sometimes falling there!

"Work—work—work
  From weary chime to chime!
Work—work—work
  As prisoners work for crime!

Band, and gusset, and seam,
　　Seam and gusset, and band,—
Till the heart is sick and the brain benumbed,
　　As well as the weary hand.

"Work—work—work
　　In the dull December light!
And work—work—work
　　When the weather is warm and bright!
While underneath the eaves
　　The brooding swallows cling,
As if to show me their sunny backs,
　　And twit me with the Spring.

"Oh but to breathe the breath
　　Of the cowslip and primrose sweet,—
With the sky above my head,
　　And the grass beneath my feet!
For only one short hour
　　To feel as I used to feel,
Before I knew the woes of want
　　And the walk that costs a meal!

"Oh but for one short hour,—
　　A respite, however brief!
No blessed leisure for love or hope,
　　But only time for grief!
A little weeping would ease my heart;
　　But in their briny bed
My tears must stop, for every drop
　　Hinders needle and thread!"

With fingers weary and worn,
　　With eyelids heavy and red,
A woman sat, in unwomanly rags,
　　Plying her needle and thread,—
　　　　Stitch—stitch—stitch!
　　In poverty, hunger, and dirt:
And still with a voice of dolorous pitch—
Would that its tone could reach the rich!—
　　She sang this "Song of the Shirt!"

JOHN KEATS (1795-1821)

On First Looking Into Chapman's Homer
Ode on a Grecian Urn
Ode to a Nightingale
Bright Star

"There is death in that hand," said Samuel Taylor Coleridge to a friend after he had greeted with a handshake a then unknown youth named John Keats. But Coleridge could not have known that before Death conquered the frail, mercurial and idealistic young man he would bequeath us some of the glories of English poetry.

The first certain indication of the orphaned Keats' poetic force was revealed in the Autumn of 1816, when he was living with his brothers in London and rapidly putting his luxuriant fancy into poetry. One October evening he visited his friend Cowden Clarke, a somewhat older man who had taught Keats his first lessons and increasingly recognized the genius of this youth of "terrier courage and great charm." They were resuming their custom of an evening's reading and talking of books. "It was a memorable night in my career," recalled Clarke, who had encountered a 1616 folio edition of George Chapman's translation of Homer. The two men pored over the volume until daybreak. Chapman's robust version of the ancient world stirred Keats as the mythologies, Latin authors and polite translations of his own day had failed to do.

While the young poet walked at sunrise the two miles from Clarke's to his own home he began to compose a poem. At ten that same morning, when Clarke came down to breakfast, he found on the table a brief note from Keats accompanied by a sonnet that Clarke read with amazement—as well he might since it was the first full flowering of the poetic genius whose growth he had nourished.

> Much have I travell'd in the realms of gold,
>   And many goodly states and kingdoms seen;
>   Round many westerns islands have I been
> Which bards in fealty to Apollo hold.
> Oft of one wide expanse had I been told
>   That deep-brow'd Homer ruled as his desmesne;
>   Yet did I never breathe its pure serene
> Till I heard Chapman speak out loud and bold:
> Then felt I like some watcher of the skies
>   When a new planet swims into his ken;

Or like stout Cortez when with eagle eyes
      He star'd at the Pacific—and all his men
Look'd at each other with a wild surmise—
      Silent upon a peak in Darien.

One of the most brilliant jewels of English poetry resulted from painter
Benjamin Robert Haydon's enthusiasm for the Elgin Marbles, a collection
of Greek sculptures he had for years studied, copied, made casts of, and induced the British Museum to acquire. In March, 1817, Haydon took his
friend John Keats to see the sculptures.

The sensitive young poet was overpowered by an art wholly different
from any he had previously known. During the next two years Keats repeatedly revisited the Museum to study the Elgin Marbles; he read a history
of Greece, pored over antique drawings, and studied other art collections—
always with his superb imagination at work.

Keats was specially stirred by the frieze of the Parthenon, which shows
the cattle being brought to the sacrifice and groups of men on horseback or
driving carts. He realized, however, that *urn* was a poetically more fitting
word than *Elgin Marbles* or *Parthenon*, and that by using *urn* he could more
effectively convey the impression made on him by the Greek sculptures.

Amy Lowell, Keats' admiring biographer, said of the "Ode on a Grecian
Urn": "The poem is well-nigh flawless . . . a picture, an experience, a
creed, all in one. It is the world without and the world within . . . a magnificent example of joy through resignation . . . written by all his many
selves working together in the complete harmony of absolute concord."

Thou still unravish'd bride of quietness!
      Thou foster-child of silence and slow time,
Sylvan historian, who canst thus express
      A flowery tale more sweetly than our rhyme:
What leaf-fring'd legend haunts about thy shape
            Of deities or mortals, or of both,
                  In Tempe or the dales of Arcady?
      What men or gods are these? What maidens loath?
What mad pursuit? What struggle to escape?
      What pipes and timbrels? What wild ecstasy?

II

Heard melodies are sweet, but those unheard
      Are sweeter; therefore, ye soft pipes, play on;
Not to the sensual ear, but more endear'd,
      Pipe to the spirit ditties of no tone:

Fair youth, beneath the trees, thou canst not leave
  Thy song, nor ever can those trees be bare;
  Bold Lover, never, never canst thou kiss,
Though winning near the goal—yet, do not grieve;
She cannot fade, though thou hast not thy bliss,
  For ever wilt thou love, and she be fair!

III

Ah, happy, happy boughs! that cannot shed
  Your leaves, nor ever bid the Spring adieu;
And, happy melodist, unwearied,
  For ever piping songs for ever new;
More happy love! more happy, happy love!
  For ever warm and still to be enjoy'd;
  For ever panting, and for ever young,
All breathing human passion far above,
    That leaves a heart high-sorrowful and cloy'd,
  A burning forehead, and a parching tongue.

IV

Who are these coming to the sacrifice?
  To what green altar, O mysterious priest,
Lead'st thou that heifer lowing at the skies,
  And all her silken flanks with garlands drest?
What little town by river or sea shore,
  Or mountain-built with peaceful citadel,
  Is emptied of this folk, this pious morn?
And, little town, thy streets for evermore
  Will silent be; and not a soul to tell
  Why thou art desolate, can e'er return.

V

O Attic shape! Fair attitude! with brede
  Of marble men and maidens overwrought,
With forest branches and the trodden weed;
  Thou, silent form, doth tease us out of thought
As doth eternity: Cold Pastoral!
  When old age shall this generation waste,
  Thou shalt remain, in midst of other woe
Than ours, a friend to man, to whom thou say'st,
  "Beauty is truth, truth beauty,"—that is all
  Ye know on earth, and all ye need to know.

Saddened by his brother's death and crushed by malevolent reviews of his poetry, Keats in the Spring of 1819 visited the Hampstead Heath home of Charles Armitage Brown, and was immediately attracted by the song of a nightingale that had built her nest near the house. Exquisitely sensitive to beauty, his nature quivered in dreamy indolence as he sat one morning for hours under a plum tree in the garden and listened to the serene joy of the bird's song. When he came into the house, Keats had two sheets of paper which he quickly thrust behind some books. With the poet's permission, Brown recovered the precious manuscript and on that May morning found upon reading those magic lines to the nightingale that Keats' melancholy had lessened—that the bird's song had somewhat eased the turbulence and pain of the tuberculous poet who was unadapted to the world in which he lived:

I

My heart aches, and a drowsy numbness pains
  My sense, as though of hemlock I had drunk,
Or emptied some dull opiate to the drains
  One minute past, and Lethe-wards had sunk:
'Tis not through envy of thy happy lot,
  But being too happy in thine happiness,—
    That thou, light-winged Dryad of the trees,
      I some melodious plot
Of beechen green, and shadows numberless,
  Singest of summer in full-throated ease.

II

O, for a draught of vintage! that hath been
  Cool'd a long age in the deep-delved earth,
Tasting of Flora and the country green,
  Dance, and Provencal song, and sunburnt mirth!
O for a beaker full of the warm South,
  Full of the true, the blushful Hippocrene,
    With beaded bubbles winking at the brim,
      And purple-stained mouth;
That I might drink, and leave the world unseen,
  And with thee fade away into the forest dim:

III

Fade far away, dissolve, and quite forget
  What thou among the leaves hast never known,

The weariness, the fever, and the fret
  Here, where men sit and hear each other groan;
Where palsy shakes a few, sad, last gray hairs,
    Where youth grows pale, and spectre-thin, and dies;
      Where but to think is to be full of sorrow
        And leaden-eyed despairs,
    Where Beauty cannot keep her lustrous eyes,
      Or new Love pine at them beyond to-morrow.

IV

Away! Away! for I will fly to thee,
  Not charioted by Bacchus and his pards,
But on the viewless wings of Poesy,
  Though the dull brain perplexes and retards:
Already with thee! tender is the night,
  And haply the Queen-Moon is on her throne,
    Cluster'd around by all her starry Fays;
      But here there is no light,
  Save what from heaven is with the breezes blown
    Through verdurous glooms and winding mossy ways.

V

I cannot see what flowers are at my feet,
  Nor what soft incense hangs upon the boughs,
But in embalmed darkness, guess each sweet
  Wherewith the seasonable month endows
The grass, the thicket, and the fruit-tree wild:
  White hawthorn, and the pastoral eglantine;
    Fast fading violets cover'd up in leaves;
      And mid-May's eldest child,
The coming musk-rose, full of dewy wine,
    The murmurous haunt of flies on summer eves.

VI

Darkling I listen; and for many a time
  I have been half in love with easeful Death,
Call'd him soft names in many a mused rhyme,
  To take into the air my quiet breath;
Now more than ever seems it rich to die,
  To cease upon the midnight with no pain,
    While thou art pouring forth thy soul abroad
      In such an ecstasy!

Still wouldst thou sing, and I have ears in vain—
   To thy high requiem become a sod.

VII

Thou wast not born for death, immortal Bird!
   No hungry generations tread thee down;
The voice I hear this passing night was heard
   In ancient days by emperor and clown:
Perhaps the self-same song that found a path
   Through the sad heart of Ruth, when, sick for home,
     She stood in tears amid the alien corn:
      The same that oft-times hath
Charm'd magic casements, opening on the foam
   Of perilous seas, in faery lands forlorn.

VIII

Forlorn! the very word is like a bell
   To toll me back from thee to my sole self!
Adieu! the fancy cannot cheat so well
   As she is fam'd to do, deceiving elf.
Adieu! adieu! thy plaintive anthem fades
   Past the near meadows, over the still stream,
     Up the hill-side; and now 'tis buried deep
      In the next valley-glades;
   Was it a vision, or a waking-dream?
   Fled is that music:—Do I wake or sleep?

One cannot speak of the tragedy of Keats without mention of the love of his life: beautiful, lively, practical Fanny Brawn, who has been characterized by some as an unfortunate factor in the poet's life. But Keats was a sick man who even in vigorous health would no doubt have been rent by the warring demons within him—love, poetry, ambition, beauty, art and a hunger for the unattainable ideals of dreaming youth. If Fanny caused the demanding and jealous poet agony, she was also the cause of his greatest moments of happiness.

In September, 1820, Keats boarded ship in England bound for Italy in a last desperate quest for health. Fanny wanted to go with him as his wife, but Keats would not subject her to what he feared would be the agony of his deathbed. Just before leaving he wrote her, "I will imagine you Venus to-night and pray, pray to your star like a Heathen."

Shortly after the vessel sailed it was becalmed off the Dorsetshire coast. One night Keats composed his beautiful "Bright Star" sonnet and wrote it out for Severen, his traveling companion, in a volume of Shakespeare's poems, on a blank page opposite the heading "A Lover's Complaint." It was poor Keats' death song. He died at Rome five months later, shortly after writing his friend Brown about Fanny: "For my sake, be her advocate for ever."

After Keats' death, Fanny seldom was able to bring herself to speak of him. She wore his ring the rest of her life. She did not marry until twelve years after the poet's death. Though tortured Keats may have doubted her constancy, she was truly his steadfast star.

> Bright star, would I were stedfast as thou art—
>   Not in lone splendour hung aloft the night
> And watching, with eternal lids apart,
>   Like nature's patient, sleepless Eremite,
> The moving waters at their priestlike task
>   Of pure ablution round earth's human shores,
> Or gazing on the new soft-fallen mask
>   Of snow upon the mountains and moors—
> No—yet still stedfast, still unchangeable,
>   Pillow'd upon my fair love's ripening breast,
>   To feel for ever its soft fall and swell,
> Awake for ever in a sweet unrest,
> Still, still to hear her tender-taken breath,
> And so live ever—or else swoon to death.

RUDYARD KIPLING (1865-1936)

Gunga Din
IF

Contrary to what many people suppose, Kipling did not live many years in India. He was born and spent his early years there, went to England for schooling, returned to India at seventeen and remained only seven years. But they were seven wonderfully interesting years that kept his fine mind fueled for a long time after he left.

When young Kipling returned to India in 1882 he obtained a position on *The Civil and Military Gazette,* and later on *The Allahabad Pioneer.* In both jobs Kipling visited various army camps and posts throughout India, lived among the British soldiers, learned the slang, manners and habits of the enlisted men and began to appreciate their problems and difficulties.

In the course of this work Kipling heard the story of Juma, a *bhisti* or water-carrier who displayed remarkable bravery in carrying water to the wounded and dying at the siege of Delhi, in 1857. Juma was with the Corps of the Guides, a highly mobile force of picked native troops, and officered by Britishers. The Guides accepted only natives "born and bred to the sword, who had faced death often, and who by instinct were brave." But the low-caste men (such as menials) were excluded from the fighting ranks, because they were believed too accustomed to being cuffed and kicked by village superiors, hence would not make good soldiers.

And yet it was Juma, a low-caste water-carrier, who during two months of blistering heat and bitter battles at Delhi ministered so calmly and so faithfully to the elite Guides that the soldiers themselves said: "This man is the bravest of the brave, for without arms or protection of any sort he is in the foremost line. If anyone deserves the star for valor, this man does." Thus the highest honor then open to a native soldier was conferred on Juma, and in response to the soldiers' petition the brave bhisti was enlisted as a soldier in The Guides.

Juma was the inspiration of Kipling's "Gunga Din." But Kipling did not carry his Gunga Din to the heights achieved by Juma, who eventually became a native officer in The Guides, and in the Afghan War of 1778 won additional honors for his great valor. Nevertheless Kipling did immortalize the Mohammedan *bhisti,* a word meaning "heavenly one," and the Hindu's "pani-wallah":

> You may talk o' gin and beer
> When you're quartered safe out 'ere,
> An' you're sent to penny-fights an' Aldershot it;
> But when it comes to slaughter
> You will do your work on water,
> An' you'll lick the bloomin' boots of 'im that's got it.
> Now in Injia's sunny clime,
> Where I used to spend my time
> A-servin' of 'Er Majesty the Queen,
> Of all them blackfaced crew
> The finest man I knew
> Was our regimental bhisti, Gunga Din.
>   He was "Din! Din! Din!
>   "You limpin' lump o' brick-dust, Gunga Din!
>   "Hi! slippery *hitherao!*
>   "Water, get it! *Panee loa!*
>   "You squidgy-nosed old idol, Gunga Din."
>
> The uniform 'e wore
> Was nothin' much before,

An' rather less than arf o' that be'ind,
For a piece of twisty rag,
An' a goatskin water-bag
Was all the field-equipment 'e could find.
When the sweatin' troop-train lay
In a sidin' through the day,
Where the 'eat would make your bloomin' eyebrows crawl
We shouted "Harry By!"
Till our throats were bricky-dry,
Then we wopped 'im 'cause 'e couldn't serve us all.
    It was "Din! Din! Din!
   "You 'eathen, where the mischief 'ave you been?
    "You put some *juldee* in it
    "Or I'll *marrow* you this minute
    "If you don't fill up my helmet, Gunga Din!"

'E would dot an' carry one
Till the longest day was done;
An' 'e didn't seem to know the use o' fear.
If we charged or broke or cut,
You could bet your bloomin' nut,
E'd be waitin' fifty paces right flank rear.
With 'is mussick on 'is back,
'E would skip with our attack,
An' watch us till the bugles made "Retire"
An' for all 'is dirty 'ide
'E was white, clear white, inside
When 'e went to tend to wounded under fire!
    It was "Din! Din! Din!"
   With the bullets kickin' dust-spots on the green
    When the cartridges ran out,
    You could hear the front-ranks shout,
   "Hi! ammunition-mules an' Gunga Din!"

I shan't forgit the night
When I dropped be'ind the fight
With a bullet where my belt-plate should a' been.
I was chokin' mad with thirst,
An' the man that spied me first
Was our good old grinnin', gruntin' Gunga Din.
'E lifted up my 'ead,
An' he plugged me where I bled,
An' 'e guv me arf-a-pint of water green:
It was crawlin' and it stunk,
But of all the drinks I've drunk,

I'm gratefullest to one from Gunga Din.
    It was "Din! Din! Din!
"'Ere's a beggar with a bullet through 'is spleen;
    "'E's chawin' up the ground,
"An' 'e's kickin' all around:
"For Gawd's sake git the water, Gunga Din!"

'E carried me away
To where a dooli lay,
An' a bullet come an' drilled the beggar clean.
'E put me safe inside
An' just before 'e died,
"I 'ope you liked your drink," sez Gunga Din.
So I'll meet 'im later on
At the place where 'e is gone—
Where it's always double drill and no canteen;
'E'll be squattin' on the coals
Givin' drinks to poor damned souls,
An' I'll get a swig in hell from Gunga Din!
    Yes, Din! Din! Din!
You Lazarushian-leather Gunga Din!
    Though I've belted you and flayed you,
    By the livin' Gawd that made you,
You're a better man than I am, Gunga Din!

In 1897 Kipling began spending his Winters at Capetown, South Africa, and on his first visit there met Dr. Sir Starr Jameson, a close friend of empire-builder Cecil Rhodes.

Kipling became a warm friend and admirer of Dr. Jameson, and since by the poet's own admission "IF" was "drawn from Jameson's character" it is interesting to see what in the man may have moved Kipling to write his most popular poem.

Kipling, according to his own creed, would be most likely to admire a man who desired only to command and direct himself. Moreover, Kipling would admire an Englishman who believed with him in a highly-organized and heavily-armed British empire, took pride in conquest, and subscribed to the aristocrat's *noblesse oblige*.

Well, Jameson at age twenty-five went to the mining camp at Kimberley, in Africa, to practice medicine. His wit and great personal charm attracted Cecil Rhodes, who told him of his plan to expand British civilization northward through Central Africa until it extended from Capetown to Cairo. Jameson joined Rhodes and became his chief instrument of policy, including dangerous missions to pacify belligerent tribal chiefs.

But Jameson's gift for leadership, great self-confidence and willingness to make daring decisions got him in serious trouble. On his own responsibility he led an invasion to take the Transvaal for Britain. He was defeated by the Boers. For this Jameson was brought to trial in London and imprisoned. When released from jail his health was shattered. However, he made a remarkable physical and political recovery, serving as Premier of South Africa from 1903 to 1907.

Unquestionably, Kipling was deeply impressed by Jameson's stout spirit, forceful personality, daring initiative, and his willingness to lead forlorn causes with no thought of personal gain. But no doubt Jameson's strong imperialism also greatly appealed to Kipling, though one finds no suggestion of it in "IF":

> If you can keep your head when all about you
> Are losing theirs and blaming it on you;
> If you can trust yourself when all men doubt you,
> But make allowance for their doubting too;
> If you can wait and not be tired by waiting,
> Or being lied about, don't deal in lies,
> Or, being hated, don't give way to hating,
> And yet don't look too good, nor talk too wise;
>
> If you can dream—and not make dreams your master;
> If you can think—and not make thoughts your aim;
> If you can meet with triumph and disaster
> And treat those two impostors just the same;
> If you can bear to hear the truth you've spoken
> Twisted by knaves to make a trap for fools,
> Or watch the things you gave your life to, broken,
> And stoop and build 'em up with wornout tools;
>
> If you can make one heap of all your winnings
> And risk it on one turn of pitch-and-toss,
> And lose, and start again at your beginnings
> And never breathe a word about your loss;
> If you can force your heart and nerve and sinew
> To serve your turn long after they are gone,
> And so hold on when there is nothing in you
> Except the Will which says to them: "Hold on";
>
> If you can talk with crowds and keep your virtue,
> Or walk with kings—nor lose the common touch;
> If neither foe nor loving friends can hurt you;
> If all men count with you, but none too much;

If you can fill the unforgiving minute
With sixty seconds' worth of distance run—
Yours is the Earth and everything that's in it,
And—which is more—you'll be a Man, my son!

WALTER SAVAGE LANDOR (1775-1864)

Rose Aylmer
Dying Speech of an Old Philosopher
To Age

When rebellious and impetuous young Landor became involved with golden-haired Nancy Jones, his wealthy father removed him from Oxford and provided him with a relatively small yearly sum. Landor thereupon began seriously to make himself a scholar, with Nancy his only recreation. In 1796 they were at Swansea, where he loved to roam the beach alone. On one of these walks the poet met a friend, the fifth Lord Aylmer, who was on the beach with his seventeen-year-old sister Rose. Nancy Jones, about to give birth, was promptly forgotten. As Landor confessed in a poem several weeks later, when he first met Rose "My courage, voice, and memory gone," "I tost and tumbled, fretted, wept."

Although Rose enjoyed Landor's company, it is improbable he made love to her. Living openly with a mistress at the time he met her, he was in no position to conduct an honorable romance. But he did see her often (apparently then breaking off with Nancy), and the beautiful girl was not indifferent to the young poet.

However, after eighteen months Rose went to India with an aunt, and a year or so later died there of cholera. When Landor learned of her death he wrote these exquisite lines, deservedly his best-known:

> Ah, what avails the sceptred race,
>   Ah, what the form divine!
> What every virtue, every grace!
>   Rose Aylmer, all were thine.

> Rose Aylmer, whom these wakeful eyes
>   May weep, but never see,
> A night of memories and of sighs
>   I consecrate to thee.

A significant postscript to the poem is that after Landor's death, at a great age, a packet of golden hair was found in his desk inscribed "Rose Aylmer's hair." It had been sent to him as a sentimental keepsake by Rose's sister.

All during his life Landor rebelled: in youth from parental authority and later in religion, politics and just about anything else that provoked his dissent. As a consequence, his was by no means a serene life, or a successful one by conventional standards. Although a superb prose writer and a vigorous political thinker, he had little influence in this field. He hoped to surpass Byron and Wordsworth in poetry, but failed in this. His marriage became a tragic fiasco and his children gave scant affection after they had succeeded in getting from him as much money as he had to dispose of. Even at age eighty-three Landor defiantly left England for good rather than submit to a court judgment he regarded as unjust.

But there was one condition Landor did not rebel at the thought of: his own death. When he reached seventy, vigorous in mind and body and with many friends who enjoyed the richness of his personality, he nevertheless wrote that it was about time he felt the effect of age, adding "Let me fold my arms across my breast, and go quietly down the current until where the current ends." And in that same year, 1846, he said of death: "I don't invite him but I shall receive him hospitably when he comes." More and more after that, Landor kept predicting he would die within a year. And on his seventy-fifth birthday, in 1850, he wrote his famous "Dying Speech of an Old Philosopher":

> I strove with none; for none was worth my strife;
> Nature I loved, and next to Nature, Art;
> I warmed both hands before the fire of life;
> It sinks, and I am ready to depart.

Two years later, still active and sending a stream of vigorous letters to the press on questions that interested him, Landor again wrote cheerful lines "To Age":

> Welcome, old friend! These many years
> Have we lived door by door;
> The Fates have laid aside their shears
> Perhaps for some few more.
>
> I was indocile at an age
> When better boys were taught,
> But thou at length hast made me sage,
> If I am sage in aught.

Little I know from other men,
    Too little they from me,
But thou hast pointed well the pen
    That writes these lines to thee.

Thanks for expelling Fear and Hope,
    One vile, the other vain;
One's scourge, the other's telescope,
    I shall not see again:

Rather what lies before my feet
    My notice shall engage—
He who hath braved Youth's dizzy heat
    Dreads not the frost of Age.

Finally, in the eighty-ninth year of his life, the old literary lion died at Florence, Italy; bent, shabby, scorned by his wife and children and cared for by Robert and Elizabeth Browning and the American artist William Wetmore Storey and his wife. Landor was glad when death approached.

SIDNEY LANIER (1842-1881)

Evening Song

Love was the keynote of Sidney Lanier's life—love that triumphed over a life of illness and poverty.

He was born in a cultured Georgia family that had a talent for love of one another. When he was released from a Union prisoner-of-war camp at the end of the Civil War he was broken in health; tuberculosis had a grip on him that gradually increased until it crushed his earthly shell.

Upon Lanier's return to Macon he fell in love with Mary Day, a slender girl of fragile beauty and delicate health, but with a heart that matched in warmth and greatness that of the aesthetic looking young man who found it difficult to decide between music and poetry. In 1867 they married—and for fourteen years lived a life of love that ennobled them and inspired those who knew them.

A summary of Lanier's difficulties can only suggest the family struggles their love survived. He taught school and then practiced law for several years, writing poetry and a novel in his spare time. But tuberculosis from time to time asserted itself and he would have to go away in quest of health.

Lanier had a few good years beginning in 1875 when his poetry found publication, he obtained a position as a flutist for the Peabody Orchestra in Baltimore and did some hack work. Again his health broke and friends had to supply the family with money. He then lectured on literature at Johns Hopkins University until April 1881, when his illness took over for its tragic victory five months later.

During these years of illness and disappointments Lanier's tenderness and devotion to his wife never abated. Friends said he was transfigured in her presence. And she, in referring to her care of him said: "This precious life I hold by so frail a tenure."

A man such as Lanier, who even wrote poetry on his deathbed, would naturally tell his love in verse. In fact, when he sent five sonnets titled "In Absence" to a publication he said "They form the beginning of a series, which I will probably be writing all my life, knowing no other method of heart's-ease for my sense of the pure worshipfulness which dwells in the Lady they celebrate." Of course he wrote many other poems celebrating their love, but none more tender than his "Evening Song":

> Look off, dear Love, across the sallow sands,
>   And mark yon meeting of the sun and sea,
> How long they kiss in sight of all the lands,
>   Ah! longer, longer, we.
>
> Now in the sea's red vintage melts the sun,
>   As Egypt's pearl dissolved in rosy wine,
> And Cleopatra night drinks all. 'Tis done,
>   Love, lay thine hand in mine.
>
> Come forth, sweet stars, and comfort heaven's heart;
>   Glimmer, ye waves, round else unlighted sands.
> O night! divorce our sun and sky apart,
>   Never our lips, our hands.

EMMA LAZARUS (1849-1887)

The New Colossus
(Inscription on the Statue of Liberty)

The inscription engraved on the pedestal of the Statue of Liberty in New York Harbor is the eloquent climax of the awakening of an American-born

Jewish woman who began life in a prosperous and protected home in New York City, and only slowly became aware of the outside world.

The Lazarus family considered themselves of the "Jewish nobility"—families from southern Europe who came to the United States many years before 1849, when Emma was born. Their children were privately tutored, sheltered from the life of the city, attended a wealthy synagogue, and were only vaguely aware that such a thing as poverty existed.

Timid, sensitive Emma lived a life of books and started to write poetry when a child. Her mind began to burgeon when she met Ralph Waldo Emerson socially in New York, sent him a copy of her privately published first poems and engaged in a long-continued correspondence with him. In 1876 she visited the Emersons at their Concord home and through him met and became friendly with William Ellery Channing.

But it was not until the Russian pogroms of 1881 that the gifted young woman broke through the wall that shut her off from the real world and the realization that America was the hope of persecuted people.

She had gone as a wealthy lady on a welfare committee to meet and help refugees who had fled Russia, and for the first time came face to face with the grief and suffering of the persecuted. From that day a new Emma Lazarus was born, as her poems spoke with more power and fire on themes she had not previously thought deeply on. In fact, she went beyond her poetry to become a vigorous defender of minorities and a denouncer of persecution and prejudice.

In 1883 a committee was formed in New York City to raise funds for the pedestal for the largest statue in the world: "Liberty Enlightening the World," a gift from France to the United States. It was to be placed on Bedloe's Island (now Liberty Island) in New York Harbor. The committee planned to auction off manuscripts of Longfellow, Whitman, Mark Twain and others, and Miss Lazarus was asked to contribute a manuscript for the auction. In November of that year she wrote and contributed a sonnet— "The New Colossus"—after examining photographs of the statue then still in Paris.

When James Russell Lowell read her lines he said the statue needed the sonnet as much as it needed the pedestal.

The Statue of Liberty was unveiled by President Grover Cleveland in October, 1886. Emma Lazarus, after a long illness, died in November, 1887. And in 1903 Georgianna Schuyler, in "loving memory" of the poet, arranged to have the sonnet engraved upon Liberty's pedestal. Few poems have been given so great a help toward immortality.

> Not like the brazen giant of Greek fame,
> With conquering limbs astride from land to land;

Here at our sea-washed, sunset gates shall stand
A mighty woman with a torch, whose flame
Is the imprisoned lightning, and her name
Mother of Exiles. From her beacon-hand
Glows world-wide welcome; her mild eyes command
The air-bridged harbor that twin cities frame.
"Keep, ancient lands, your storied pomp!" cries she
With silent lips. "Give me your tired, your poor,
Your huddled masses yearning to breathe free,
The wretched refuse of your teeming shore.
Send these, the homeless, tempest-tost to me,
I lift my lamp beside the golden door!"

VACHEL LINDSAY (1879-1931)

The Congo

One Sunday in October, 1913, Vachel Lindsay sat with his parents in the family pew at the First Christian Church, in Springfield, Illinois. Brother Burnham, the minister, spoke of his sorrow over the loss of an old college friend, Brother Ray Eldred, who had drowned in the River Congo while engaged in missionary work.

Something that Brother Burnham said ignited the volatile imagination and made vivid certain memories of the thirty-four-year-old poet, according to Eleanor Ruggles in her biography of Lindsay. He thought of one of the favorite books of his youth, Stanley's *Darkest Africa*, with a map of Africa all in black except for a twisting gold line representing the River Congo. He recalled the religious ecstasies of one of the Lindsay family's Negro cooks, the Hampton Singers' rendering of *Swing Low, Sweet Chariot*, the frenzied dancing of Negroes he had seen on stage and street, and no doubt he remembered, from his several walking-tours of the nation, Negroes he had seen under the spell of religious emotion at revival meetings and gospel missions and obscure rural churches.

Vachel Lindsay was a man who saw meaning, beauty, color and poetry where others merely looked; a visionary who lived the brotherhood he preached, stopping as a grateful guest in the homes of poor Negroes when he roamed virtually penniless through the South and other parts of the nation, reciting and selling or giving away copies of his poems. Lindsay loved all men and dreamed that they could be united in a religious brotherhood without diluting their loyalty to disparate churches.

Brother Burnham had somehow stirred this poet to deeper thoughts about a race of people he knew and liked—from the Negroes who lived in a tenement on the corner across from his Springfield home, to the wise and witty *Uncle Remus* his father used to read to him; from the massive black men he met in his travels to the tormented souls he had seen terrorized and lynched during a race riot that caused him to storm the press with letters of protest.

In this mood and with these thoughts he left the church that day and immediately began to write his "The Congo," wherein he hoped to show that the Negro's ill-fate is at first alleviated by his capacity for expressing joy and ultimately redeemed by his religious faith. Seven or eight weeks passed before the poem had the courageous content and arresting rhythm he believed it should have.

If public acceptance is a valid criterion, it was time well-spent. It is Lindsay's most famous poem, two-thirds of which is all that we have been able to reprint.

I. THEIR BASIC SAVAGERY

Fat black bucks in a wine-barrel room,
Barrel-house kings, with feet unstable,

A deep rolling bass   Sagged and reeled and pounded on the table,
Pounded on the table,
Beat an empty barrel with the handle of a broom,
Hard as they were able,
Boom, boom, BOOM.
With a silk umbrella and the handle of a broom,
Boomlay, boomlay, boomlay, BOOM.
Then I had religion. THEN I had a vision.
I could not turn from their revel in derision.

More deliberate.   THEN I SAW THE CONGO, CREEPING
Solemnly chanted.   THROUGH THE BLACK,
CUTTING THROUGH THE FOREST WITH A
    GOLDEN TRACK.
Then along that riverbank
A thousand miles
Tatooed cannibals danced in files;
Then I heard the boom of the blood-lust song

A rapidly piling climax And a thigh-bone beating on a tin-pan gong.
of speed and racket.   And "BLOOD" screamed the whistles and the fifes
    of the warriors,
"BLOOD" screamed the skull-faced, lean witch-
    doctors,
"Whirl ye the deadly voo-doo rattle,
Harry the uplands,

Steal all the cattle,
Rattle-rattle, rattle-rattle,
Bing.
Boomlay, boomlay, boomlay, BOOM,"

With a philosophic
pause.

A roaring, epic, rag-time tune
From the mouth of the Congo
To the Mountains of the Moon.

Shrilly and with a
heavily accented metre.

Death is an Elephant,
Torch-eyed and horrible,
Foam-flanked and terrible.
BOOM, steal the pgymies,
BOOM, kill the Arabs,
BOOM, kill the white men,

Like the wind in the
chimney.

HOO, HOO, HOO.
Listen to the yell of Leopold's ghost
Burning in Hell for his hand-maimed host.
Hear how the demons chuckle and yell
Cutting his hands off, down in Hell.
Listen to the creepy proclamation,
Blown through the lairs of the forest-nation,
Blown past the white-ants' hill of clay,

All the "o" sounds very
golden. Heavy accents
very heavy. Light
accents very light.
Last line whispered.

Blown past the marsh where the butterflies play:
"Be careful what you do,
Or Mumbo-Jumbo, God of the Congo,
And all of the other
Gods of the Congo,
Mumbo-Jumbo will hoo-doo you,
Mumbo-Jumbo will hoo-doo you,
Mumbo-Jumbo will hoo-doo you."

* * * * * * * *

III. THE HOPE OF THEIR RELIGION

Heavy bass. With a
literal imitation of camp
meeting racket, and
trance

A good old negro in the slums of the town
Preached at a sister for her velvet gown.
Howled at a brother for his low-down ways,
His prowling, guzzling, sneak-thief days.
Beat on the Bible till he wore it out
Starting the jubilee revival shout.
And some had visions, as they stood on chairs,
And sang of Jacob, and the golden stairs,
And they all repented, a thousand strong,
From their stupor and savagery and sin and wrong,
And slammed with their hymn books till they shook
      the room

With "Glory, glory, glory,"
And "Boom, boom, BOOM."

Exactly as in the first section. Begin with terror and power, and with joy.

THEN I SAW THE CONGO, CREEPING
    THROUGH THE BLACK,
CUTTING THROUGH THE JUNGLE WITH
    A GOLDEN TRACK.
And the gray sky opened like a new-rent veil
And showed the Apostles with their coats of mail.
In bright white steel they were seated round
And their fire-eyes watched where the Congo wound.
And the Twelve Apostles, from their thrones on high,
Thrilled all the forest with their heavenly cry:—

Sung to the tune of "Hark, ten thousand harps and voices."

"Mumbo-Jumbo will die in the jungle;
Never again will he hoo-doo you,
Never again will he hoo-doo you."
Then along that river, a thousand miles,
The vine-snarled trees fell down in files.

With growing deliberation and joy.

Pioneer angels cleared the way
For a Congo paradise, for babes at play,
For sacred capitals, for temples clean.
Gone were the skull-faced witch-men lean.

In rather higher key— as delicately as possible.

There, where the wild-ghost-gods had wailed
A million boats of the angels sailed
With oars of silver, and prows of blue
And silken pennants that the sun shone through.
'Twas a land transfigured, 'twas a new creation.
Oh, a singing wind swept the negro nation
And on through the backwoods clearing flew:—

To the tune of "Hark, ten thousand harps and voices."

"Mumbo-Jumbo is dead in the jungle.
Never again will he hoo-doo you.
Never again will he hoo-doo you."
Redeemed were the forests, the beasts and the men,
And only the vulture dared again
By the far, lone mountains of the moon

Dying down into a penetrating, terrified whisper.

To cry, in the silence, the Congo tune:—
"Mumbo-Jumbo will hoo-doo you,
Mumbo-Jumbo will hoo-doo you.
Mumbo . . . Jumbo . . . will . . . hoo-doo . . . you."

HENRY WADSWORTH LONGFELLOW (1807-1882)

A Psalm of Life
The Village Blacksmith
The Wreck of the Hesperus
The Bridge
The Children's Hour
The Cross of Snow

Although it has become fashionable during the past thirty or forty years to dismiss Longfellow as a poetic preacher and a singer of saccharine songs, nevertheless he still speaks appealingly to those who cling to the homely virtues and cherish a quiet faith in God and country. He was, in fact, much more of a scholar and a poet of genuine ability than his deceptively simple verse suggests. The restraint—the lack of emotion—in his poetry is characteristic of the gentle, dignified man who lived a life of reflection. Moreover, he was simply practicing his belief that the function of poetry was "to charm, to strengthen, to teach."

It is surprising to realize that at the time of its publication in 1838 "A Psalm of Life" had a freshness and energy that familiarity has dissipated for many of us. Not that it was a contrived piece of didactic morality. Longfellow said "I kept it some time in manuscript, unwilling to show it to anyone, it being a voice from my inmost heart at a time when I was rallying from depression." He wrote it one summer day in 1828, on the blank parts of a note of invitation. But it could not have been so casually arrived at as this suggests, since it was the formulation of moral truths the poet had for some time been seeking; the lesson life had already taught him. It was the end of a period of grief and distress following the death of his first wife three years previously.

Whereas today the poem may meet with an indifferent or even scoffing reception, when it was first published it stirred people, especially the young, to aspire higher and to an appreciation of the nobility of life. It was reprinted all over the world, even translated into Chinese and woven into a fan that was sent to the poet. But Longfellow tells how the "conceit was taken out of me" when the poem was quoted at length during a sermon. Later that day a woman remarked that the sermon was good but no one seemed to know what poem the preacher quoted from.

A PSALM OF LIFE
*What the Heart of the Young
Man Said to the Psalmist*

Tell me not, in mournful numbers,
    Life is but an empty dream!—
For the soul is dead that slumbers,
    And things are not what they seem.

Life is real! Life is earnest!
    And the grave is not its goal:
Dust thou art, to dust returnest,
    Was not spoken of the soul.

Not enjoyment, and not sorrow,
    Is our destined end or way;
But to act, that each tomorrow
    Finds us farther than today.

Art is long, and Time is fleeting,
    And our hearts, though stout and brave,
Still, like muffled drums, are beating
    Funeral marches to the grave.

In the world's broad field of battle,
    In the bivouac of Life,
Be not like dumb, driven cattle!
    Be a hero in the strife!

Trust no Future, howe'er pleasant!
    Let the dead Past bury its dead!
Act,—act in the living Present!
    Heart within, and God o'erhead!

Lives of great men all remind us
    We can make our lives sublime,
And departing, leave behind us
    Footprints on the sands of time;

Footprints, that perhaps another,
    Sailing o'er life's solemn main,
A forlorn and shipwrecked brother,
    Seeing, shall take heart again.

Let us, then, be up and doing,
    With a heart for any fate;
Still achieving, still pursuing,
    Learn to labor and to wait.

On Brattle Street in Cambridge, Massachusetts, there stood a horse chest-nut tree beneath which was the shop of the village's blacksmith. Longfellow passed this spot twice each day on his way to and from his home in Cam-bridge and Harvard College. Certainly the handsome and dapper young professor must have become acquainted with the smithy and on occasion stopped to watch the man wield his hammer.

In October, 1839, the poet recorded in his journal: "Wrote a new Psalm of Life. It is 'The Village Blacksmith.'" Later he wrote his father: "There will be a kind of ballad on a Blacksmith in the next *Knickerbocker*, which you may consider, if you please, as a song in praise of your ancestor in Newbury." This was a reference to Stephen Longfellow, who became a blacksmith when orphaned, and later was a schoolmaster and the town clerk of Portland, Maine.

The poem became so famous that there was strong protest thirty-seven years later when the chestnut tree was cut down because its branches en-dangered drivers who passed beneath it. But portions of the wood were kept and used to make an elaborate chair, which was paid for by contributions from the school children of Cambridge, and presented by them to Long-fellow on his seventy-second birthday. A brass plate on the chair bore the inscription:

> To the Author of The Village Blacksmith
>
> This Chair made from the wood of the spreading
> chestnut tree, is presented as an expression of grateful
> regard and veneration by the children of Cambridge, who
> with their friends join in best wishes and congratulations
> on this anniversary.

Longfellow wrote and had printed for children who called at his home to see and sit in the chair, the following:

> "Only your love and remembrance could
>   Give life to this dead wood,
> And make these branches, leafless now so long,
>   Blossom again in song."

The line "Blossom again in song" referred to a phrase from the poem carved at the base of the chair.

> Under a spreading chestnut-tree
>   The village smithy stands;

The smith, a mighty man is he,
  With large and sinewy hands;
And the muscles of his brawny arms
  Are strong as iron bands.

His hair is crisp, and black, and long,
  His face is like the tan;
His brow is wet with honest sweat,
  He earns whate'er he can,
And looks the whole world in the face,
  For he owes not any man.

Week in, week out, from morn till night,
  You can hear his bellows blow;
You can hear him swing his heavy sledge,
  With measured beat and slow,
Like a sexton ringing the village bell,
  When the evening sun is low.

And children coming from school
  Look in at the open door;
They love to see the flaming forge,
  And hear the bellows roar,
And catch the burning sparks that fly
  Like chaff from a threshing floor.

He goes on Sunday to the church,
  And sits among his boys;
He hears the parson pray and preach,
  He hears his daughter's voice,
Singing in the village choir,
  And it makes his heart rejoice.

It sounds to him like her mother's voice,
  Singing in Paradise!
He needs must think of her once more,
  How in the grave she lies:
And with his hard, rough hand he wipes
  A tear out of his eyes.

Toiling—rejoicing—sorrowing,
  Onward through life he goes;
Each morning sees come task begin,
  Each evening sees it close;
Something attempted, something done,
  Has earned a night's repose.

Thanks, thanks to thee, my worthy friend,
  For the lesson thou has taught!
Thus at the flaming forge of life
  Our fortunes must be wrought;
Thus on its sounding anvil shaped
  Each burning deed and thought.

On the night of December 15, 1839, the New England coast was lashed by one of the wildest northwest gales it had experienced in years, snow and sleet compounding the work of the high winds. Gloucester, Massachusetts, was one of the ports hit hardest. The Boston papers stated that sixty vessels took refuge in Gloucester's outer harbor, twenty of which were wrecked on an exposed reef called Norman's Woe. Seventeen bodies were washed ashore, said the papers, including "a female who was lashed to the bitt [timber holding the windlass] of the windlass of a Castine schooner, two others of the crew also perishing."

The name of the schooner proved to be the "Favorite," out of Wiscasset, Maine, and the "female" was Mrs. Sally Hilton, aged fifty-five.

Two days after the storm Longfellow recorded in his Diary: "News of shipwrecks horrible on the coast. Twenty bodies washed ashore near Gloucester, one lashed to a piece of wreckage. There is a reef called Norman's Woe where many of these took place, among them a schooner *Hesperus*. I must write a ballad on this."

Two weeks later the poet wrote his famous poem, recording in his Journal: "I sat still till twelve o'clock by the fire, smoking, when suddenly it came into my mind to write 'The Ballad of the Schooner *Hesperus*,' which I accordingly did. Then I went to bed, but could not sleep. New thoughts were running in my mind, and I got up to add them to the ballad. It was three by the clock when I fell asleep. I feel pleased with the ballad. It hardly cost me an effort. It did not come into my mind by lines, but by stanzas." When the poem was published two weeks later Longfellow was paid $25.00 for it.

Thirty-five years ago Henry Beston, in *The Bookman*, pointed out that no schooner *Hesperus* was wrecked at Gloucester. The *Hesperus*, from Gardiner, Maine, was in fact anchored in Boston Harbor during the storm, and was torn from its mooring and against another vessel and then into a dock. The *Hesperus* was damaged but no lives aboard it were lost. Mr. Beston observed that the poet just liked the sound of the name *Hesperus,* and had used it on other occasions.

It was the schooner Hesperus,
  That sailed the wintry sea;

And the skipper had taken his little daughter,
  To bear him company.

Blue were her eyes as the fairy-flax,
  Her cheeks were like the dawn of day,
And her bosom white as the hawthorn buds,
  That ope in the month of May.

The skipper he stood beside the helm,
  His pipe was in his mouth,
And he watched how the veering flaw did blow
  The smoke now West, now South.

Then up and spake an old Sailor,
  Had sailed to the Spanish Main,
"I pray thee, put into yonder port,
  For I fear a hurricane.

"Last night, the moon had a golden ring,
  And tonight no moon we see!"
The skipper, he blew a whiff from his pipe,
  And a scornful laugh laughed he.

Colder and louder blew the wind,
  A gale from the Northeast,
The snow fell hissing in the brine,
  And the billows frothed like yeast.

Down came the storm, and smote amain
  The vessel in its strength;
She shuddered and paused, like a frighted steed,
  Then leaped her cable's length.

"Come hither! come hither! my little daughter,
  And do not tremble so;
For I can weather the roughest gale
  That ever wind did blow."

He wrapped her warm in his seaman's coat
  Against the stinging blast;
He cut a rope from a broken spar,
  And bound her to the mast.

"O father! I hear the church-bells ring,
  Oh say, what may it be?"

'Tis a fog-bell on a rock-bound coast!"—
And he steered for the open sea.

"O father! I hear the sound of guns,
Oh say, what may it be?"
"Some ship in distress, that cannot live
In such an angry sea!"

O father! I see a gleaming light,
Oh say, what may it be?"
But the father answered never a word,
A frozen corpse was he.

Lashed to the helm, all stiff and stark,
With his face turned to the skies,
The lantern gleamed through the gleaming snow
On his fixed and glassy eyes.

Then the maiden clasped her hands and prayed
That savèd she might be;
And she thought of Christ, who stilled the wave,
On the Lake of Galilee.

And fast through the midnight dark and drear,
Through the whistling sleet and snow,
Like a sheeted ghost, the vessel swept
Tow'rds the reef of Norman's Woe.

And ever the fitful gusts between
A sound came from the land;
It was the sound of the trampling surf
On the rocks and the hard sea-sand.

The breakers were right beneath her bows,
She drifted a dreary wreck,
And a whooping billow swept the crew
Like icicles from her deck.

She struck where the white and fleecy waves
Looked soft as carded wool,
But the cruel rocks, they gored her side
Like the horns of an angry bull.

Her rattling shrouds, all sheathed in ice,
With the masts went by the board;

> Like a vessel of glass, she stove and sank,
> Ho! ho! the breakers roared!

> At day-break, on the bleak sea-beach,
> A fisherman stood aghast,
> To see the form of a maiden fair,
> Lashed close to a drifting mast.

> The salt sea was frozen on her breast,
> The salt tears in her eyes;
> And he saw her hair, like the brown sea-weed,
> On the billows fall and rise.

> Such was the wreck of the Hesperus,
> In the midnight and the snow!
> Christ save us all from a death like this,
> On the reef of Norman's Woe!

When Longfellow's first wife died in Europe four years after their marriage, the poet remained abroad for another year. During this period he met and was attracted to Frances Appleton, a Boston girl ten years younger than himself.

Longfellow established bachelor quarters in Cambridge, in 1836, took up his academic duties at Harvard and persistently began to court Miss Appleton, who gave no encouragement to the poet with the beautiful voice. During the seven years that elapsed before his beloved Fanny relented, Longfellow experienced the despair, indecision and inner conflict of the ardent lover who was frustrated.

He spoke in his Journal of Fanny holding "his reason captive" and said "my pride has written hic jacet of that passion" and that he "lives alone, grim as Death, with only one great thought in my mind."

When the poet called on Miss Appleton he crossed over the bridge between Cambridge and Boston, and recorded in his Journal that "I always stop on the bridge." These were memorable moments to him, recaptured in "The Bridge," written in 1845, ten years after he had married Fanny, as he reflected on his moods and feelings during the years of uncertain courtship now become triumphant:

> I stood on the bridge at midnight,
> As the clocks were striking the hour,
> And the moon rose o'er the city,
> Behind the dark church-tower.

I saw her bright reflection
In the waters under me,
Like a golden goblet falling
And sinking into the sea.

And far in the hazy distance
Of that lovely night in June,
The blaze of the flaming furnace
Gleamed redder than the moon.

Among the long, black rafters
The wavering shadows lay,
And the current that came from the ocean
Seemed to lift and bear them away;

As, sweeping and eddying through them,
Rose the belated tide,
And, streaming into the moonlight,
The seaweed floated wide.

And like those waters rushing
Among the wooden piers,
A flood of thoughts came o'er me
That filled my eyes with tears.

How often, oh, how often,
In the days that had gone by,
I had stood on that bridge at midnight
And gazed on that wave and sky!

How often, oh, how often,
I had wished that the ebbing tide
Would bear me away on its bosom
O'er the ocean wild and wide!

For my heart was hot and restless,
And my life was full of care,
And the burden laid upon me
Seemed greater than I could bear.

But now it has fallen from me,
It is buried in the sea;
And only the sorrow of others
Throws its shadow over me.

Yet whenever I cross the river
　　On its bridge with wooden piers,
Like the odor of brine from the ocean
　　Comes the thought of other years.

And I think how many thousands
　　Of care-encumbered men,
Each bearing his burden of sorrow,
　　Have crossed the bridge since then.

I see the long procession
　　Still passing to and fro,
The young heart hot and restless,
　　And the old subdued and slow!

And forever and forever,
　　As long as the river flows,
As long as the heart has passions,
　　As long as life has woes;

The moon and its broken reflection
　　And its shadows shall appear,
As the symbol of love in heaven,
　　And its wavering image here.

Knowledge of Longfellow's life and personality suggests it was almost inevitable that he should celebrate in verse the happiness his five children gave
him. (Another child died in infancy.) His own childhood in a comfortable
Maine home was happy. His life with Fanny Appleton was an exceptionally
happy one. His temperament was best suited to the intimacies of family life,
and he wrote that "Homekeeping hearts are the happiest."

But evidently his three daughters most delighted him. About the time he
composed "The Children's Hour" he wrote Charles Sumner: "It is Sunday
afternoon. You know, then, how the old home looks,—the shadows in the
library, and the sunshine in the study, where I stand at my desk to write
you this. Two little girls are playing about the room. Allegra counting with
great noise the brass handles on my secretary, 'nine, eight, five, one,' and
Edith insisting upon having some paper box, long promised but never found,
and informing me that I am not a man of my word." And from their summer
home at Nahant he wrote: "Here come the three girls bursting into the room,
fresh from a bath. Well, I have kissed them all, and written them a little
letter apiece, and turned them all out; and now proceed." During the same
summer he wrote a child correspondent: "I am passing the summer with

my three little girls. The oldest is about your age. . . . Her name is Alice. . . . She is a nice girl and loves poetry. . . . The second is Edith, with blue eyes, and beautiful golden locks. . . . She is a very busy little woman. . . . The youngest is Allegra, which, you know, means merry; and she is the merriest little thing you ever saw,—always singing and laughing all over the house. . . . I do not say anything about the boys. They are such noisy fellows it is of no use to talk about them."

Several years later Longfellow wrote: "My little girls are flitting about my study as birds. . . . What a beautiful world this child-world is! So instinct with life, so illuminated with imagination. I take infinite delight in seeing it go on around and feel all the tenderness of the words that fell from blessed lips, 'Suffer these little children to come unto me.' After that benediction how can any one dare to deal harshly with a child."

Obviously "The Children's Hour" came from a warm and loving heart:

> Between the dark and the daylight,
>   When the night is beginning to lower,
> Comes a pause in the day's occupations,
>   That is known as the Children's Hour.
>
> I hear in the chamber above me
>   The patter of little feet,
> The sound of a door that is opened,
>   And voices soft and sweet.
>
> From my study I see in the lamplight,
>   Descending the broad hall stair,
> Grave Alice, and laughing Allegra,
>   And Edith with golden hair.
>
> A whisper, and then a silence:
>   Yet I know by their merry eyes
> They are plotting and planning together
>   To take me by surprise.
>
> A sudden rush from the stairway,
>   A sudden raid from the hall!
> By three doors left unguarded
>   They enter my castle wall!
>
> They climb up into my turret
>   O'er the arms and back of my chair;
> If I try to escape, they surround me;
>   They seem to be everywhere.

They almost devour me with kisses,
　　Their arms about me entwine,
Till I think of the Bishop of Bingen
　　In his Mouse-Tower on the Rhine!

Do you think, O blue-eyed banditti,
　　Because you have scaled the wall,
Such an old mustache as I am
　　Is not a match for you all!

I have you fast in my fortress,
　　And will not let you depart,
But put you down into the dungeon
　　In the round-tower of my heart.

And there I will keep you forever,
　　Yes, forever and a day,
Till the walls shall crumble to ruin,
　　And moulder in dust away!

Incidentally, Longfellow's son Ernest said that the famous doggerel:

There was a little girl
Who had a little curl
　　Right in the middle of her forehead;
And when she was good
She was very, very good,
　　But when she was bad she was horrid

was composed by the poet while walking up and down with his infant Alice
in his arms. Blanche R. Tucker in her biography of Longfellow said the
lines were written when the poet's daughter Edith did not want to have her
hair curled. Edward Wagenknecht, Longfellow's most recent biographer, says
the evidence of the poet's authorship of the stanza is far from conclusive. At
any rate, it *sounds* like Longfellow.

After years of idyllic married life, tragedy struck Longfellow in July,
1861, when his beloved Fanny's dress caught fire from a match that had been
dropped on the floor of the library in their home. She died the next day
and was buried three days later, on the eighteenth anniversary of her wedding. The poet was still in bed from burns suffered when he went to her
rescue.

This bereavement almost crushed the man, who aged as a consequence
and for months was unable to speak of his loss. "With me all deep feelings

are silent ones," he once said. "The thoughts that are in my heart and brain I cannot record." When a friend expressed the hope to Longfellow that he would be able to "bear his cross" with patience, the poet replied *"Bear* the cross, yes; but what if one is stretched upon it?"

Eighteen years after his wife's death Longfellow was looking through a book of western scenery and encountered a picture of the mountain in Colorado where the snow lies in long furrows which from a distance form the clear image of a great cross.

That evening the seventy-two-year-old poet looked at his wife's picture on the wall of his bedroom, thought of the picture of the remarkable Colorado mountainside, and wrote "The Cross of Snow," the only love-poem about his wife that he wrote, except for his "The Evening Star" which was composed in 1845. The lines given below were found in Longfellow's portfolio when he died three years later:

> In the long, sleepless watches of the night,
> A gentle face—the face of one long dead—
> Looks at me from the wall, where round its head
> The night-lamp casts a halo of pale light.
> Here in this room she died; and soul never more white
> Never through martyrdom of fire was led
> To its repose; nor can in books be read
> The legend of a life more benight.
> There is a mountain in the distant West
> That, sun-defying, in its deep ravines
> Displays a cross of snow upon its side.
> Such is the cross I wear upon my breast
> These eighteen years, through all the changing scenes
> And seasons, changeless since the day she died.

RICHARD LOVELACE (1618-1658)

To Althea From Prison
To Lucasta, Going to the Wars

Richard Lovelace, son of an old and distinguished family, was all one expects to find in a Cavalier in the time of Charles I of England: handsome, gay, engaging, writer of fine lyrics and ambitious to be a soldier and courtier. Moreover, he had the necessary sentimental and traditional love of country and was ready to defend the monarchy and the country's ancient institutions.

When Lovelace left Oxford he became a favorite at the Court, and when King Charles decided to war against the Scots the young poet enthusiastically joined the expedition that most of the nobles viewed with apathy.

It was a dull war, terminated by an uneasy truce. But more troubles were brewing for Charles in Parliament, where the King's increasing enemies were active. Lovelace and some friends strolled into Parliament, interjected themselves into the debate, tore up and strewed the floor with documents against the King that Parliament planned to put into effect. For this Lovelace was imprisoned in The Gatehouse for seven weeks. During this time he wrote his noted "To Althea From Prison," a charming expression of not infrequently voiced sentiments. Althea has never been identified, but since Lovelace was young, handsome, not indifferent to feminine charms and often quite serious in his poetry, it is improbable that these lines were addressed to a purely imaginary beloved:

>   When Love with unconfinèd wings
>   Hovers within my gates,
>   And my divine Althea brings
>   To whisper at the grates;
>   When I lie tangled in her hair
>   And fettered to her eye,
>   The birds that wanton in the air
>   Know no such liberty.
>
>   When flowing cups run swiftly round
>   With no allaying Thames,
>   Our careless heads with roses bound,
>   Our hearts with loyal flames;
>   When thirst grief in wine we steep,
>   When healths and draughts go free—
>   Fishes that tipple in the deep
>   Know no such liberty.
>
>   When, like committed linnets, I
>   With shriller throat shall sing
>   The sweetness, mercy, majesty,
>   And glories of my King;
>   When I shall voice aloud how good
>   He is, how great should be,
>   Enlargèd winds, that curl the flood,
>   Know no such liberty.
>
>   Stone walls do not a prison make,
>   Nor iron bars a cage;

Minds innocent and quiet take
　That for an hermitage;
If I have freedom in my love
　And in my soul am free,
Angels alone, that soar above,
　Enjoy such liberty.

Four years after the poem to Althea, Lovelace was able to get out of London to join the King's forces during the Civil War. By this time the poet had apparently ended his romance with "Althea"; now he was addressing poems to "Lucasta." Some early writers said "Lucasta" was one Lucy Sacherverell, a woman of about Lovelace's age then living in London. Others, including William Hazlitt, said "Lucasta" represented a real person, but not Lucy Sacherverell. However, after Lovelace was erroneously reported killed in battle, Lucy married. Later Lovelace addressed a poem to "Lucasta" asking her to release him from the faith he vowed in her, since she had married in his absence. It is difficult to dismiss "Lucasta" as a mere romantic fiction of the poet's brain, especially when one reads the tender poem to her written just before Lovelace joined the King's army during the rebellion of the 1640's:

Tell me not, Sweet, I am unkind,
　That from the nunnery
Of thy chaste breast and quiet mind,
　To wars and arms I fly.

True, a new mistress now I chase,
　The first foe in the field;
And with a stronger faith embrace
　A sword, a horse, a shield.

Yet this inconstancy is such
　As you too shalt adore;
I could not love thee, Dear, so much,
　Loved I not Honour more.

There is no record that Lovelace ever married. He died penniless and despondent, at the age of forty in 1658, nine years after the Puritans beheaded his King.

JAMES RUSSELL LOWELL (1819-1891)

My Love
She Came and Went
"And What is so Rare as a Day in June"

One day in his twentieth year James Russell Lowell, who had complacently asserted he was "not made for anything but to loiter through life," left his Cambridge, Massachusetts, home to call on a Harvard classmate, William A. White, who lived in adjoining Watertown. There the aimless youth met and was attracted to nineteen-year-old Maria White, a delicate, beautiful, serene-spirited girl of lofty standards who was herself a poet of ability. During their five-year courtship Maria, in her quiet way, encouraged the poet to become influential in public affairs and to cultivate only the true and beautiful. Through her Lowell met a group of young people whose company he enjoyed and whose interest in social causes enlisted his sympathies. Because of Maria, Lowell began to devote more time to the writing of poetry, including the tender "My Love," written a year after the smitten youth met her:

Not as all other women are
Is she that to my soul is dear;
Her glorious fancies come from far,
Beneath silver evening-star,
And yet her heart is ever near.

Great feelings hath she of her own,
Which lesser souls may never know;
God giveth them to her alone,
And sweet they are as any tone
Wherewith the wind may choose to blow.

Yet in herself she dwelleth not,
Although no home were half so fair;
No simplest duty is forgot,
Life hath no dim and lowly spot
That doth not in her sunshine share.

She doeth little kindnesses,
Which most leave undone, or despise;
For naught that sets one heart at ease,
And giveth happiness or peace,
Is low-esteemèd in her eyes.

She hath no scorn of common things,
And, though she seem of other birth,
Round us her heart entwines and clings,
And patiently she folds her wings
To tread the humble paths of earth.

Blessing she is: God made her so,
And deeds of weekday holiness
Fall from her noiseless as the snow,
Nor hath she ever chanced to know
That aught were easier than to bless.

She is most fair, and thereunto
Her life doth rightly harmonize;
Feeling or thought that was not true
Ne'er made less beautiful the blue
Unclouded heaven of her eyes.

She is a woman: one in whom
The spring-time of her childish years
Hath never lost its fresh perfume,
Though knowing well that life hath room
For many blights and many tears.

I love her with a love as still
As a broad river's peaceful might,
Which, by high tower and lowly mill,
Goes wandering at its own will,
And yet doth ever flow aright.

And, on its full, deep breast serene,
Like quiet isles my duties lie;
It flows around them and between,
And makes them fresh and fair and green,
Sweet homes wherein to live and die.

Lowell and Maria White were married in 1844 and made their home in Elmwood, his father's massive home in Cambridge, the center of most of the poet's joys and sorrows, and one of the great influences in his life. Here Lowell's occult-minded mother and his sister both suffered mental breakdowns. And here, too, a girl, Blanche, was born to the adoring couple. But their joy was short-lived; the baby died fourteen months after birth. This first poignant personal sorrow was commemorated in Lowell's "The Changeling" and in his "The First Snowfall," but perhaps most touching in "She Came and Went":

As a twig trembles, which a bird
  Lights on to sing, then leaves unbent,
So is my memory thrilled and stirred;—
  I only know she came and went.

As clasps some lake, by gusts unriven,
  The blue dome's measureless content,
So my soul held that moment's heaven;—
  I only know she came and went.

As, at one bound, our swift spring heaps
  The orchards full of bloom and scent,
So clove her May my wintry sleeps;—
  I only know she came and went.

An angel stood and met my gaze,
  Through the low doorway of my tent;
The tent is struck, the vision stays;—
  I only know she came and went.

O, when the room grows slowly dim,
  And life's last oil is nearly spent,
One gush of light these eyes will brim,
  Only to think she came and went.

Lowell had what he called the "mystic side" of his nature, the dreamy idealism of his *The Vision of Sir Launfal.* He seldom talked about this poem to friends, probably because it expressed the heroic life he had once dreamed of living, and also because its loveliest lines—the tribute to June— voiced his hopes for his beloved Maria, who was suffering from a persistent cough.

The famous lines to June were written during the bitterness of a New England winter at Elmwood—which Lowell described as "a complete Temple of the Winds . . . Through every chink the blasts are talking to each other . . . every one telling a different story of his prowess among the rotten boughs and loose shingles without." The poet yearned for Spring to dispel the damp and drafts from the old mansion's dark halls and rooms, in the hope Maria's failing health would improve. He thought, too, of Spring as a time of relief from "manhood's tenser strain" when one could return at least briefly to the carefree outlook of youth.

But his "beautiful and good" Maria continued gradually to decline, and died in 1857.

And what is so rare as a day in June?
    Then, if ever, come perfect days;
Then Heaven tries the earth if it be in tune,
    And over it softly her warm ear lays:
Whether we look, or whether we listen,
We hear life murmur, or see it glisten;
Every clod feels a stir of might,
    An instinct within it that reaches and towers,
And, groping blindly above it for light,
    Climbs to a soul in grass and flowers;
The flush of life may well be seen
Thrilling back over hills and valleys; . . .

Now is the high tide of the year,
    And whatever of life hath ebbed away
Comes flooding back with a ripply cheer,
    Into every bare inlet and creek and bay;
Now the heart is so full that a drop overfills it,
We are happy now because God wills it;
No matter how barren the past may have been,
'Tis enough for us now that the leaves are green. . . .

Joy comes, grief goes, we know not how;
Everything is happy now,
    Everything is upward striving;
'Tis as easy now for the heart to be true
As for grass to be green or skies to be blue,—
    'Tis the natural way of living:
Who knows whither the clouds have fled?
    In the unscarred heaven they leave no wake;
And the eyes forget the tears they have shed,
    The heart forgets its sorrow and ache.

(From Prelude to Part First)

EDWIN MARKHAM (1852-1940)

The Man With the Hoe

Edwin Markham's outraged indignation against the brutalization of the laboring man, as represented by "The Man With the Hoe," was not the protest of a bookish social reformer, but the cry of an American who from early youth had known the meaning of hard work.

His parents had pioneered across the nation to Oregon. When Edwin was five his improvident father died, and soon thereafter his mother and her two children moved to a wild section of central California. Here the growing boy snatched fragments of education thrown out by rural schools, and he worked at farming and ranching. Determined to get an education, Markham went to San Jose High School and provided for himself by working in a blacksmith shop. Then he taught school and later studied at Teachers Training College in Oakland.

While at the college in Oakland, Markham began reading Fourier and other social reformers whose writings aroused him against man's greedy exploitation of man. On one of those days in 1886 a friend showed him a copy of *Scribner's Magazine* containing a black and white reproduction of Millet's painting "The Man with the Hoe," a broken peasant symbolical of all toilers crushed by poverty.

Markham later said the picture "held my soul." Convinced that this man's problem was humanity's problem, he jotted down the first stanza of the poem: "to nail down my purpose to write a poem that should cry up the lost rights of the toiling multitude."

One April afternoon thirteen years later Markham visited an art exhibit in the San Francisco home of Mrs. Richard Crocker and for the first time he saw the original of the Millet painting. He looked at it for two hours, his soul stunned by its majesty and terror. At five o'clock that Saturday afternoon the poet sat down in his home to put into vibrant lines a plea to humanity for brotherhood through social justice. His indignation was not against work or labor or even the poverty he always knew and cheerfully accepted. Rather, his was an anguished and ringing condemnation of the drudgery and soul-shriveling treatment of labor then common throughout the world. On the fourth day Markham completed one of the most controversial and influential poems ever published in the United States. In fact, it swept the world with its eloquent challenge to the smug and heartless.

> *God made man in His own image,*
> *in the image of God made He him.—Genesis.*

> Bowed by the weight of centuries he leans
> Upon his hoe and gazes on the ground,
> The emptiness of ages in his face,
> And on his back the burden of the world.
> Who made him dead to rapture and despair,
> A thing that grieves not and that never hopes,
> Stolid and stunned, a brother to the ox?
> Who loosened and let down this brutal jaw?

Whose was the hand that slanted back this brow?
Whose breath blew out the light within this brain?

Is this the Thing the Lord God made and gave
To have dominion over sea and land;
To trace the stars and search the heavens for power;
To feel the passion of Eternity?
Is this the dream He dreamed who shaped the suns
And markt their ways upon the ancient deep?
Down all the caverns of Hell to their last gulf
There is no shape more terrible than this—
More tongued with censure of the world's blind greed—
More filled with signs and portents for the soul—
More packt with danger to the universe.

What gulfs between him and the seraphim!
Slave of the wheel of labor, what to him
Are Plato and the swing of Pleiades?
What the long reaches of the peaks of song,
The rift of dawn, the reddening of the rose?
Through this dread shape the suffering ages look;
Time's tragedy is in that aching stoop;
Through this dread shape humanity betrayed,
Plundered, profaned and disinherited,
Cries protest to the Powers that made the world,
A protest that is also prophecy.

O masters, lords and rulers in all lands,
Is this the handiwork you give to God,
This monstrous thing distorted and soul-quencht?
How will you ever straighten up this shape;
Touch it again with immortality;
Give back the upward looking and the light;
Rebuild in it the music and the dream;
Make right the immemorial infamies,
Perfidious wrongs, immedicable woes?

O masters, lords and rulers in all lands,
How will the future reckon with this man?
How answer his brute question in that hour
When whirlwinds of rebellion shake all shores?
How will it be with kingdoms and with kings—
With those who shaped him to the thing he is—
When this dumb Terror shall rise to judge the world,
After the silence of the centuries?

CHRISTOPHER MARLOWE (1564-1593)

from Faustus

Christopher Marlowe is but a shadowy figure of the Elizabethan age, but enough is known about him to explain how it happened that he reached the height of his poetic powers in his *The Tragical History of Dr. Faustus.*

Marlowe's brief life of turbulence began in Canterbury, February, 1564, two months before Shakespeare's birth. His father, a prosperous business man and church-warden, pointed his son toward the ministry—a career he was temperamentally unsuited for. Nevertheless, at the age of seventeen, Marlowe began a six-year stay at Cambridge, a gateway to a Church career.

But to the fiery youth these were years of religious disillusionment, of doubts and skepticism, perhaps of the then dangerous derision of Christianity. They were years when the young man secretly spurned the profound tomes of required reading, and turned with greedy delight to the forbidden fruits in the pages of Ovid, translating them and others into an idiom of his own. He became a poet. And apparently he was also a man of action—possibly secret and ulterior—since he was often absent from Cambridge for considerable periods of time.

It was presumably while in college that Marlowe began his great *Tamburlaine,* introducing a flame-tipped lyricism into English poetic drama. In any event, in 1587 he left Cambridge for London and the world of the theater, light-heartedly cynical and made audacious by the wine of freedom after the fetters of Cambridge.

His *Tamburlaine* was an immediate success on the London stage.

Two years later Marlowe was living in the Liberty of Norton Folgate, north of London. One day Marlowe, according to a dramatic reconstruction by Charles Norman in his *The Muses' Darling,* went into the city to rummage through the bookstalls against the sides of St. Paul's Cathedral, stopped at Edward White's at the Sign of the Guns and there found a faded gem he would transmute into a brilliant jewel. It was an eighty-page pamphlet: "THE HISTORIE of the damnable life, and deserved death of *Doctor Iohn Faustus,*" translated from the German.

With quickened interest the impulsive young poet read the "argument" of the book: that Faustus of Wittenberg, Germany, was a Conjurer and Necromancer who saw and did many strange things in the earth and the air. He read on and learned that Faustus, like Marlowe, had been a divinity student, and like Marlowe, Faustus "being of a naughty mind . . . applied not to his studies, but took to himself other studies." When the fascinated young man read that "Doctor Faustus began to practice in his devilish Art and conjured the Devil" he bought the book and strode away in elation. No doubt the great play was even then beginning to germinate in his quick mind. Faustus was a character upon whom he, Marlowe, could work his literary magic.

And when he did so, within a few months, his Faustus began with a soliloquy much like those the poet indulged in during his doubting days at Cambridge. But unlike other versions of Faustus, Marlowe's preached no sermons, taught no lessons. Rather he was his author's hero—Marlowe's other self, perhaps—speaking in glowing verse.

For example, when Faustus' compact with the Devil came to an end, he pleaded with Satan for one last pleasure,

> "That I might have unto my paramour,
> That heavenly *Helen* which I saw of late."

The wish is granted:
Enter Helen:

> Was this the face that launch'd a thousand ships,
> And burnt the topless towers of Ilium?—
> Sweet Helen, make me immortal with a kiss.—
> Her lips suck forth my soul: see, where it flies!—
> Come, Helen, come, give me my soul again.
> Here will I dwell, for heaven is in these lips,
> And all is dross that is not Helena.
> I will be Paris, and for love of thee,
> Instead of Troy, shall Wittenberg be sack'd;
> And I will combat with weak Menelaus,
> And wear thy colours on my plumèd crest;
> Yea, I will wound Achilles in the heel,
> And then return to Helen for a kiss.
> O, thou art fairer than the evening air
> Clad in the beauty of a thousand stars;
> Brighter thou art than flaming Jupiter
> When he appear'd to hapless Semele;
> More lovely than the monarch of the sky
> In wanton Arethusa's azur'd arms;
> And none but thou shalt be my paramour!

And when Faustus finally must face his doom his agony begins:

> O Faustus,
> Now hast thou but one bare hour to live,
> And then thou must be damnèd perpetually!

Stand still, you ever-moving spheres of heaven,
That time may cease, and midnight never come;
Fair Nature's eye, rise, rise again, and make
Perpetual day; or let this hour be but
A year, a month, a week, a natural day,
That Faustus may repent and save his soul!
O *lente, lente currite, noctis equi!*
The stars move still, time runs, the clock will strike,
The devil will come, and Faustus must be damn'd.
O, I'll leap up to heaven!—Who pulls me down?—
See, where Christ's blood streams in the firmament!
One drop of blood will save me: O my Christ!—
Rend not my heart for naming of my Christ;
Yet will I call on him; O, spare me, Lucifer!—
Where is it now? 'tis gone:
And, see, a threatening arm, an angry brow!
Mountains and hills, come, come, and fall on me,
And hide me from the heavy wrath of heaven!
No!
Then will I headlong run into the earth:
Gape, earth! O, no, it will not harbour me!
You stars that reigned at my nativity,
Whose influence hath allotted death and hell,
Now draw up Faustus, like a foggy mist,
Into the entrails of yon labouring cloud,
That, when you vomit forth into the air,
My limbs may issue from your smoky mouths;
But let my soul mount and ascend to heaven!
O, half the hour is past! 'twill all be past anon.
O, if my soul must suffer for my sin,
Impose some end to my incessant pain;
Let Faustus live in hell a thousand years,
A hundred thousand, and at last be sav'd!
No end is limited to damnèd souls.
Why were thou not a creature wanting soul?
Or why is this immortal that thou hast?
O, Pythagoras' metempsychosis, were that true,
This soul should fly from me, and I be chang'd
Into some brutish beast! all beasts are happy,
For, when they die,
Their souls are soon dissolv'd in elements;
But mine must live still to be plagu'd in hell.
Curst be the parents than engender'd me!
No, Faustus, curse thyself, curse Lucifer
That hath depriv'd thee of the joys of heaven.

It strikes, it strikes! Now, body turn to air,
Or Lucifer will bear thee quick to hell!
O soul, be chang'd into small water-drops,
And fall into the ocean, ne'er be found!

GEORGE MEREDITH (1828-1913)

From Modern Love

Poetry has sometimes been called a catharsis—a medium that purifies the poet's emotions. Certainly it proved to be such in the case of proud and sensitive George Meredith who never discussed his disastrous marriage after he had told the story of his first passion and its miserable ending in his powerful and grim sonnet sequence *Modern Love*.

Meredith was twenty-one, handsome, without means or income but possessing great undeveloped literary talent when he married Mary Peacock. He was enthralled by this beautiful, witty, sophisticated, literary-minded woman of great charm and physical appeal. She accepted him because she loved him, and in spite of his lack of means and his uncertain prospects. He dismissed the fact of her being seven years older than he was, and apparently was blind to her waspish, argumentative and unyielding nature. In the vernacular of today, all they had going for them was *love;* events proved it was not enough.

The facts of their nine years of life together are briefly told. The first three and one-half years of their marriage the couple—always desperately in need of money—spent in various lodgings, boarding houses and at the country home of Mrs. Meredith's comfortably fixed father, the noted author Thomas Love Peacock. In 1853 the Merediths' son was born. In 1855 Meredith's first novel was published but returned scant income. At the end of 1856 Meredith mentioned in a letter that his wife was spending Christmas away from him, while he worked on his *Richard Feverel*. In 1858 Mrs. Meredith went to Capri with Henry Wallis, a noted artist, and a year later she returned to England with a baby. After two years of bitter loneliness and illness Mrs. Meredith died of a kidney disease. Meredith ignored her dying plea that he come and see her.

Behind this bare recital is the story of a man and woman united in little more than a physical passion that did not last more than a few years and could not overcome the perhaps inevitable clash of their temperaments. Both of them were skilled in and quick to employ sharp-tongued satire and ridicule in controversy. She was a tireless arguer. He was not an easy man to live with: vain, jealous, demanding, unforgiving, and capable of deliberate cruelty.

But within months after his wife's death, which moved him deeply, Meredith had written a long poem—fifty sixteen-line sonnets—wherein he tells the story of their marriage, with some changes of the actual experiences. Apart from its literary excellence, the poem is a remarkable baring of his heart in which he neither spares himself nor blames his wife. Both of them were wrong, concluded Meredith, in not realizing that the sensuality of first love must mature to a more adult and less torrid plane. Never again did he write of this unhappy private history. Having forgiven and become reconciled to the woman in death, he apparently felt no need to revert to it. Here are three memorable passages from the poem:

"Am I Failing?"

Am I failing? For no longer can I cast
A glory round about this head of gold.
Glory she wears, but springing from the mould;
Not like the consecration of the Past!
Is my soul beggared? Something more than earth
I cry for still: I cannot be at peace
In having Love upon a mortal lease.
I cannot take the woman at her worth!
Where is the ancient wealth wherewith I clothed
Our human nakedness, and could endow
With spiritual splendour a white brow
That else had grinned at me the fact I loathed?
A kiss is but a kiss now! and no wave
Of great flood that whirls me to the sea.
But, as you will! we'll sit contentedly,
And eat our pot of honey on the grave.

"Mark Where the Pressing Wind"

Mark where the pressing wind shoots javelin-like
Its skeleton shadow on the broad-backed wave!
Here is a fitting spot to dig Love's grave;
Here where the ponderous breakers plunge and strike,
And dart their hissing tongues high up the sand:
In hearing of the ocean, and in sight
Of those ribbed wind-streaks running into white.
If I the death of Love had deeply planned,
I never could have made it half so sure,
As by the unblest kisses which upbraid
The full-waked sense; or failing that, degrade!

'Tis morning; but no morning can restore
What we have forfeited. I see no sin:
The wrong is mixed. In tragic life, God wot,
No villain need be! Passions spin the plot:
We are betrayed by what is false within.

"Thus Piteously Love Closed"
Thus piteously Love closed what he begat:
The union of this ever-diverse pair!
These two were rapid falcons in a snare,
Condemned to do the flitting of the bat.
Lovers beneath the singing sky of May,
They wandered once; clear as the dew on flowers:
But they fed not on the advancing hours:
Their hearts held cravings for the buried day.
Then each applied to each that fatal knife,
Deep questioning, which probes to endless dole.
Ah, what a dusty answer gets the soul
When hot for certainties in this our life!—
In tragic hints here see what evermore,
Moves dark as yonder midnight ocean's force,
Thundering like ramping hosts of warrior horse,
To throw that faint thin line upon the shore!

JOAQUIN MILLER (CINCINNATUS HINER MILLER) (1839-1913)

Exodus for Oregon

Those familiar with the life of Joaquin Miller are entitled to view with suspicion anything he might have told as happening to himself. He was an incurable romanticizer of his life, a shrewd self-promoter, and on the most inappropriate occasions he could be an obnoxious boor.

Nevertheless, at the age of fourteen he did have an authentic experience that he put into excellent verse twenty-one years later. It was the kind of adventure certain to remain vividly in a man's mind.

It began in Indiana on March 17, 1852, when the Miller family set out for Oregon to homestead on six hundred and forty acres offered free by Congress to all who made the perilous trek. The Millers were well-equipped, with two covered wagons, sixteen head of oxen and four horses. Traveling at two miles an hour, they crossed Indiana and Illinois, and reached St.

Joseph, Missouri, on the Missouri River, in two months. That was the
easiest part of their journey. From St. Joseph they went northwest to the
Platte River, followed its winding course and along the Oregon Trail to
Laramie, Wyoming. They were just a single group in a vast westward caravan that met with rain, mud, dust, storms, mountain slopes and peaks, pitiless
plains, searing deserts and occasional Indians that Miller afterwards said he
dispersed with dime-novel heroism. They also encountered covered wagons
returning East with gaunt remains of families decimated by cholera, and
sometimes found by the trailside bleached skeletons of settlers whose dreams
were tragically terminated.

From Laramie the Millers went through the foothills of the Rockies, along
the Sweetwater River to South Pass, where they sold one wagon in order
to have more oxen to take the remaining wagon over the summit without
difficulty. They detoured to Salt Lake City to sell excess baggage at a profit.
In mid-Summer they went on to Pocatello, Idaho, following the Snake River
through desolate canyons and reached Oregon on September 26th—seven
months after leaving Indiana!

Whatever exaggerations and fictions Joaquin Miller felt were necessary
to his reputation or expected by his audience, the trip to Oregon needed no
embellishments either for entertainment or because of a failure to recall it.
To the poet's credit he adhered to essential truth in his admirable "Exodus
for Oregon":

> A tale half told and hardly understood;
> The talk of bearded men that chanced to meet,
> That lean'd on quaint rifles in the wood,
> That look'd in fellow faces, spoke discreet
> And low, as half in doubt and in defeat
> Of hope; a tale it was of lands of gold
> That lay below the sun. Wild-wing'd and fleet
> It spread among the swift Missouri's bold
> Unbridled men, and reach'd to where Ohio roll'd.
>
> Then long chain'd lines of yoked and patient steers;
> Then long white trains that pointed to the west,
> Beyond the savage west; the hopes and fears
> Of blunt, untutor'd men, who hardly guess'd
> Their course; the brave and silent women, dress'd
> In homely spun attire, the boys in bands,
> The cheery babes that laugh'd at all, and bless'd
> The doubting hearts, with laughing lifted hands! . . . .
> What exodus for far untraversed lands!

The Plains! The shouting drivers at the wheel;
The crash of leather whips; the crush and roll
Of wheels; the groan of yokes and grinding steel
And iron chain, and lo! at last the whole
Vast line, that reach'd as if to touch the goal,
Began to stretch and stream away and wind
Toward the west as if with one control;
Then hope loom'd fair, and home lay far behind;
Before, the boundless plain, and fiercest of their kind.

At first the way lay green and fresh as seas,
And far away as any reach of wave;
The sunny streams went by in belt of trees;
And here and there the tassel'd tawny brave
Swept by on horse, look'd back, stretch'd forth and gave
A yell of warn, and then did wheel and rein
Awhile, and point away, dark-brow'd and grave,
Into the far and dim and distant plain
With signs and prophecies, and then plunged on again.

Some hills at last began to lift and break;
Some streams began to fail of wood and tide,
The somber plain began betime to take
A hue of weary brown, and wild and wide
It stretch'd its naked breast on every side.
A babe was heard at last to cry for bread
Amid the deserts; cattle low'd and died,
And dying men went by with broken tread,
And left a long black serpent line of wreck and dead.

Strange hunger'd birds, black-wing'd and still as death,
And crown'd of red with hooked beaks, blew low
And close about, till we could touch their breath—
Strange unnamed birds, that seem'd to come and go
In circles now, and now direct and slow,
Continual, yet never touch the earth;
Slim foxes slid and shuttled to and fro
At times across the dusty weary dearth
Of life, look'd back, then sank like crickets in a hearth.

Then dust arose, a long dim line like smoke
From out of riven earth. The wheels went groaning by,
Ten thousand feet in harness and in yoke,
They tore the ways of ashen alkali,

And desert winds blew sudden, swift and dry.
The dust! it sat upon and fill'd the train!
It seem'd to fret and fill the very sky.
Lo! dust upon the beasts, the tent, the plain,
And dust, alas! on breasts that rose not up again.

They sat in desolation and in dust
By dried-up desert streams; the mother's hands
Hid all her bended face; the cattle thrust
Their tongues and faintly call'd across the lands.
The babes, that knew not what this way through sands
Could mean, did ask if it would end to-day—
The panting wolves slid by, red-eyed, in bands
To pools beyond. The men look'd far away,
And, silent, saw that all a boundless desert lay.

They rose by night; they struggled on and on
As thin and still as ghosts; then here and there
Beside the dusty way before the dawn,
Men silent laid them down in their despair,
And died. But woman! Woman, frail as fair,
May man have strength to give to you your due;
You falter'd not, nor murmured anywhere,
You held your babes, held to your course, and you
Bore on through burning hell your double burdens through.

Men stood at last, the decimated few,
Above a land of running streams, and they?
They push'd aside the boughs, and peering through
Beheld afar the cool, refreshing bay;
Then some did curse, and some bend hands to pray;
But some look'd back upon the desert, wide
And desolate with death, then all the day
They mourned. But one, with nothing left beside
His dog to love, crept down among the ferns and died.

JOHN MILTON (1608-1674)

On His Blindness

John Milton was as complex and paradoxical as the seventeenth century
in which he lived. It was a time of factional conflicts and strife in which

strong convictions were brutally expressed by a people becoming aware of their personal rights and liberties.

Milton, despite his learning and his classicism and romanticism, could hardly have remained aloof to the turbulence of his day. He was convinced of his great powers, believed he was destined for greatness and determined to achieve it. Consequently, he was not a serene man.

Although we think of Milton as a poet, he actually spent a great deal of time pamphleteering on various controversial questions: advocating divorce, denouncing the clergy, defending Parliament, opposing the monarchy and supporting the Puritan cause.

His eyesight, never strong, had been failing for several years. While in the pay of the Puritan Government writing his *Defense of the English People* in 1650 he lost the sight of his left eye. Warned that continued close work would destroy the other eye he persisted in his "supreme duty" to "render the greatest service to the common weal it was in my power to render." Two years later, at the age of forty-three, Milton was totally blind.

This, though foreshadowed, was nevertheless a terrible blow to one whose life was devoted to scholarly pursuits. At first black despair seized him, but gradually he began the fight to make himself submit to the condition. It was the beginning of his magnificent triumph over total darkness: *Paradise Lost* and *Samson Agonistes*. He indicated this winning battle with his sonnet on his blindness:

> When I consider how my light is spent,
>> Ere half my days, in this dark world and wide,
>> And that one talent, which is death to hide,
>> Lodged with me useless, though my soul more bent
> To serve therewith my Maker, and present
>> My true account, lest He returning chide,
>> "Doth God exact day-labor, light denied?"
>> I fondly ask. But Patience, to prevent
> That murmur, soon replies, "God doth not need
>> Either man's work or His own gifts; who best
>> Bear his mild yoke, they serve Him best: His state
> Is kingly; thousands at His bidding speed
>> And post o'er land and ocean without rest;
>> They also serve who only stand and wait."

WILLIAM VAUGHAN MOODY (1869-1910)

Gloucester Moors

Some of William Vaughan Moody's finest poems are, in effect, testimony to the durability of his mid-Western origin against the allurements of genteel Harvard University and the cultural attractions of the Europe he visited for protracted periods.

Moody was raised in the traditions of a pioneer Indiana family and steeped in that area's intense patriotism and democratic ideals. The serious, reticent youth enjoyed the academic serenity of Harvard when he arrived there in 1889, with money saved from teaching and borrowed from an uncle, supplemented by income from tutoring and other work. He was an outstanding student, dedicated himself to poetry, and spent a year traveling in Europe.

In 1895 Moody, with considerable reluctance but evidently realizing the necessity and value of the experience, left the ultra-refinements of Harvard for the more robust life of Chicago, where he joined the English department of the University of Chicago. It was not the Mid-west of his Indiana boyhood and youth. The city's crudity and harshness made him yearn for the soft charm of Cambridge. He was bitter at the "phantasmagoric ugliness," the "spectacle of Gospel-peddling comfort," with "nothing to relieve the gaseous tedium of mushroom intellectuality." But then he began to see things differently, and "to discover more clearly what is worthy in human motive and admirable in human achievement." "I pick up," he said, "shreds of comfort out of this or that one of God's ash-barrels." His sympathy for unfortunates and his fundamental respect for his fellowman were gaining ascendancy over his instinctive dislike of the metropolis and the "sick perfume of the masses." Moreover, his soul protested against greedy commercialism and the inhumanity of ruthless industrialization.

It was in this rebellious state of mind that Moody left Chicago in May, 1900, for Gloucester, Massachusetts, to complete work on a History of English Literature. And there, when Gloucester Harbor and its picturesque surroundings were at their loveliest, Moody worked and walked and enjoyed himself in this "bewitching place."

But more important, this idyllic respite from the grime and grind of commerce and industry recalled vividly to him the barren and unhappy life of the industrialized man. Thus, amid scenes remote from his subject, he wrote his protest against the glaring sins of capitalism at the turn of the century. The poet found himself by finding life as it really was, and in the fires of that life forged these powerful lines:

A mile behind is Gloucester town
Where the fishing fleets put in,
A mile ahead the land dips down
And the woods and farms begin.
Here, where the moors stretch free
In the high blue afternoon,
Are the marching sun and talking sea,
And the racing winds that wheel and flee
On the flying heels of June.

Jill-o'er-the-ground is purple blue,
Blue is the quaker-maid,
The wild geranium holds its dew
Long in the boulder's shade.
Wax-red hangs the cup
From the huckleberry boughs,
In barberry bells the grey moths sup
Or where the choke-berry lifts high up
Sweet bowls for their carouse.

Over the shelf of the sandy cove
Beach-peas blossom late.
By copse and cliff the swallows rove
Each calling to its mate.
Seaward the sea-gulls go,
And the land-birds all are here;
The green-gold flash was a vireo,
And yonder flame where the marsh-flags grow
Was a scarlet tanager.

This earth is not the steadfast place
We landsmen build upon;
From deep to deep she varies pace,
And while she comes is gone.
Beneath my feet I feel
Her smooth bulk heave and dip;
With velvet plunge and soft upreel
She swings and steadies to her keel
Like a gallant, gallant ship.

These summer she sets for sail,
The sun is her masthead light,
She tows the moon like a pinnace frail
Where her phosphor wake churns bright.
Now hid, now looming clear,

On the face of the dangerous blue
The star fleets tack and wheel and veer,
But on, but on does the old earth steer
As if her port she knew.

God, dear God! Does she know her port,
Though she goes so far about?
Or blind astray, does she make her sport
To brazen and chance it out?
I watched when her captains passed:
She were better captainless.
Men in the cabin, before the mast,
But some were reckless and some aghast,
And some sat gorged at mess.

By her battened hatch I leaned and caught
Sounds from the noisome hold,—
Cursing and sighing of souls distraught
And cries too sad to be told.
Then I strove to go down and see;
But they said, "Thou art not of us!"
I turned to those on the deck with me
And cried, "Give help!" But they said, "Let be:
Our ship sails faster thus."

Jill-o'er-the-ground is purple blue,
Blue is the quaker-maid,
The alder-clump where the brook comes through
Breeds cresses in its shade.
To be out of the moiling street
With its swelter and its sin!
Who has given to me this sweet,
And given my brother dust to eat?
And when will his wage come in?

Scattering wide or blown in ranks,
Yellow and white and brown,
Boats and boats from the fishing banks
Come home to Gloucester town.
There is cash to pursue and spend,
There are wives to be embraced,
Hearts to borrow and hearts to lend,
And hearts to take and keep to the end,—
O little sails, make haste!

But thou, vast outbound ship of souls,
What harbor town for thee?
What shapes, when thy arriving tolls,
Shall crowd the banks to see?
Shall all the happy shipmates then
Stand singing brotherly?
Or shall a haggard ruthless few
Warp her over and bring her to,
While the many broken souls of men
Fester down in the slaver's pen,
And nothing to say or do?

THOMAS MOORE (1779-1852)

Oh! Breathe Not His Name
She is Far From the Land

Dublin in 1796 was a town tense with plots and conspiracies against its English rulers. When Thomas Moore entered Trinity College that year he soon became friendly with, and fascinated by, a youth who was destined before long to become one of the famous martyrs to Ireland's freedom: Robert Emmet, brilliant, eloquent, and passionately devoted to the revolutionary cause.

But Emmet did not permit friendship with Moore to blind him to the immensely likeable young man's lack of fitness for the stern demands of dangerous schemes and actions. He did not question Moore's loyalty to Ireland's cause and his hatred of injustice, but he shrewdly recognized Moore as primarily a creator and singer of songs, a witty and accomplished drawing room darling who would never entirely grow up.

Moore idolized Emmet, thrilled to Dublin's turbulent political atmosphere and was not afraid to take his stand on the side of freedom. Nevertheless, after college he left Ireland for the influential world of London society. And there, to the still existent scorn of some of the Irish, Moore charmed lords, ladies and lesser lights with his mostly Irish poems and songs.

However, Moore never abandoned his Irish sympathies. When the English captured, tried and hung Emmet for his leadership of an abortive uprising, Moore, then in England, read Emmet's celebrated speech from the dock asking the world "the charity of silence" and requesting "Let no man write my epitaph." The poet, deeply impressed, wrote a poem that echoed his martyred hero's plea:

Oh! breathe not his name, let it sleep in the shade,
Where cold and unhonor'd his relics are laid:
Sad, silent, and dark, be the tears that we shed,
As the night-dew that falls on the grass o'er his head.

But the night-dew that falls, though in silence it weeps,
Shall brighten with verdure the grave where he sleeps;
And the tear that we shed, though in secret it rolls,
Shall long keep his memory green in our souls.

Lovely Sarah Curran, daughter of John Philpot Curran, Dublin lawyer, orator and wit, was no less a tragic figure than her lover, Robert Emmet. Although aware of his revolutionary activities, she took no part in them. But when Emmet was arrested the English suspected her participation and immediately searched the Curran home and questioned her.

The authorities placed no charges against Sarah. But her father, fearful of losing profitable government preference, cravenly begged that his name be not mentioned and insanely denounced his daughter, declared he never wanted to see her again and was rumored to have given her a fearful beating. The stricken girl eventually recovered from delirium, lived for a while with a family at Newmarket and later married a British Army officer. But she never really recovered from Emmet's execution and her father's brutal bitterness. Five years after Emmet's death, Sarah died. Moore, who knew her, sang of Sarah's love for Emmet in his beautiful "She is Far From the Land":

She is far from the land where her young hero sleeps,
    And lovers are round her, sighing:
But coldly she turns from their gaze, and weeps,
    For her heart in his grave is lying.

She sings the wild songs of her dear native plains,
    Every note which he loved awaking;—
Ah! little they think, who delight in her strains,
    How the heart of the minstrel is breaking.

He had lived for his love, for his country he died,
    They were all that to life had entwined him;
Nor soon shall the tears of his country be dried,
    Nor long will his love stay behind him.

Oh! make her a grave where the sunbeams rest,
    When they promise a glorious morrow;
They'll shine o'er her sleep, like a smile from the West,
    From her own loved island of sorrow.

THEODORE O'HARA (1820-1867)

The Bivouac of the Dead

William Cory once asked if death was invented so that there might be poetry, and concluded that if so it was not a senseless arrangement.

Certainly if death had not been a subject of frequent contemplation to Theodore O'Hara he might have written some verse, but hardly anything approaching the single poem that has kept his name alive.

Even as a young man this Kentucky-born son of Irish parents was disposed to spells of melancholy meditation, and would often seek solitude for his ruminations in the Frankfort (Kentucky) Cemetery. But he was otherwise sociable and active as a newspaperman, and quick to join in military adventures.

When the War with Mexico began in 1846 O'Hara volunteered, became an Army Captain, participated in the Battle of Chapultepec and was badly wounded at Contreras.

In the Fall of 1847 O'Hara returned to Frankfort for convalescence and soon was taking occasional strolls through Frankfort Cemetery. On one of these meditative walks the handsome veteran came upon the graves of some Kentucky comrades who had been killed in the Battle of Buena Vista. He sat on the ground near these graves and wrote the first draft of his moving tribute to his comrades-in-arms.

The poem is often erroneously attributed to the Civil War, possibly because O'Hara saw much action as a Colonel in the Confederate Army. He died in Alabama in 1867, but seven years later the Kentucky legislature resolved that his body be removed to his beloved Frankfort Cemetery, which was ceremoniously done.

> The muffled drum's sad roll has beat
>   The soldier's last tattoo!
> No more on life's parade shall meet
>   The brave and fallen few.
> On Fame's eternal camping ground
>   Their silent tents are spread,
> And glory guards with solemn round
>   The bivouac of the dead.
>
> No rumor of the foe's advance
>   Now swells upon the wind,
> Nor troubled thought at midnight haunts
>   Of loved ones left behind;

No vision of the morrow's strife
    The warrior's dream alarms,
No braying horn nor screaming fife
    At dawn shall call to arms.

Their shivered swords are red with rust,
    Their plumèd heads are bowed,
Their haughty banner, trailed in dust,
    Is now their martial shroud—
And plenteous funeral tears have washed
    The red stains from each brow,
And the proud forms by battle gashed
    Are free from anguish now.

The neighing troop, the flashing blade,
    The bugle's stirring blast,
The charge,—the dreadful cannonade,
    The din and shout, are passed;
Nor war's wild notes, nor glory's peal
    Shall thrill with fierce delight
Those breasts that nevermore shall feel
    The rapture of the fight.

Like the fierce Northern hurricane
    That sweeps his great plateau,
Flushed with the triumph yet to gain,
    Come down the serried foe,
Who heard the thunder of the fray
    Break o'er the field beneath,
Knew well the watchword of that day
    Was "Victory or death!"

Rest on, embalmed and sainted dead!
    Dear as the blood you gave—
No impious footstep here shall tread
    The herbage of your grave.
Nor shall your glory be forgot
    While Fame her record keeps,
Or honor points the hallowed spot
    Where valor proudly sleeps.

Yon marble minstrel's voiceless stone
    In deathless song shall tell,
When many a vanquished year hath flown,
    The story how ye fell.

> Nor wreck nor change, nor winter's blight,
> Nor time's remorseless doom,
> Can dim one ray of holy light
> That gilds your glorious tomb.

WILFRED OWEN (1893-1918)

Strange Meeting

One cannot read Wilfred Owen's World War I poems—generally conceded to be the greatest written during that holocaust—without recognizing them as the eloquent cry of a heart stricken by war's slaughter, filth and suffering.

When gently-reared, serious, shy young Owen joined the British Army in 1915 he had neither delusions that it was a glorious adventure nor convictions that war was an obscene spectacle. In fact, when he first arrived in France during the bitter winter of 1917 and was sent to the Somme battlefield, he wrote home of the "excitement" and of "the fine heroic feeling about being in France."

But this lighthearted attitude could not continue in the face of the experiences he encountered: slogging through miles of trenches in which the water averaged a depth of two feet; four days in an advanced post dug-out between the opposing lines; shell craters full of water in which men drowned; men so badly stuck in mud that they escaped only by leaving their clothes and boots in it; dead soldiers left unburied for weeks among the still-living; twelve days without even washing his face or removing his boots.

Whereas months of this degrading existence may make some men brutal and callous, it aroused the pity that was the keynote of Owen's character. He felt that when he could not alleviate human suffering he must share it with his fellow-man. He wrote that an army encampment was "a kind of paddock where the beasts are kept a few days before the shambles." He spoke of the look on the faces of soldiers: not fear or gloom, but "a blindfold look, and without expression like a dead rabbit's." Worst of all to his sensitive nature was "the universal pervasion of *Ugliness*. Hideous landscapes, vile noises, foul language, and nothing but foul, even from one's own mouth (for all are devil-ridden)—everything unnatural, broken, blasted."

And yet out of all this blood and squalor Wilfred Owen created poems that trumpeted in exalted lines the terrible things he saw and the passionate convictions they engendered. He died in battle one week before the fighting ended. Among his papers was found this last and unfinished poem, perhaps his finest, but in any case more intimate and serene than the others:

It seemed that out of battle I escaped
Down some profound dull tunnel, long since scooped
Through granites which titanic wars had groined.
Yet also there encumbered sleepers groaned,
Too fast in thought or death to be bestirred.
Then, as I probed them, one sprang up, and stared
With piteous recognition in fixed eyes,
Lifting distressful hands as if to bless.
And by his smile, I knew that sullen hall,
By his dead smile I knew we stood in Hell.
With a thousand pains that vision's face was grained;
Yet no blood reached there from the upper ground,
And no guns thumped, or down the flues made moan.
"Strange friend," I said, "here is no cause to mourn."
"None," said the other, "save the undone years,
The hopelessness. Whatever hope is yours,
Was my life also; I went hunting wild
After the wildest beauty in the world,
Which lies not calm in eyes, or braided hair,
But mocks the steady running of the hour,
And if it grieves, grieves richlier than here.
For by my glee might many men have laughed,
And of my weeping something had been left,
Which must die now. I mean the truth untold,
The pity of war, the pity war distilled.
Now men will go content, with what we spoiled.
Or, discontent, boil bloody, and be spilled.
They will be swift with swiftness of the tigress,
None will break ranks, though nations trek from progress.
Courage was mine, and I had mystery,
Wisdom was mine, and I had mastery;
To miss the march of this retreating world
Into vain citadels that are not walled.
Then, when much blood had clogged their chariot-wheels
I would go up and wash them from sweet wells,
Even with truths that lie too deep for taint.
I would have poured my spirit without stint
But not through wounds; not on the cess of war.
Foreheads of men have bled where no wounds were.
I am the enemy you killed, my friend.
I knew you in this dark; for so you frowned
Yesterday through me as you jabbed and killed.
I parried; but my hands were loath and cold.
Let us sleep now . . ."

COVENTRY PATMORE (1823-1896)

The Married Lover
Preludes *to* The Angel in the House
Departure
The Toys

It would be easy and true enough to say that Coventry Patmore earned the epithet of "the poet of matrimony" simply because he was a poet with a strong erotic temperament.

But there is more to it than that. Coventry was the favorite son and constant companion of a father who continuously analyzed the subject of love, allowed the boy's mind to take whatever bent it preferred, and encouraged him in his poetical ambitions. However, the young man's sensuous and passionate nature was kept under control because of his deeply religious nature and his mother's stern Puritan principles.

The handsome twenty-one-year-old explored aspects of love in his first volume of poems, which gained him a measure of attention. Then he contracted the malady himself when he fell madly in love with and married learned Emily Andrews, the beautiful orphaned daughter of a Congregationalist minister.

Life with this charming woman proved to be all that young Patmore envisioned in his romantic day-dreams, and he saw their marriage as an earthly symbol of the union between God and the Soul. Even after years of marriage Patmore was recording private reminders to himself that he must "become more chaste, affectionate, tender, just, courtly" to his beloved Emily.

Poets have always celebrated the freshness and ecstasy of love in anticipation or in initial consummation. Patmore sang in praise of the bonds of matrimony, and particularly so in his famous "The Married Lover":

Why, having won her, do I woo?
  Because her spirit's vestal grace
Provokes me always to pursue,
  But, spirit-like, eludes embrace;
Because her womanhood is such
  That, as on court-days subjects kiss
The Queen's hand, yet so near a touch
  Affirms no mean familiarness;
Nay, rather marks more fair the height
  Which can with safety so neglect
To dread, as lower ladies might,

That grace could meet with disrespect;
Thus she with happy favour feeds
   Allegiance from a love so high
That thence no false conceit proceeds
   Of difference bridged, or state put by;
Because, although in act and word
   As lowly as a wife can be,
Her manner, when they call me lord,
   Remind me 'tis by courtesy;
Not with her least consent of will.
   Which would my proud affection hurt,
But by the noble style that still
   Imputes an unattained desert;
Because her hair and lofty brows,
   When all is won which hope can ask,
Reflect a light of hopeless snows
   That bright in virgin ether bask;
Because, though free of the outer court
   I am, this Temple keeps its shrine
Sacred to heaven; because, in short,
   She's not and never can be mine.

Patmore, however, was at work on a far more ambitious tribute to married love; a long poem titled "The Angel in the House." In this epic of married love in all its aspects the poet demonstrated that marriage is not the end but the fulfillment and enrichment of love, and that its very bonds can bring delights and joys not otherwise possible. He wrote with confident happiness because his own marriage was the proof of the poet's argument. It was in fact his song in honor of Emily—the earthly angel in his house—who was overjoyed with the poem, which had a huge sale. Although the lengthy poem has the Victorian atmosphere of a society no longer recognizable to people today, its several Preludes remain untouched by the passage of Time:

UNTHRIFT

Ah, wasteful woman, she that may
   On her sweet self set her own price,
Knowing man cannot choose but pay,
   How has she cheapened paradise;
How given for nought her priceless gift,
   How spoiled the bread, and spilled the wine,
Which, spent with due, respective thrift,
   Had made brutes men, and men divine.

HONOUR AND DESERT

O Queen, awake to thy renown,
   Require what 'tis our wealth to give,
And comprehend and wear the crown
   Of thy despised prerogative!

I, who in manhood's name at length
   With glad songs come to abdicate
The gross regality of strength,
   Must yet in this thy praise abate,
That, through thine erring humbleness
   And disregard of thy degree,
Mainly, has man been so much less
   Than fits his fellowship with thee.

High thoughts had shaped the foolish brow,
   The coward had grasped the hero's sword,
The vilest had been great, hadst thou,
   Just to thyself, been worth's reward.
But lofty honours undersold
   Seller and buyer both disgrace;
And favours that make folly bold
   Banish the light from virtue's face.

THE TRIBUTE

Boon Nature to the woman bows;
   She walks in earth's whole glory clad,
And, chiefest far herself of shows,
   All others help her and are glad:
No splendour 'neath the sky's proud dome
   But serves her for familiar wear;
The far-fetched diamond finds its home
   Flashing and smouldering in her hair;
For her the seas their pearls reveal;
   Art and strange lands her pomp supply
With purple, chrome, and cochineal,
   Ochre, and lapis lazuli;
The worm its golden woof presents;
   Whatever runs, flies, dives, or delves,
All doff for her their ornaments,
   Which suit her better than themselves;
And all, by this their power to give,
   Proving her right to take, proclaim
Her beauty's clear prerogative
   To profit so by Eden's blame.

While Patmore was writing his "The Angel in the House" Emily over-taxed her strength in caring for their six children on a meagre income. In 1857 she contracted tuberculosis. The poet, confident she would conquer the disease, spared no effort or resource in her behalf. But after four years, when it became evident the battle would be lost, the devoted couple courageously faced their last year together and gave to each other love and tenderness exceeding that of their earliest days.

When Emily died at the age of thirty-eight, Patmore found this touching last message to him in her will: "I leave my wedding ring to your second wife with my love and blessing. . . . also I leave you my grateful acknowl-edgement of your goodness and love to me, my last prayer that God may bless you and console you, my first and last love."

The stricken husband told of Emily's last day of life in his poignant "Departure":

It was not like your great and gracious ways!
Do you, that have naught other to lament,
Never, my love, repent
Of how, that July afternoon,
You went
With sudden, unintelligible phrase,
And frighten'd eye,
Upon your journey of so many days
Without a single kiss, or a good-bye?
I knew, indeed, that you were parting soon;
And so we sate, within the low sun's rays,
You whispering to me, for your voice was weak,
Your harrowing praise.
Well, it was well
To hear you such things speak,
And I could tell
What made your eyes a growing gloom of love,
As a warm South-wind sombres a March grove.

And it was like your great and gracious ways
To turn your talk on daily things, my Dear,
Lifting the luminous, pathetic lash
To let the laughter flash,
Whilst I drew near,
Because you spoke so low that I could scarcely hear.
But all at once to leave me at the last,
More at the wonder than the loss aghast,
With huddled, unintelligible phrase,
And frighten'd eye,

And go your journey of all days
With not one kiss, or a good-bye,
And the only loveless look the look with which you pass'd:
'Twas all unlike your great and gracious ways.

Patmore had the full responsibility and care of his six motherless children,
work to which he immediately devoted himself however ill-equipped for it
by temperament. He was, in fact, often intolerant of the irritating shortcomings of children, impatient with their trivial complaints and demands,
and lacking in understanding of their special needs in new and different
circumstances. But he truly loved his children, tried to enter into their life
and was aware that he fell far short of the ideal father. Moreover, his out-
bursts of anger and unreasonableness would be followed by remorse over his
failure to understand and sympathize with a child's world.

Shortly after the death of his wife, and when his oldest son Milne was a
cadet on the *Brittania*, something caused the poet to recall an early instance
of his impulsive cruelty to this boy, and in his lingering sorrow he wrote his
most touching poem, "The Toys":

My little Son, who looked from thoughtful eyes
And moved and spoke in quiet grown-up wise,
Having my law the seventh time disobeyed,
I struck him, and dismissed
With hard words and unkissed,
—His Mother, who was patient, being dead.
Then, fearing lest his grief should hinder sleep,
I visited his bed,
But found him slumbering deep,
With darkened eyelids, and their lashes yet
From his late sobbing wet.
And I, with moan,
Kissing away his tears, left others of my own;
For, on a table drawn beside his head,
He had put, within his reach,
A box of counters and a red-veined stone,
A piece of glass abraded by the beach,
And six or seven shells,
A bottle with bluebells,
And two French copper coins, ranged there with careful art,
To comfort his sad heart.
So when that night I prayed
To God, I wept, and said:
Ah, when at last we lie with trancèd breath,
Not vexing Thee in death,

And Thou rememberest of what toys
We made our joys,
How weakly understood
Thy great commanded good,
Then, fatherly not less
Than I whom Thou has moulded from the clay,
Thou'lt leave Thy wrath, and say,
"I will be sorry for their childishness."

EDWARD COOTE PINKNEY (1802-1828)

A Health

"A Health" is precisely the kind of poem one would expect from the pen of Pinkney. At thirteen he was commissioned a midshipman in the U.S. Navy, an action facilitated because an uncle of his was a commodore and his father a prominent diplomat. But the son was not diplomatic: at least twice during his nine years in the U.S. Navy he got into serious disputes with his superior officers. It has been said, but not proved, that he once challenged his ship's captain to a duel and when the latter refused, Pinkney posted him in the press as a coward. This handsome man's punctilio in matters of honor involved him in several other duel challenges.

When Pinkney resigned from the Navy in 1824 he already had quite a reputation as a poet, and his verse was as romantic as his life. Several of his earlier poems were dedicated to his first serious love, Mary Hawkins. But when he met a graceful and beautiful "sweet promiser" named Georgiana McCausland of Baltimore he married her in 1824, and during that year addressed to her his best-known poem. After Pinkney's death in 1828 several other women claimed, without convincing anyone, that the spirited lines of "A Health" were addressed to them. It's the kind of poem women like to imagine themselves the subject of:

I fill this cup to one made up of loveliness alone,
A woman, of her gentle sex the seeming paragon;
To whom the better elements and kindly stars have given
A form so fair, that, like the air, 'tis less of earth than heaven.

Her every tone is music's own, like those of morning birds,
And something more than melody dwells ever in her words;
The coinage of her heart are they, and from her lips each flows
As one may see the burthened bee forth issue from the rose.

Affections are as thoughts to her, the measure of her hours;
Her feelings have the fragrancy, the freshness of young flowers;
And lovely passion, changing oft, so fill her, she appears
The image of themselves by turns,—the idol of past years!

Of her bright face one glance will trace a picture of the brain,
And of her voice in echoing hearts a sound must long remain,
But memory such as mine of her so very much endears,
When death is nigh my latest sigh will not be life's but hers.

I fill this cup to one made up of loveliness alone,
A woman, of her gentle sex the seeming paragon—
Her health! and would on earth there stood some more of such a frame,
That life might be all poetry, and weariness a name.

EDGAR ALLAN POE (1809-1849)

To Helen
The Raven
Annabel Lee
The Bells

It was an important day for poetry when Robert Stanard invited his older
schoolmate Edgar Allan Poe to his gracious Richmond, Virginia, home; apparently so that his mother, Jane Stith Stanard, could meet the teen-age poet
whose charm and brilliance he had told her of.

It was, too, a day of awakening—the beginning of adult emotion—for the
sensitive, precocious youth. Mrs. Stanard's classic beauty, its antique grandeur
enhanced by the statuesque style of dress of the day, held the budding poet
spellbound. The glow of her personality and the warmth of her hospitality
gave substance to the ecstatic dream her beauty evoked in Poe. He would
ever after think of her as one who radiated an ethereal light—a flame from
antiquity, newly lighted. She was Poe's first love—idealized as only a youthful
worshipper of beauty can exalt.

Tradition tells us that in Mrs. Stanard the orphaned Poe found the comforting friend he so desperately needed; one who listened understandingly
as he read his poems, giving gentle criticism and needed encouragement.
In later years the Stanard family recalled Poe's frequent visits and the bond
that linked the beautiful lady and the bright-burning youth.

But after a year or so impenetrable clouds of melancholy enveloped Jane

Stith Stanard, as they were eventually to enshroud the poet. Poe's "Helen" died insane at the age of thirty-one. It was said Poe haunted her grave, even weeping there on lonely nights. It is known, from his friends of the period, that the poet was grief-stricken.

Four years later Poe wrote in his first book "I have been happy, tho' in a dream." It was the dream made immortal when he wrote—at age fifteen, said Poe—these lines:

> Helen, thy beauty is to me
>   Like those Nicean barks of yore,
> That gently, o'er a perfumed sea,
>   The weary, wayworn wanderer bore
>   To his own native shore.
>
> On desperate seas long wont to roam,
>   Thy hyacinth hair, thy classic face,
> Thy Naiad airs, have brought me home
>   To the glory that was Greece
>   And the grandeur that was Rome.
>
> Lo! in yon brilliant window-niche
>   How statue-like I see thee stand,
> The agate lamp within thy hand!
>   Ah, Psyche, from the regions which
>   Are Holy Land!

Poe may have contemplated the theme of "The Raven" earlier, but was in any case stimulated by Dickens' *Barnaby Rudge,* which he reviewed in 1841. In commenting on the novel, in which an idiot youth has as his companion a very knowing and talking raven, Poe suggested that a raven might also have been used in the story instead of a prophetic owl that makes a midnight visit.

Two years later Poe, beginning his final poetical resurgence, went to the editors of a Philadelphia magazine, explained that his wife and her mother were starving, and he destitute, and asked them to buy a poem he would read to them. It was apparently an early version of "The Raven," which the editors rejected. But they collected fifteen dollars around the office and shop for Poe.

During the summer and autumn of 1844 the Poes were living in an old farmhouse overlooking the Hudson River on the outskirts of New York. Here the tormented author took "The Raven," originally planned as a short poem, and worked long hours over it. Into it went not only his technical genius and his superb imaginative powers, but also the innate melancholy, frustration and despair that led to much of the tragedy of his life, and in turn fed on it. Poe worked in a large room, over the door of which was a shelf on which rested a small plaster cast—the "pallid bust of Pallas."

When Poe completed the poem he read it to a friend and told him it was the greatest poem ever written. Even if deliberately exaggerating, the poet was extremely proud of it and usually had a copy with him which he would read—with great beauty and effect—without too much urging. The poem was published in 1845 and its immediate popularity put poor Poe into a fever of expectations never to be realized. Still, he kept tinkering with the poem, ending with its sixteenth version in September 1849, a few weeks before he died.

Once upon a midnight dreary, while I pondered, weak and weary,
Over many a quaint and curious volume of forgotten lore,—
While I nodded, nearly napping, suddenly there came a tapping,
As of some one gently rapping—rapping at my chamber door.
"'Tis some visitor," I muttered, "tapping at my chamber door—
      Only this and nothing more."

Ah, distinctly I remember, it was in the bleak December,
And each separate dying ember wrought its ghost upon the floor.
Eagerly I wished the morrow;—vainly I had sought to borrow
From my books surcease of sorrow—sorrow for the lost Lenore—
For the rare and radiant maiden whom the angels name Lenore—
      Nameless here for evermore.

And the silken sad uncertain rustling of each purple curtain
Thrilled me—filled me with fantastic terrors never felt before;
So that now, to still the beating of my heart, I stood repeating
"'Tis some visitor entreating entrance at my chamber door—
Some late visitor entreating entrance at my chamber door;
      This it is and nothing more."

Presently my soul grew stronger; hesitating then no longer,
"Sir," said I, "or Madam, truly your forgiveness I implore;
But the fact is I was napping, and so gently you came rapping,
And so faintly you came tapping—tapping at my chamber door—
That I scarce was sure I heard you"—here I opened wide the door:—
      Darkness there and nothing more.

Deep into that darkness peering, long I stood there wondering, fearing,
Doubting, dreaming dreams no mortal ever dared to dream before;
But the silence was unbroken, and the darkness gave no token,
And the only word there spoken was the whispered word, "Lenore!"
This I whispered, and an echo murmured back the word, "Lenore!"
      Merely this and nothing more.

Back into the chamber turning, all my soul within me burning,
Soon I heard again a tapping, somewhat louder than before;
"Surely," said I, "surely there is something at my window lattice;
Let me see, then, what thereat is, and this mystery explore,—
Let my heart be still a moment, and this mystery explore;—
            'Tis the wind and nothing more."

Open here I flung the shutter, when, with many a flirt and flutter,
In there stepped a stately Raven of the saintly days of yore;
Not the least obeisance made he; not an instant stopped or stayed he;
But with mien of lord or lady, perched above my chamber door,—
Perched upon a bust of Pallas just above my chamber door,—
            Perched and sat, and nothing more.

Then this ebony bird beguiling my sad fancy into smiling,
By the grave and stern decorum of the countenance it wore,
"Though thy crest be shorn and shaven, thou," I said, "art sure no craven,
Ghastly grim and ancient Raven wandering from the Nightly shore—
Tell me what thy lordly name is on the Night's Plutonian shore!"
            Quoth the Raven, "Nevermore."

Much I marveled this ungainly fowl to hear discourse so plainly,
Though its answer little meaning—little relevancy bore;
For we can not help agreeing that no living human being
Ever yet was blessed with seeing bird above his chamber door—
Bird or beast upon the sculptured bust above his chamber door,
            With such name as "Nevermore."

But the Raven, sitting lonely on that placid bust, spoke only
That one word, as if his soul in that one word he did outpour.
Nothing further then he uttered—not a feather then he fluttered—
Till I scarcely more than muttered, "Other friends have flown before—
On the morrow *he* will leave me, as my hopes have flown before."
            Then the bird said, "Nevermore."

Startled at the silence broken by reply so aptly spoken,
"Doubtless," said I, "what it utters is its only stock and store,
Caught from some unhappy master whom unmerciful Disaster
Followed fast and followed faster till his songs one burden bore,—
Till the dirges of his Hope the melancholy burden bore
            Of—'Never—nevermore!'"

But the Raven still beguiling all my sad soul into smiling,—
Straight I wheeled a cushioned seat in front of bird and bust and door;
Then, upon the velvet sinking, I betook myself to linking

Fancy unto fancy, thinking what this ominous bird of yore—
What this grim, ungainly, ghastly, gaunt, and ominous bird of yore
Meant in croaking "Nevermore!"

This I sat engaged in guessing, but no syllable expressing
To the fowl whose fiery eyes now burned into my bosom's core;
This and more I sat divining with my head at ease reclining
On the cushion's velvet lining that the lamplight gloated o'er,
But whose velvet violet lining with the lamplight gloating o'er,
She shall press, ah, nevermore!

Then, methought, the air grew denser, perfumed from an unseen censer
Swung by Seraphim whose footfalls tinkled on the tufted floor.
"Wretch," I cried, "thy God hath lent thee—by these angels he hath sent thee
Respite—respite and nepenthe from thy memories of Lenore!
Quaff, oh quaff this kind nepenthe, and forget this lost Lenore!"
Quoth the Raven, "Nevermore."

"Prophet!" said I, "thing of evil!—prophet still, if bird or devil!
Whether Tempter sent, or whether tempest tossed thee here ashore,
Desolate yet all undaunted, on this desert land enchanted—
On this home by Horror haunted—tell me truly, I implore—
Is there—*is* there balm in Gilead?—tell me—tell me, I implore!"
Quoth the Raven, "Nevermore."

"Prophet!" said I, "thing of evil!—prophet still, if bird of devil!
By that Heaven that bends above us—by that God we both adore—
Tell this soul with sorrow laden if, within the distant Aidenn,
It shall clasp a sainted maiden whom the angels name Lenore—
Clasp a rare and radiant maiden whom the angels name Lenore."
Quoth the Raven, "Nevermore."

"Be that word our sign of parting, bird or fiend!" I shrieked, upstarting—
"Get thee back into the tempest and the Night's Plutonian shore!
Leave no black plume as a token of that lie thy soul hath spoken!
Leave my loneliness unbroken!—quit the bust above my door!
Take thy beak from out my heart, and take thy form from off my door!"
Quoth the Raven, "Nevermore."

And the Raven, never flitting, still is sitting, still is sitting
On the pallid bust of Pallas just above my chamber door;
And his eyes have all the seeming of a demon's that is dreaming,
And the lamplight o'er him streaming throws his shadow on the floor;
And my soul from out that shadow that lies floating on the floor
Shall be lifted—nevermore!

After twelve bitter years of failure and wandering Edgar Allan Poe, his consumption-wracked little wife, Virginia, and her strong, valiant mother Maria Clemm, made their last home together in a humble cottage at Fordham, outside New York City.

Poe had chosen the place in desperate hope the country air would yet spare to him the tragically delicate cousin he had marrried in secret when she was thirteen, and he was twenty-five.

That summer of 1846 the devoted husband saw the fatal shadows closing in on his sweet, gentle Virginia—whose waxen features were faintly rouged by fever.

The poverty-haunted poet must have thought remorsefully of her many hours of unspoken worry over his financial difficulties, drinking and recurring melancholia. He recognized her tragedy as a part of his tragedy. In his great sorrow, in the midst of his beautiful tenderness to the frail creature, he would recall their happier moments—more memorable because so few. In this anguish of mind, and in poverty and hunger, Poe began to write his lyric of their love, foreseeing that death was destined soon to call her—and perhaps him, too.

As Fall and Winter came on Poe withdrew from unnecessary human contacts to be with and minister to his uncomplaining "Sis," as she grew thinner and weaker on her straw mattress wrapped in her "Eddie's" cloak. Neighbors gave them food and fuel; friends later sent Virginia a feather bed and ample bed clothes. Desperately the sweet, immature girl clung to the lonely genius the world was quick to ridicule and calumniate. Finally, on January 29, 1847, she died, her ill and half-crazed husband at her side.

In a last burst of poetical fervor, Poe completed this touching dirge-like memoir, in March, 1849, seven months before he joined his "Annabel Lee" in death.

It was many and many a year ago,
    In a kingdom by the sea,
That a maiden there lived whom you may know
    By the name of Annabel Lee;
And this maiden she lived with no other thought
    Than to love and be loved by me.

I was a child and *she* was a child,
    In this kingdom by the sea;
But we loved with a love that was more than love—
    I and my Annabel Lee;
With a love that the winged seraphs of heaven
    Coveted her and me.

And this was the reason that, long ago,
In this kingdom by the sea,
A wind blew out of a cloud, chilling
My beautiful Annabel Lee;
So that her highborn kinsmen came
And bore her away from me,
To shut her up in a sepulcher
In this kingdom by the sea.

The angels, not half so happy in heaven,
Went envying her and me—
Yes! that was the reason (as all men know,
In this kingdom by the sea)
That the wind came out of a cloud by night,
Chilling and killing my Annabel Lee.

But our love it was stronger by far than the love
Of those who were older than we—
Of many far wiser than we—
And neither the angels in heaven above,
Nor the demons down under the sea,
Can ever dissever my soul from the soul
Of the beautiful Annabel Lee.

For the moon never beams without bringing me dreams
Of the beautiful Annabel Lee;
And the stars never rise but I see the bright eyes
Of the beautiful Annabel Lee;
And so, all the night-tide, I lie down by the side
Of my darling, my darling, my life and my bride,
In her sepulcher there by the sea—
In her tomb by the side of the sea.

Although Poe had been vaguely planning to do a poem on bells, he never got around to it until about a year after Virginia's death, when he was visiting the Philadelphia home of Mrs. Shew. He and his hostess were having tea in a little conservatory overlooking the garden. Poe remarked that he had to write a poem, perhaps mentioning the subject of bells, but complained he had neither inspiration nor strength for the task. When the church bells sounded in the air he protested they jarred him, and pushed away the paper Mrs. Shew had provided him with. His hostess then wrote "The bells, the little silver bells" and Poe completed the stanza. Then Mrs. Shew wrote "The heavy iron bells" and urged the poet on. He finished two more stanzas, but could do no more. That evening he fell into a coma. The doctor summoned by Mrs. Shew feared the patient was dying.

During the remainder of the year the poem was revised at least four times before its publication a month after Poe's death. Hervey Allen, Poe's exhaustive biographer, pointed out that the poet had long contemplated the poem, and that the word "Tintinnabulation"—hailed as coined by Poe—was derived by the poet from Pliny's observation that long before the Christian era the pagans used bells and called them "tintinnabula." A clipping to this effect from an obscure publication was found among Poe's papers.

It is ironic that one of the least mournful of Poe's poems should have been written after the death of Virginia and during the months the poet moved inexorably toward his sad ending in Baltimore following a drinking spree, apparently accompanied by drugging, manhandling and robbery in the saloon the delirious genius was found in.

Hear the sledges with the bells,
Silver bells!
What a world of merriment their melody foretells!
How they tinkle, tinkle, tinkle,
In the icy air of night!
While the stars, that oversprinkle
All the heavens, seem to twinkle
With a crystalline delight;
Keeping time, time, time,
In a sort of Runic rhyme,
To the tintinnabulation that so musically wells
From the bells, bells, bells, bells,
Bells, bells, bells—
From the jingling and the tinkling of the bells.

Hear the mellow wedding bells,
Golden bells!
What a world of happiness their harmony foretells!
Through the balmy air of night
How they ring out their delight!
From their molten-golden notes,
And all in tune,
What a liquid ditty floats
To the turtle-dove that listens, while she gloats
On the moon!
Oh, from out the sounding cells,
What a gush of euphony voluminously wells!
How it swells!
How it dwells
On the Future! how it tells
Of the rapture that impels

To the swinging and the ringing
Of the bells, bells, bells,
Of the bells, bells, bells, bells,
Bells, bells, bells—
To the rhyming and the chiming of the bells!

Hear the loud alarum bells,
Brazen bells!
What a tale of terror, now, their turbulency tells!
In the startled ear of night
How they scream out their affright!
Too much horrified to speak,
They can only shriek, shriek,
Out of tune,
In a clamorous appealing to the mercy of the fire,
In a mad expostulation with the deaf and frantic fire,
Leaping higher, higher, higher,
With a desperate desire,
And a resolute endeavor
Now—now to sit, or never,
By the side of the pale-faced moon.
Oh, the bells, bells, bells!
What a tale their terror tells
Of Despair!
How they clang, and clash, and roar!
What a horror they outpour
On the bosom of the palpitating air!
Yet the ear, it fully knows,
By the twanging
And the clanging,
How the danger ebbs and flows;
Yet the ear distinctly tells,
In the jangling
And the wrangling,
How the danger sinks and swells,—
By the sinking or the swelling in the anger of the bells,
Of the bells,
Of the bells, bells, bells, bells,
Bells, bells, bells—
In the clangor and the clamor of the bells!

Hear the tolling of the bells,
Iron bells!
What a world of solemn thought their monody compels!
In the silence of the night
How we shiver with affright

At the melancholy menace of their tone!
  For every sound that floats
  From the rust within their throats
        Is a groan.
And the people—ah, the people,
They that dwell up in a steeple,
        All alone,
And who, tolling, tolling, tolling,
In that muffled monotone,
Feel a glory in so rolling
On the human heart a stone—
They are neither man nor woman,
They are neither brute nor human,
        They are Ghouls:
And their king it is who tolls;
And he rolls, rolls, rolls,
        Rolls
A paen from the bells;
And his merry bosom swells
With the paen of the bells,
And he dances, and he yells.
Keeping time, time, time,
In a sort of Runic rhyme,
To the paen of the bells,
        Of the bells:
Keeping time, time, time,
In a sort of Runic rhyme,
To the throbbing of the bells,
Of the bells, bells, bells—
To the sobbing of the bells;
Keeping time, time, time,
As he knells, knells, knells,
In a happy Runic rhyme,
To the rolling of the bells,
Of the bells, bells, bells:
To the tolling of the bells,
Of the bells, bells, bells, bells,
        Bells, bells, bells—
To the moaning and the groaning of the bells.

SIR WALTER RALEIGH (1552?-1618)

The Passionate Man's Pilgrimage
The Conclusion

Many men in high positions—perhaps even most of them—eventually discover how hollow is the vanity of pride of place and power. But few of them have learned this lesson so thoroughly and so painfully as did Sir Walter Raleigh.

Raleigh, one of the more remarkable men of Elizabethan England, lived many lives: explorer, New World colonizer, naval strategist and hero, the darling of powerful Queen Elizabeth, statesman, poet, historian, and a lavish liver at the expense of the State. His courage and wit combined with his strong personality and tremendous energy to lift him almost as high as his ruthless ambition and selfish egotism could desire.

But suddenly the career of this paradoxical man—patriot and plotter, benefactor and greedy, Puritan in mind and habits yet with a Pagan delight in gestures and poses—was halted when enemies conspired to have him arrested on a charge of treason at the age of fifty-two. At a trial that degraded English justice, Raleigh was sentenced to death and stripped of all his property and wealth.

It was apparently during the two or three weeks between sentence and the execution date that Raleigh wrote his magnificent "The Passionate Man's Pilgrimage"—a cry of disillusionment, but also one of confidence that the Heavenly Court would reverse his fellowman's verdict against him based on malice.

> Give me my Scallop shell of quiet,
>   My staff of Faith to walk upon,
> My Script of Joy, Immortal diet,
>   My bottle of salvation:
> My Gown of Glory, hope's true gage,
>   And thus I'll take my pilgrimage.
>
> Blood must be my body's balmer,
>   No other balm will there be given
> Whilst my soul like a white Palmer
>   Travels to the land of heaven,
> Over the silver mountains,
> Where spring the Nectar fountains:
> And there I'll kiss
> The Bowl of bliss,

And drink my eternal fill
On every milken hill.
My soul will be a-dry before,
But after it, will ne'er thirst more.

And by the happy blissful way
   More peaceful Pilgrims I shall see,
That have shook off their gowns of clay,
   And go appareled fresh like me.
I'll bring them first
To slake their thirst,
   And then to taste those Nectar suckets
At the clear wells
Where sweetness dwells,
   Drawn up by Saints in Christall buckets.

And when our bottles and all we,
Are filled with immortality:
Then the holy paths we'll travel
Strewed with Rubies thick as gravel,
Ceilings of Diamonds, Sapphire floors,
High walls of Coral and Pearl Bowers.

From thence to heaven's Bribeless hall
Where no corrupted voices brawl,
No Conscience molten into gold,
Nor forged accusers bought and sold,
No cause deferred, nor vain spent Journey,
For there Christ is the King's Attorney:
Who pleads for all without degrees,
And he hath Angels, but no fees.

When the grand twelve million Jury,
Of our sins with sinful fury,
Gainst our soul's black verdicts give,
Christ pleads His death, and then we live,
Be thou my speaker taintless pleader,
Unblotted Lawyer, true proceeder,
Thou movest salvation even for alms:
Not with a bribed Lawyer's palms.

And this is my eternal plea,
To Him that made Heaven, Earth and Sea,
Seeing my flesh must die so soon,
And want a head to dine next noon,

Just at the stroke when my veins start and spread
Set on my soul an everlasting head.
Then am I ready like a palmer fit,
To tread those blest paths which before I writ.

A few days before the day set for Raleigh's execution King James suspended sentence but kept the once powerful man confined in the Tower of London for thirteen years—bitter years of reflection on the emptiness of pride of position and power.

Finally Raleigh was released from The Tower at age sixty-five, to lead an expedition to Guinea in South America, where he insisted to the King there was gold. When he returned without gold he was attacked, slandered, and again tried for treason and again condemned to death—this time without any last-minute reprieve. The night before he was beheaded Raleigh again put into immortal lines the truth that vain and inordinately ambitious men will only learn from life itself:

Even such is Time, that takes in trust
    Our youth, our joys, our all we have,
And pay us but with earth and dust;
    Who in the dark and silent grave,
    When we have wandered all our ways,
Shuts up the story of our days;
    But from this earth, this grave, this dust,
My God shall raise me up, I trust.

EDWIN ARLINGTON ROBINSON (1869-1935)

Mr. Flood's Party

Robinson spent the first twenty-seven years of his life, except for two years at Harvard University, in Gardiner, Maine, a town of 4,500 people on the Kennebec River. This is the "Tilbury Town" of many of his poems; a community small and varied enough for the shy young man to observe and study the men and women who became the subjects for poems. And here was the conflict between an older colonial culture and the pressures of modernity, found in much of his poetry.

As a young man in Gardiner, Robinson spoke of the "mental tragedies" to be discovered in the lives of apparently happy people. He believed that people often live deeper lives than we realize, and he hoped his poetry would lead us to a more sympathetic understanding of our fellow man when we realize there is usually not a great difference between individuals.

This attitude explains in good part why the poet is preoccupied with failures—both spiritual and material—and with lives of frustration. Besides, Robinson's New England conscience constantly prodded him that he was a failure. Thus he was sympathetic to failures and anxious to find their moments of triumph.

One of the many Gardiner personalities that interested Robinson, and in whom perhaps the poet years later recognized a kindred spirit because of his own solitary heavy drinking, was the father of Harry Smith, a friend of the poet.

Smith's father was an eccentric farmer and ship's caulker who amused young Robinson with his custom of proposing and drinking toasts to himself. He became the Mr. Flood of the poem, who stood on a hill looking down on the town, raised his jug of liquor and drank a salutation to his dear friends in the village. Eben Flood's story, told with gentle humor and an understanding of man's tragedy, is one of the most successful of the poet's "failures":

> Old Eben Flood, climbing alone one night
> Over the hill between the town below
> And the forsaken upland hermitage
> That held as much as he should ever know
> On earth again of home, paused warily.
> The road was his with not a native near;
> And Eben, having leisure, said aloud,
> For no man else in Tilbury Town to hear:
>
> "Well, Mr. Flood, we have the harvest moon
> Again, and we may not have many more;
> The bird is on the wing, the poet says,
> And you and I have said it here before.
> Drink to the bird." He raised up to the light
> The jug that he had gone so far to fill,
> And answered huskily: "Well, Mr. Flood,
> Since you propose it, I believe I will."
>
> Alone, as if enduring to the end
> A valiant armor of scarred hopes outworn,
> He stood there in the middle of the road
> Like Roland's ghost winding a silent horn.
> Below him, in the town among the trees,
> Where friends of other days had honored him,
> A phantom salutation of the dead
> Rang thinly till old Eben's eyes were dim.

Then, as a mother lays her sleeping child
Down tenderly, fearing it may awake,
He set the jug down slowly at his feet
With trembling care, knowing that most things break;
And only when assured that on firm earth
It stood, as the uncertain lives of men
Assuredly did not, he paced away,
And with his hand extended paused again:

"Well, Mr. Flood, we have not met like this
In a long time; and many a change has come
To both of us, I fear, since last it was
We had a drop together. Welcome home!"
Convivially returning with himself,
Again he raised the jug up to the light;
And with an acquiescent quaver said:
"Well, Mr. Flood, if you insist, I might.

"Only a very little, Mr. Flood—
For auld lang syne. No more, sir; that will do."
So, for the time, apparently it did,
And Eben evidently thought so too;
For soon amid the silver loneliness
Of night he lifted up his voice and sang,
Secure, with only two moons listening,
Until the whole harmonious landscape rang—

"For auld lang syne." The weary throat gave out,
The last word wavered, and the song was done.
He raised again the jug regretfully
And shook his head, and was again alone.
There was not much that was ahead of him,
And there was nothing in the town below—
Where strangers would have shut the many doors
That many friends had opened long ago.

CHRISTINA ROSSETTI (1830-1894)

"When I am Dead, My Dearest"
A Birthday
Love Lies Bleeding
Up-Hill

It may be surprising, but it is understandable, that some of our most charming love lyrics came from the hand of a frail, sweet un-married woman of sturdy religious convictions and strong sensibilities.

High-strung, graceful Christina Rossetti could hardly have escaped activity in one of the arts, given her talent and the intellectual atmosphere of the closely knit Rossetti family. She began to write verse at eleven and for a brief while painted in water-colors. But poetry soon won out.

Educated entirely at home by her mother, to whom she was unusually devoted for fifty-six years, Christina met many of the visitors who called at the London home of her scholarly and artistic father and brothers. But her shyness, and illnesses that arrived and disappeared with puzzling rapidity, prevented her becoming aware that some of the younger men were notic-ing her.

However, when she was seventeen Christina was attracted to James Collinson, a twenty-three-year-old painter, reasonably prosperous, good-natured, introverted and by no means an Apollo. Before long she was in love with this socially awkward little man, encouraged him to write religious poetry, and dreamed of sharing poetry and life with him.

But Collinson had become a Roman Catholic. To a strict and devout Anglican, such as Christina, this was a barrier to their marriage. Collinson, assailed by doubts and by love, renounced his Catholicism to become an Anglican, and the engagement was announced. Their peace and happines was short-lived; Collinson had new doubts—about the Church of England, marriage conflicting with his ambition as an artist, and worry that he had been wrong in leaving Catholicism.

While others scoffed at Collinson, Christina was sympathetic and understanding, but coldly determined that no matter how great her love she would not marry him if he returned to the Roman Catholic Church, which he did when Christina was nineteen.

The delicate young poet never entirely recovered from this blow, suffering a lifelong melancholia and frequent illness as a consequence.

It is no accident that Christina wrote the following poem shortly before the engagement was broken, perhaps in anticipation of the romance's collapse:

When I am dead, my dearest,
　Sing no sad songs for me;
Plant thou no roses at my head,
　Nor shady cypress tree:
Be the green grass above me
　With showers and dewdrops wet:
And if thou wilt, remember,
　And if thou wilt, forget.

I shall not see the shadows,
　I shall not feel the rain;
I shall not hear the nightingale
　Sing on as if in pain:
And dreaming through the twilight
　That doth rise nor set,
Haply I may remember,
　And haply may forget.

Five years after the break with Collinson, a new man entered the poet's
life: Charles Bagot Cayley, a scholarly, lonely, shy and mildly eccentric
man of considerable learning but of no means whatever. Christina enjoyed
this wistful gentleman's company and was charmed by the many odd ways
in which the gentle day-dreamer tried to tell her of his love; such as the
gift of a rare sea mouse with a dissertation on the species. She grew to love
him, and perhaps for a time dreamed of a gay and light-hearted romance,
as expressed in her lilting "A Birthday":

My heart is like a singing bird
　Whose nest is in a watered shoot:
My heart is like an apple-tree
　Whose boughs are bent with thickset fruit;
My heart is like a rainbow shell
　That paddles in a halcyon sea;
My heart is gladder than all these
　Because my love is come to me.

Raise me a dais of silk and down;
　Hang it with vair and purple dyes;
Carve it in doves and pomegranates,
　And peacocks with a hundred eyes;
Work it in gold and silver grapes,
　In leaves and silver fleurs-de-lys;
Because the birthday of my life
　Is come, my love is come to me.

However, Christina never married poor, faithful Cayley, although she gave him her deepest love to the day of her death, and in her last years reproached herself for leading him on only to disappointment. His agnosticism stood in the way of their full happiness, but did not otherwise exclude him from the role of constant lover who, year after year, gave her great pleasure with his frequent visits.

There is the further fact that this frail little man did not stir Christina as had Collinson, whose effect on her was such that she fainted when she saw him on the street a year after their engagement was ended. Another twenty years later the poet again was stricken when she met, but did not speak to, Collinson on a London street. Instead her heart spoke in the dramatic "Love Lies Bleeding":—

> Love, that is dead and buried, yesterday
> > Out of his grave rose up before my face;
> > No recognition in his look, no trace
> Of memory in his eyes dust-dimmed and grey;
> While I, remembering, found no word to say,
> > But felt my quickening heart leap in its place;
> > Caught afterglow thrown back from long-set days,
> Caught echoes of all music past away.
> Was this indeed to meet?—I mind me yet
> > In youth we met when hope and love were quick,
> > We parted with hope dead but love alive:
> I mind me how we parted then heart-sick,
> > Remembering, loving, hopeless, weak to strive:—
> Was this to meet? Not so, we have not met.

Collinson died poor and obscure in 1881; Cayley died in 1883 as gently and quietly as he had lived; Christina had yet eleven more years of life, much of it in pain.

The spiritual travail of her final years was realistically foreshadowed by the poet in 1858 in her famous "Up-Hill"; a summation of her philosophy of life as a struggle for Christian perfection with comforting peace at its end. She needed this assurance because her last months were clouded by doubts as to the worthiness of her life—a doubt not shared by those who know her history:

> Does the road wind up-hill all the way?
> > Yes, to the very end.
> Will the day's journey take the whole long day?
> > From morn to night, my friend.

But is there for the night a resting-place?
    A roof for when the slow dark hours begin.
May not the darkness hide it from my face?
    You cannot miss that inn.

Shall I meet other wayfarers at night?
    Those who have gone before.
Then must I knock, or call when just in sight?
    They will not keep you standing at that door.

Shall I find comfort, travel-sore and weak?
    Of labour you shall find the sum.
Will there be beds for me and all who seek?
    Yea, beds for all who come.

ABRAM JOSEPH RYAN (1834-1886)

The Conquered Banner

At the opening of the Civil War, Virginia-born Father Abram Ryan resigned his teaching post with St. John's College in Brooklyn, New York, because he could not bear the hatred of the South he encountered, and he would not tolerate Southerners being called rebels and traitors.

He went to St. Louis and from there he and his sixteen-year-old brother David traveled South and joined the Confederate Army—Father Ryan as a chaplain, his brother as a soldier. The two brothers remained together as a part of Jeb Stuart's daring forces. When David was killed in battle at Chancellorsville his pale, rather scholarly brother was crushed. Never robust, shortly afterwards he became ill and was sent to a military hospital in Richmond, where he met and became friendly with Jefferson Davis.

As the tide turned and Union Armies penetrated the South, Father Ryan was placed in charge of a mission church at Edgefield, outside Nashville, Tennessee. For him the war was over, as he moved into his tiny room back of the small church.

And on Palm Sunday, April 9, 1865, as he sat reading his breviary Father Ryan heard from a neighbor that the war was over for everyone—Lee had surrendered! Though he feared this would happen, nevertheless the news shocked and saddened him. Lee was his hero, and would continue to be.

That night the twenty-seven-year-old priest slept fitfully, alternately thinking and dreaming of his comrades-in-arms, of his dead brother, of Lee. But one dream was more vivid than the others: an old soldier pointing despairingly to a blood-stained Stars and Bars—the flag of the Confederacy—that hung in disarray on a fence. The spectral soldier seemed to be saying that the banner would never wave again.

During the morning Father Ryan could not get that dream out of his mind. Finally he went to his desk and, in a surge of controlled emotion, began to write a poem. Upon completion he doubted that it did justice to the nobility of his subject. The next day he read it to a wounded soldier who stopped in for a visit, and before long it had swept the South and made the author famous.

In subsequent years Father Ryan traveled extensively in behalf of the South and continued to write. He was in New Orleans in 1878 when a yellow fever epidemic struck the city. Generous aid from the North was rushed to the stricken town. Happy at this demonstration of good-will, the Southern poet wrote *Reunited*. But *The Conquered Banner* is the poem of his that still waves.

> Furl that Banner, for 'tis weary;
> Round its staff 'tis drooping dreary;
> Furl it, fold it, it is best;
> For there's not a man to wave it,
> And there's not a sword to save it,
> And there's no one left to lave it
> In the blood which heroes gave it;
> And its foes now scorn and brave it;
> Furl it, hide it—let it rest!
>
> Take that Banner down! 'tis tattered;
> Broken is its staff and shattered;
> And the valiant hosts are scattered
> Over whom it floated high.
> Oh! 'tis hard for us to fold it;
> Hard to think there's none to hold it;
> Hard that those, who once unrolled it,
> Now must furl it might a sigh.
>
> Furl that Banner! furl it sadly!
> Once ten thousand hailed it gladly,
> And ten thousand wildly, madly,
> Swore it should forever wave;
> Swore that foeman's sword should never
> Hearts like theirs entwined dissever,
> Till that flag should float forever
> O'er their freedom, or their grave.

Furl it; for the hands that grasped it,
And the hearts that fondly clasped it,
Cold and dead are lying low;
And that Banner—it is trailing!
While around it sounds the wailing
Of its people in their woe.

For, though conquered, they adore it!
Love the cold, dead hands that bore it!
Weep for those who fell before it!
Pardon those who trailed and tore it!
But, oh! wildly they deplore it,
Now who furl and fold it so.

Furl that Banner! True, 'tis gory,
Yet 'tis wreathed around with glory,
And 'twill live in song and story,
Though its folds are in the dust;
For its fame on brightest pages,
Penned by poets and by sages,
Shall go sounding down the ages—
Furl its folds though now we must.

Furl that Banner, softly, slowly!
Treat it gently—it is holy—
For it droops above the dead.
Touch it not—unfold it never,
Let it droop there, furled forever,
For its peoples' hopes are dead.

ALAN SEEGER (1888-1916)

I Have a Rendezvous with Death

Alan Seeger was the voice of idealistic youth in a War and a day that
now seem far more remote than the forty-five years which have elapsed
since then.

In early 1915 the War still excited and thrilled many soldiers; their ideals
were as yet untarnished by the suffering, death and desolation that multiplied
during the ensuing months and years.

Seeger dashed into the War with the exuberant spirit of a reckless adventurer, rather than as the carefully reared son of wealthy parents of old New England families; a youth who after completing college at Harvard went to France in 1912. He loved that country so, that two weeks after the War began in 1914, he enlisted in the French Foreign Legion. In explaining his enlistment he revealed his high ideals and fatalistic acceptance of war and its consequences: "Without renouncing their nationality they [Americans in the Foreign Legion] had yet chosen to make their homes here [Paris] beyond any other city in the world. Did not the benefits and blessings they had received point them a duty that heart and conscience could not deny? . . . It was unthinkable to leave the danger to them and accept only the pleasures oneself. . . . The same fate that makes him surrender himself to the impulses of normal living and of love, forces him now to make himself the instrument through which a greater force works out its inscrutable ends. . . . He shoulders arms and marches forth with haste."

This was not cheap posturing or the world-weariness of a twenty-eight-year-old poet. It was a man of vitality who was glad to dice with death for his ideals; ideals he believed would endure even if death won. Seeger cried "Yea" to life and to War with the realization—perhaps the intuition—that War might cut him down.

Nor did actual soldiering and combat disillusion him. His letters from the front in France spoke of "the magnificent orchestra of battle," and he said "I think we are marching to victory too, but wherever we are going we are going triumphantly." Never did he express regret for the choice he made.

After eight months on the firing line Seeger wrote his mother that his chances of returning were about one in ten, but urged her to be proud of his contribution adding "I could not have done better. Death is nothing terrible after all. . . . Had I the choice I would be nowhere else in the world than where I am. . . . If I do not come out I will share the good fortune of those who disappear at the pinnacle of their careers."

Alan Seeger had his "Rendezvous With Death" on the night of July first, 1916, when the Foreign Legion was ordered to clear the Germans out of the village of Belloy-en-Santerre. His squad, in the first attack, was swept by machine gun fire. Seeger and most of his comrades were struck down. When daylight came it was found that his life of high aspirations had ended as he predicted in his poem, and as he seemed almost to invite:

> I have a rendezvous with Death
> At some disputed barricade,
> When Spring comes back with rustling shade
> And apple-blossoms fill the air—
> I have a rendezvous with Death
> When Spring brings back blue days and fair.

It may be he shall take my hand
And lead me into his dark land
And close my eyes and quench my breath—
It may be I shall pass him still.
I have a rendezvous with Death
On some scarred slope of battered hill
When Spring comes round again this year
And the first meadow-flowers appear.

God knows 'twere better to be deep
Pillowed in silk and scented down,
Where Love throbs out in blissful sleep,
Pulse night to pulse, and breath to breath,
Where hushed awakenings are dear . . .
But I've a rendezvous with Death
At midnight in some flaming town,
When Spring trips north again this year,
And I to my pledged word am true,
I shall not fail that rendezvous.

KARL SHAPIRO (1913-   )

Elegy for a Dead Soldier

Few fine poems so clearly and graphically reveal the circumstances leading to their creation as does this one. One need hardly say more than that Karl Shapiro, one of America's leading contemporary poets, served in the South Pacific from 1941 to 1945, and this powerful but compassionate commentary no doubt epitomizes the feelings of a sensitive and understanding man toward his fallen comrades in arms. It is one of the few superb poems that have come to us out of World War II:

A white sheet on the tail-gate of a truck
Becomes an altar; two small candlesticks
Sputter at each side of the crucifix
Laid round with flowers brighter than the blood,
Red as the red of our apocalypse,
Hibiscus that a marching man will pluck
To stick into his rifle or his hat,
And great blue morning-glories pale as lips
That shall no longer taste or kiss or swear.

The wind begins a low magnificat,
The chaplain chats, the palm trees swirl their hair,
The columns come together through the mud.

II

We too are ashes as we watch and hear
The psalm, the sorrow, and the simpler praise
Of one whose promised thoughts of other days
Were such as ours, but now wholly destroyed,
The service record of his youth wiped out,
His dream dispersed by shot, must disappear.
What can we feel but wonder at a loss
That seems to point at nothing but the doubt
Which flirts our sense of luck into the ditch?
Reader of Paul who prays beside this fosse,
Shall we believe our eyes or legends rich
With glory and rebirth beyond the void?

III

For this comrade is dead, dead in the war,
A young man out of millions yet to live,
One cut away from all that war can give,
Freedom of self and peace to wander free.
Who mourns in all this sober multitude
Who did not feel the bite of it before
The bullet found its aim? This worthy flesh,
This boy laid in a coffin and reviewed—
Who had not wrapped himself in this same flag,
Heard the light fall of dirt, his wound still fresh,
Felt his eyes closed, and heard the distant brag
Of the last volley of humanity?

IV

By chance I saw him die, stretched on the ground,
A tatooed arm lifted to take the blood
Of someone else sealed in a tin. I stood
During the last delirium that stays
The intelligence a tiny moment more,
And then the strangulation, the last sound.
The end was sudden, like a foolish play,
A stupid fool slamming a foolish door,
The absurd catastrophe, half-prearranged,

And all the decisive things still left to say.
So we disbanded, angrier and unchanged,
Sick with the utter silence of dispraise.

V

We ask for no statistics of the killed,
For nothing political impinges on
This single casualty, or all those gone,
Missing or healing, sinking or dispersed,
Hundreds of thousands counted, millions lost.
More than an accident and less than willed
Is every fall, and this one like the rest.
However others calculate the cost,
To us the final aggregate is *one,*
One with a name, one transferred to the blest;
And though another stoops, and takes the gun,
We cannot add the second to the first.

VI

I would not speak for him who could not speak
Unless my fear were true: he was not wronged,
He knew to which decision he belonged
But let it choose itself. Ripe in instinct,
Neither the victim nor the volunteer,
He followed and the leaders could not seek
Beyond the followers. Much of this he knew;
The journey was a detour that would steer
Into the Lincoln Highway of a land
Remorselessly improved, excited, new,
And that was that he wanted. He had planned
To earn and drive. He and the world had winked.

VII

No history deceived him, for he knew
Little of times and armies not his own;
He never felt that peace was but a loan,
Had never questioned the idea of gain.
Beyond the headlines once or twice he saw
The gathering of a power by the few
But could not tell their names; he cast his vote,
Distrusting all the elected but not the law.
He laughed at socialism; *on mourrait*

Pour les industriels? He shed his coat
And not for brotherhood, but for his pay.
To him the red flag marked the sewer main.

VIII

Above all else he loathed the homily,
The slogan and the ad. He paid his bill
But not for Congressmen at Bunker Hill.
Ideals were few and those there were not made
For conversation. He belonged to church
But never spoke of God. The Christmas tree,
The Easter egg, baptism, he observed,
Never denied the preacher on his perch,
And would not sign Resolved That or Whereas.
Softness he had and hours and nights reserved
For thinking, dressing, dancing to the jazz.
His laugh was real, his manners were home made.

IX

Of all men poverty pursued him least;
He was ashamed of all the down and out,
Spurned the panhandler like an uneasy doubt,
And saw the unemployed as a vague mass
Incapable of hunger or revolt.
He hated other races, south or east,
And shoved them to the margin of his mind.
He could recall the justice of the Colt,
Take interest in a gang-war like a game,
His ancestry was somewhere far behind
And left him only his peculiar name.
Doors opened, and he recognized no class.

X

His children would have known a heritage,
Just or unjust, the richest in the world,
The quantum of all art and science curled
In the horn of plenty, bursting from the horn,
A people bathed in honey, Paris come,
Vienna transferred with the highest wage,
A World's Fair spread to Phoenix, Jacksonville,
Earth's capitol, the new Byzantium,
Kingdom of man—who know? Hollow or firm,

No man can ever prophesy until
Out of death some undiscovered germ,
Whole toleration or pure peace is born.

XI

The time to mourn is short that best becomes
The military dead. We lift and fold the flag,
Lay bare the coffin with its written tag,
And march away. Behind, four others wait
To lift the box, the heaviest of loads.
The anesthetic afternoon benumbs,
Sickens our senses, forces back our talk.
We know that others on tomorrow's roads
Will fall, ourselves perhaps, the man beside,
Over the world the threatened, all who walk:
And could we mark the grave of him who died
We would write this beneath his name and date:

Epitaph

Underneath this wooden cross there lies
A Christian killed in battle. You who read,
Remember that this stranger died in pain;
And passing here, if you can lift your eyes
Upon a peace kept by a human creed,
Know that one soldier has not died in vain.
New Guinea, 1944

PERCY BYSSHE SHELLEY (1792-1822)

Indian Serenade
Ode to the West Wind
Adonais

In November, 1819, an unsophisticated and rather sentimental young lady named Sophia Stacey arrived in Florence, Italy, from England. She was the ward of one of Shelley's favorite uncles, who had told her just enough about the poet to quicken her curiosity and perhaps stimulate her romantic imagination. Two days after her arrival she called on the Shelleys and the next day she and a friend traveling with her took lodgings in the same house the poet and his wife lived in.

The two new arrivals became quite intimate with the Shelleys, particularly with the poet, whom Sophia found "mysterious" and "interesting." Shelley usually had a romantic effect upon women who met him and in the present case apparently did nothing to discourage the impression.

Shelley appears to have been chiefly attracted by Sophia's trained and appealing voice, being especially delighted when she accompanied herself on the harp. When she asked the poet for a poem that could be put to music he sent her "To Sophia" ("Thou art fair and few are fairer") and "To a Faded Violet," and it is possible he may have composed "Good-Night," "Love's Philosophy" and "Time Long Past" for her, since he did write them out and give them to her.

But the first poem he gave Sophia Stacey was the more famous and more passionate "Indian Serenade." Newman Ivy White points out that these lyrics for Sophia have often been misunderstood and suspiciously interpreted, as have other of his poems addressed to several other women.

Sophia obviously charmed Shelley but there is no evidence and no reason to suppose that the poems were any more than tributes to the power of music. Other beautiful singing voices similarly affected him. Sophia's voice just happened to evoke a more impassioned response. She, incidentally, was in Florence less than two months and seems not to have caused Mrs. Shelley any concern.

I arise from dreams of thee
In the first sweet sleep of night,
When the winds are breathing low,
And the stars are shining bright:
I arise from dreams of thee,
And in a spirit in my feet
Hath led me—who knows how?—
To thy chamber window, Sweet!

The wandering airs they faint
On the dark, the silent stream—
The Champak odours fail
Like sweet thoughts in a dream;
The nightingale's complaint,
It dies upon her heart;
As I must on thine,
Oh, beloved as thou art!

Oh lift me from the grass!
I die! I faint! I fail!

Let thy love in kisses rain
On my lips and eyelids pale.
My cheek is cold and white, alas!
My heart beats loud and fast;—
Oh! press it to thine own again,
Where it will break at last.

As a youth Shelley was rebellious, non-conforming and the sworn enemy
of tyranny. When he matured he regarded the poet as "the unacknowledged
legislator of the world" and believed his own mission as a poet was not to
teach, but to inspire—to "lift the veil from the hidden beauty of the world."
He believed, moreover, that poetry—including his own—must make its contribution to a great human revolution that he considered necessary.

The romantic and visionary nature of this "beautiful and ineffectual
angel" (to quote Matthew Arnold) is indicated by the fact that the revolution he urged would amount to anarchy kept in control by goodness, truth
and a love of the beautiful and sublime.

When we realize the intensity of these fanciful convictions and desires,
it is easy to appreciate the poet's dejection when he became convinced his
voice was not reaching an audience. This personal despondency is found in
a number of his poems.

One morning Shelley went on a sight-seeing boat in the Bay of Naples.
It was a clear day and the sea was so calm that the seaweed on the floor of
the Bay could be seen distinctly by those on the boat. This impressed Shelley.
He thought again of the deeply imbedded and undying impulses for good
that lay dormant in mankind, and which if aroused would conquer evil in
the world. It was a thought that would recur again and again.

Later, at sunset on an Autumn day in a wood by the river Arno, near
Florence, amid hail and rain accompanied by thunder and lightning, Shelley
was moved to think of the mild but tempestuous West Wind as the symbolic
destroyer of the old order, which would also sow the seeds that Spring would
bring to birth. In seeing the cycle of growth, destruction and regeneration
as both a natural and social force, Shelley saw himself as a poet playing a
role in it.

I

O Wild West Wind, thou breath of Autumn's being,
Thou, from whose unseen presence the leaves dead
Are driven, like ghosts from an enchanter fleeing,

Yellow, and black, and pale, and hectic red,
Pestilence-stricken multitudes: O thou,
Who chariotest to their dark wintry bed

The wingèd seeds, where they lie cold and low,
Each like a corpse within its grave, until
Thine azure sister of the Spring shall blow

Her clarion o'er the dreaming earth, and fill
(Driving sweet buds like flocks to feed in air)
With living hues and odours plain and hill:

Wild Spirit, which art moving everywhere;
Destroyer and preserver; hear, oh, hear!

II

Thou on whose stream, mid the steep sky's commotion,
Loose clouds like earth's decaying leaves are shed,
Shook from the tangled boughs of Heaven and Ocean,

Angels of rain and lightning: there are spread
On the blue surface of thine aëry surge,
Like the bright hair uplifted from the head

Of some fierce Maenad, even from the dim verge
Of the horizon to the zenith's height,
The locks of the approaching storm. Thou dirge

Of the dying year, to which this closing night
Will be the dome of a vast sepulchre,
Vaulted with all thy congregated might

Of vapours, from whose solid atmosphere
Black rain, and fire, and hail will burst: oh, hear!

III

Thou who didst waken from his summer dreams
The blue Mediterranean, where he lay,
Lulled by the coil of his crystàlline streams,

Beside a pumice isle in Baiae's bay,
And saw in sleep old palaces and towers
Quivering within the wave's intenser day,

All overgrown with azure moss and flowers
So sweet, the sense faints picturing them! Thou
For whose path the Atlantic's level powers

Cleave themselves into chasms, while far below
The sea-blooms and the oozy woods which wear
The sapless foliage of the ocean, know

Thy voice, and suddenly grow gray with fear,
And tremble and despoil themselves: oh, hear!

IV

If I were a dead leaf thou mightest bear,
If I were a swift cloud to fly with thee;
A wave to pant beneath thy power, and share

The impulse of thy strength, only less free
Than thou, O uncontrollable! If even
I were as in my boyhood, and could be

The comrade of thy wanderings over Heaven,
As then, when to outstrip thy skiey speed
Scarce seem'd a vision; I would ne'er have striven

As thus with thee in prayer in my sore need.
Oh, lift me as a wave, a leaf, a cloud!
I fall upon the thorns of life! I bleed!

A heavy weight of hours has chained and bowed
One too like thee: tameless, and swift, and proud.

V

Make me thy lyre, even as the forest is:
What if my leaves are falling like its own!
The tumult of thy mighty harmonies

Will take from both a deep, autumnal tone,
Sweet though in sadness. Be thou, Spirit fierce,
My spirit! Be thou me, impetuous one!

Drive my dead thoughts over the universe
Like withered leaves to quicken a new birth!
And by the incantation of this verse,

Scatter, as from an unextinguished hearth
Ashes and sparks, my words among mankind!
Be through my lips to unawakened earth

The trumpet of a prophecy! O, Wind,
If Winter comes, can Spring be far behind?

Shelley and John Keats had met several times in England, but did not become close friends. When Shelley, who went to Italy in 1818, learned that Keats' health was failing rapidly, he promptly invited the ailing man to take up residence with the Shelley's at Pisa for his better recovery.

However, Keats and his devoted artist friend Joseph Severn went instead to Rome in late 1820, and five months later the twenty-six-year-old tuberculous poet died there.

Shelley heard the news on April 19th and immediately began to write his glorious tribute to one whose "fate and fame shall be an echo and a light unto eternity!"

When Shelley sent Byron a copy of the completed elegy, he conceded that while his praise of Keats as a poet was sincere, it might be excessive. "But if I have erred," he added, "I console myself with reflecting that it is in defense of the weak—not in conjunction with the powerful."

Shelley, of course, would regret the death of any creator of fine poetry, but Keats' passing inspired him to such great heights because he believed that "the savage criticism" of Keats' poetry was the principal cause of his death. These critics, said Shelley, "scatter their insults and their slanders without heed as to whether the poisoned shaft lights on a heart made callous by many blows or one like Keats's composed of more penetrable stuff . . . Miserable man! you, one of the meanest, have wantonly defaced one of the noblest specimens of the workmanship of God."

Shelley's emotion in behalf of Keats seems due not only to his belief that Keats was pilloried by the critics, but also because Shelley considered himself a victim of literary persecution—a poet grievously injured by the reviewers. One of his biographers said Shelley's instinct to fight back was inhibited by his belief that revenge was one of the greatest of human errors. Consequently, in "Adonais" he identifies his own fate with that of Keats as "a herd-abandoned deer, struck by the hunter's dart," and one "who in another's fate now wept his own." Thus, in defending Keats, Shelley was at least subconsciously defending himself; in mourning Keats he was in a sense lamenting his own ultimate dissolution, nearer at hand than he could have anticipated. (He drowned at sea sixteen months later, a copy of Keats' poems in his pocket.) But since to Shelley Intellectual Beauty was the only reality, he transmuted his despair into the belief that human life survives by joining "the soul of Adonais" where "the one remains, the many change and pass."

Although Shelley had little hope his "Adonais" would "excite any attention," he did feel it was "the least imperfect of my compositions, and, as the image of my regret and honour for poor Keats, I wish it to be so." In thus honoring Keats, Shelley increased his own fame:

I weep for Adonais—he is dead!
Oh weep for Adonais! though our tears
Thaw not the frost which binds so dear a head!
And thou, sad Hour, selected from all years
To mourn our loss, rouse thy obscure compeers,
And teach them thine own sorrow, say: "With me
Died Adonais; till the Future dares
Forget the Past, his fate and fame shall be
An echo and a light unto eternity!"

Where wert thou, mighty Mother, when he lay,
When thy Son lay, pierced by the shaft which flies
In darkness? Where was lorn Urania
When Adonais died? With veilèd eyes,
'Mid listening Echoes, in her Paradise
She sate, while one, with soft enamoured breath,
Rekindled all the fading melodies,
With which, like flowers that mock the corse beneath,
He had adorned and hid the coming bulk of Death.

O weep for Adonais—he is dead!
Wake, melancholy Mother, wake and weep!
Yet wherefore? Quench within their burning bed
Thy fiery tears, and let thy loud heart keep
Like his, a mute and uncomplaining sleep;
For he is gone, where all things wise and fair
Descend;—oh, dream not that the amorous Deep
Will yet restore him to the vital air;
Death feeds on his mute voice, and laughs at our despair.

Most musical of mourners, weep again!
Lament anew, Urania!—He died,
Who was the Sire of an immortal strain,
Blind, old, and lonely, when his country's pride,
The priest, the slave, and the liberticide,
Trampled and mocked with many a loathèd rite
Of lust and blood; he went, unterrified,
Into the gulf of death; but his clear Sprite
Yet reigns o'er earth; the third among the sons of light.

Most musical of mourners, weep anew!
Not all to that bright station dared to climb;
And happier they their happiness who knew,
Whose tapers yet burn through that night of time

In which suns perished; others more sublime,
Struck by the envious wrath of man or god,
Have sunk, extinct in their refulgent prime;
And some yet live, treading the thorny road,
Which leads, through toil and hate, to Fame's serene abode.

But now, thy youngest, dearest one, has perished—
The nursling of thy widowhood, who grew,
Like a pale flower by some sad maiden cherished,
And fed with true-love tears, instead of dew;
Most musical of mourners, weep anew!
Thy extreme hope, the loveliest and the last,
The bloom, whose petals, nipped before they blew
Died on the promise of the fruit, is waste;
The broken lily lies—the storm is overpast.

To that high Capital, where kingly Death
Keeps his pale court in beauty and decay,
He came; and bought, with price of purest breath,
A grave among the eternal.—Come away!
Haste, while the vault of blue Italian day
Is yet his fitting charnel-roof! while still
He lies, as if in dewy sleep he lay;
Awake him not! surely he takes his fill
Of deep and liquid rest, forgetful of all ill.

He will awake no more, oh, never more!—
Within the twilight chamber spreads apace
The shadow of white Death, and at the door
Invisible Corruption waits to trace
His extreme way to her dim dwelling-place;
The eternal Hunger sits, but pity and awe
Soothes her pale rage, nor dares she to deface
So fair a prey, till darkness, and the law
Of change, shall o'er his sleep the mortal curtain draw.

Oh, weep for Adonais!—the quick Dreams,
The passion-wingèd Ministers of thought,
Who were his flocks, whom near the living streams
Of his young spirit he fed, and whom he taught
The love which was its music, wander not,—
Wander no more, from kindling brain to brain,
But droop there, whence they sprung; and mourn their lot
Round the cold heart, where, after their sweet pain,
They ne'er will gather strength, or find a home again.

And one with trembling hands clasps his cold head,
And fans him with her moonlight wings, and cries;
"Our love, our hope, our sorrow, is not dead;
See, on the silken fringe of his faint eyes,
Like dew upon a sleeping flower, there lies
A tear some Dream has loosened from his brain."
Lost Angel of a ruined Paradise!
She knew not 'twas her own; as with no stain
She faded, like a cloud which had outwept its rain.

One from a lucid urn of starry dew
Washed his light limbs as if embalming them;
Another clipped her profuse locks, and threw
The wreath upon him, like an anadem,
Which frozen tears instead of pearls begem;
Another in her wilful grief would break
Her bow and wingèd reeds, as if to stem
A greater loss with one which was more weak;
And dull the barbèd fire against his frozen cheek.

Another Splendour on his mouth alit,
That mouth, whence it was wont to draw the breath
Which gave it strength to pierce the guarded wit,
And pass into the panting heart beneath
With lightning and with music; the damp death
Quenched its caress upon his icy lips;
And as a dying meteor stains a wreath
Of moonlight vapour, which the cold night clips,
It flushed through his pale limbs, and passed to its eclipse.

And others came . . . Desires and Adorations,
Wingèd Persuasions and veiled Destinies,
Splendours, and Glooms, and glimmering Incarnations
Of hopes and fears, and twilight Phantasies;
And Sorrow, with her family of Sighs,
And Pleasure, blind with tears, led by the gleam
Of her own dying smile instead of eyes,
Came in slow pomp;—the moving pomp might seem
Like pageantry of mist on an autumnal stream.

All he had loved, and moulded into thought,
From shape, and hue, and odour, and sweet sound,
Lamented Adonais. Morning sought
Her eastern watch-tower, and her hair unbound,
Wet with the tears which should adorn the ground,

Dimmed the aereal eyes that kindle day;
Afar the melancholy thunder moaned,
Pale Ocean in unquiet slumber lay,
And the wild Winds flew round, sobbing in their dismay.

Lost Echo sits amid the voiceless mountains,
And feeds her grief with his remembered lay,
And will no more reply to winds or fountains,
Of amorous birds perched on the young green spray,
Or herdsman's horn, or bell at closing day;
Since she can mimic not his lips, more dear
Than those for whose disdain she pined away
Into a shadow of all sounds:—a drear
Murmur, between their songs, is all the woodmen hear.

Grief made the young Spring wild, and she threw down
Her kindling buds, as if she Autumn were,
Or they dead leaves; since her delight is flown,
For whom should she have waked the sullen year?
To Phoebus was not Hyacinth so dear
Nor to himself Narcissus, as to both
Thou, Adonais: wan they stand and sere
Amid the faint companions of their youth,
With dew all turned to tears; odour, to sighing ruth.

Thy spirit's sister, the lorn nightingale
Mourns not her mate with such melodious pain;
Not so the eagle, who like thee could scale
Heaven, and could nourish in the sun's domain
Her mighty youth with morning, doth complain,
Soaring and screaming round her empty nest,
As Albion wails for thee: the curse of Cain
Light on his head who pierced thy innocent breast,
And scared the angel soul that was its earthly guest!

Ah, woe is me! Winter is come and gone,
But grief returns with the revolving year;
The airs and streams renew their joyous tone;
The ants, the bees, the swallows reappear;
Fresh leaves and flowers deck the dead Season's bier;
The amorous birds now pair in every brake,
And build their mossy homes in field and brere;
And the green lizard, and the golden snake,
Like unimprisoned flames, out of their trance awake.

Through wood and field and stream and hill and Ocean,
A quickening life from the Earth's heart has burst
As it has ever done, with change and motion,
From the great morning of the world when first
God dawned on Chaos; in its stream immersed,
The lamps of Heaven flash with a softer light;
All baser things pant with life's sacred thirst;
Diffuse themselves and spend in love's delight,
The beauty and the joy of their renewèd might.

The leprous corpse, touched by this spirit tender,
Exhales itself in flowers of gentle breath;
Like incarnations of the stars, when splendour
Is changed to fragrance, they illumine death
And mock the merry worm that wakes beneath;
Nought we know, dies. Shall that alone which knows
Be as a sword consumed before the sheath
By sightless lightning?—the intense atom glows
A moment, then is quenched in a most cold repose.

Alas! that all we loved of him should be,
But for our grief, as if it had not been,
And grief itself be mortal! Woe is me!
Whence are we, and why are we? of what scene
The actors or spectators? Great and mean
Meet massed in death, who lends what life must borrow.
As long as skies are blue, and fields are green,
Evening must usher night, night urge the morrow,
Month follows month with woe, and year wake year to sorrow.

He will awake no more, oh, never more!
"Wake thou," cried Misery, "childless Mother, rise
Out of thy sleep, and slake, in thy heart's core,
A wound more fierce than his, with tears and sighs."
And all the Dreams that watched Urania's eyes,
And all the Echoes whom their sister's song
Had held in holy silence, cried: "Arise!"
Swift as Thought by the snake Memory stung,
From her ambrosial rest the fading Splendour sprung.

She rose like an autumnal Night, that springs
Out of the East, and follows wild and drear
The golden Day, which, on eternal wings,
Even as a ghost abandoning a bier,
Had left Earth a corpse. Sorrow and fear

So struck, so roused, so rapped Urania;
So saddened round her like an atmosphere
Of stormy mist; so swept her on her way
Even to the mournful place where Adonais lay.

Out of her secret Paradise she sped,
Through camps and cities rough with stone, and steel,
And human hearts, which to her aery tread
Yielding not, wounded the invisible
Palms of her tender feet where'er they fell:
And barbèd tongues, and thoughts more sharp than they,
Rent the soft Form they never could repel,
Whose sacred blood, like the young tears of May,
Paved with eternal flowers that undeserving way.

In the death-chamber for a moment Death,
Shamed by the presence of that living Might,
Blushed to annihilation, and the breath
Revisited those lips, and Life's pale light
Flashed through those limbs, so late her dear delight.
"Leave me not wild and drear and comfortless,
As silent lightning leaves the starless night!
Leave me not!" cried Urania: her distress
Roused Death: Death rose and smiled, and met her vain caress.

"Stay yet awhile! speak to me once again;
Kiss me, so long but as a kiss may live;
And in my heartless breast and burning brain
That word, that kiss, shall all thoughts else survive,
With food of saddest memory kept alive,
Now thou art dead, as if it were a part
Of thee, my Adonais! I would give
All that I am to be as thou now art!
But I am chained to Time, and cannot thence depart!

"O gentle child, beautiful as thou wert,
Why didst thou leave the trodden paths of men
Too soon, and with weak hands though mighty heart
Dare the unpastured dragon in his den?
Defenseless as thou wert, oh, where was then
Wisdom the mirrored shield, or scorn the spear?
Or hadst thou waited full cycle, when
Thy spirit should have filled its crescent sphere,
The monsters of life's waste had fled from thee like deer.

"The herded wolves, bold only to pursue;
The obscene ravens, clamorous o'er the dead;
The vultures to the conqueror's banner true
Who feed where Desolation first has fed,
And whose wings rain contagion;—how they fled,
When, like Apollo, from his golden bow
The Pythian of the age one arrow sped
And smiled!—The spoilers tempt no second blow,
They fawn on the proud feet that spurn them lying low.

"The sun comes forth, and many reptiles spawn;
He sets, and each ephemeral insect then
Is gathered into death without a dawn,
And the immortal stars awake again;
So is it in the world of living men:
A godlike mind soars forth, in its delight
Making earth bare and veiling heaven, and when
It sinks, the swarms that dimmed or shared its light
Leaves to its kindred lamps the spirit's awful night."

Thus ceased she: and the mountain shepherds came,
Their garlands sere, their magic mantles rent;
The Pilgrim of Eternity, whose fame
Over his living head like Heaven is bent,
An early but enduring monument,
Came, veiling all the lightnings of his song
In sorrow; from her wilds Ierne sent
The sweetest lyrist of her saddest wrong,
And Love taught Grief to fall like music from his tongue.

'Midst others of less note, came one frail Form,
A phantom among men; companionless
As the last cloud of an expiring storm
Whose thunder is its knell; he, as I guess,
Had gazed on Nature's naked loveliness,
Actaeon-like, and now he fled astray
With feeble steps o'er the world's wilderness,
And his own thoughts, along that rugged way,
Pursued, like raging hounds, their father and their prey.

A pard-like Spirit beautiful and swift—
A Love in desolation masked;—a Power
Girt round with weakness;—it can scarce uplift
The weight of the superincumbent hour;
It is a dying lamp, a falling shower,

A breaking billow;—even whilst we speak
Is it not broken? On the withering flower
The killing sun smiles brightly: on a cheek
The life can burn in blood, even while the heart may break.

His head was bound with pansies overblown,
And faded violets, white, and pied, and blue;
And a light spear topped with a cypress cone,
Round whose rude shaft dark ivy-tresses grew
Yet dripping with the forest's noonday dew,
Vibrated, as the ever-beating heart
Shook the weak hand that grasped it; of that crew
He came the last, neglected and apart;
A herd-abandoned deer struck by the hunter's dart.

All stood aloof, and at his partial moan
Smiled through their tears; well knew that gentle band
Who in another's fate now wept his own,
As in the accents of an unknown land
He sung new sorrow; sad Urania scanned
The Stranger's mien, and murmured: "Who art thou?"
He answered not, but with a sudden hand
Made bare his branded and ensanguined brow,
Which was like Cain's or Christ's—oh! that it should be so!

What softer voice is hushed over the dead?
Athwart what brow is that dark mantle thrown?
What form leans sadly o'er the white death-bed,
In mockery of monumental stone,
The heavy heart heaving without a moan?
If it be He, who, gentlest of the wise,
Taught, soothed, loved, honoured the departed one,
Let me not vex, with inharmonious sighs,
The silence of that heart's accepted sacrifice.

Our Adonais has drunk poison—oh!
What dead and viperous murderer could crown
Life's early cup with such a draught of woe?
The nameless worm would now itself disown:
It felt, yet could escape, the magic tone
Whose prelude held all envy, hate, and wrong,
But what was howling in one breast alone,
Silent with expectation of the song,
Whose master's hand is cold, whose silver lyre unstrung.

Live thou, whose infamy is not thy fame!
Live; fear no heavier chastisement from me,
Thou noteless blot on a remembered name!
But be thyself, and know thyself to be!
And ever at thy season be thou free
To spill the venom when thy fangs o'erflow:
Remorse and Self-contempt shall cling to thee;
Hot Shame shall burn upon thy secret brow,
And like a beaten hound tremble thou shalt—as now.

Nor let us weep that our delight is fled
Far from these carrion kites that scream below;
He wakes or sleeps with the enduring dead;
Thou canst not soar where he is sitting now—
Dust to the dust! but the pure spirit shall flow
Back to the burning fountain whence it came,
A portion of the Eternal, which must glow
Through time and change, unquenchably the same,
Whilst thy cold embers choke the sordid hearth of shame.

Peace, peace! he is not dead, he doth not sleep—
He hath awakened from the dream of life—
'Tis we, who lost in stormy visions, keep
With phantoms an unprofitable strife,
And in mad trance, strike with our spirit's knife
Invulnerable nothings.—*We* decay
Like corpses in a charnel; fear and grief
Convulse us and consume us day by day,
And cold hopes swarm like worms within our living clay.

He has outsoared the shadow of our night;
Envy and calumny and hate and pain,
And that unrest which men miscall delight,
Can touch him not and torture not again;
From the contagion of the world's slow stain
He is secure, and now can never mourn
A heart grown cold, a head grown gray in vain;
Nor, when the spirit's self has ceased to burn,
With sparkless ashes load an unlamented urn.

He lives, he wakes—'tis Death is dead, not he;
Mourn not for Adonais.—Thou young Dawn,
Turn all thy dew to splendour, for from thee
The spirit thou lamentest is not gone;
Ye caverns and ye forests, cease to moan!

Cease, ye faint flowers and fountains, and thou Air,
Which like a mourning veil thy scarf hadst thrown
O'er the abandoned Earth, now leave it bare
Even to the joyous stars which smile on its despair!

He is made one with Nature: there is heard
His voice in all her music, from the moan
Of thunder, to the song of the night's sweet bird;
He is a presence to be felt and known
In darkness and in light, from herb and stone,
Spreading itself where'er that Power may move
Which has withdrawn his being to its own;
Which wields the world with never-wearied love,
Sustains it from beneath, and kindles it above.

He is a portion of the loveliness
Which once he made more lovely: he doth bear
His part, while the one Spirit's plastic stress
Sweeps through the dull dense world, compelling there,
All new successions to the forms they wear;
Torturing th' unwilling dross that checks its flight
To its own likeness, as each mass may bear;
And bursting in its beauty and its might
From trees and beasts and men into the Heaven's light.

The splendours of the firmament of time
May be eclipsed, but are extinguished not;
Like stars to their appointed height they climb,
And death is a low mist which cannot blot
The brightness it may veil. When lofty thought
Like a young heart above its mortal lair,
And love and life contend in it, for what
Shall be its earthly doom, the dead live there
And move like winds of light on dark and stormy air.

The inheritors of unfulfilled renown
Rose from their thrones, built beyond mortal thought,
Far in the Unapparent. Chatterton
Rose pale,—his solemn agony had not
Yet faded from him; Sidney, as he fought
And as he fell and as he lived and loved
Sublimely mild, a Spirit without spot,
Arose; and Lucan, by his death approved:
Oblivion as they rose shrank like a thing reproved.

And many more, whose names on Earth are dark,
But whose transmitted effluence cannot die
So long as fire outlives the parent spark,
Rose, robed in dazzling immortality.
"Thou art become as one of us," they cry,
"It was for thee yon kingless sphere has long
Swung blind in unascended majesty,
Silent alone amid an Heaven of Song.
Assume thy wingèd throne, thou Vesper of our throng!"

Who mourns for Adonais? Oh, come forth,
Fond wretch! and know thyself and him aright.
Clasp with thy panting soul the pendulous Earth;
As from a centre, dart thy spirit's light
Beyond all worlds, until its spacious might
Satiate the void circumference: then shrink
Even to a point within our day and night;
And keep thy heart light lest it make thee sink
When hope has kindled hope, and lured thee to the brink.

Or go to Rome, which is the sepulchre,
Oh, not of him, but of our joy: 'tis nought
That ages, empires, and religions there
Lie buried in the ravage they have wrought;
For such as he can lend,—they borrow not
Glory from those who made the world their prey;
And he is gathered to the kings of thought
Who waged contention with their time's decay,
And of the past are all that cannot pass away.

Go thou to Rome,—at once the Paradise,
The grave, the city, and the wilderness;
And where its wrecks like shattered mountains rise,
And flowering weeds, and fragrant copses dress
The bones of Desolation's nakedness
Pass, till the spirit of the spot shall lead
Thy footsteps to a slope of green access
Where, like an infant's smile, over the dead
A light of laughing flowers along the grass is spread.

And gray walls moulder round, on which dull Time
Feeds, like slow fire upon a hoary brand;
And one keen pyramid with wedge sublime,
Pavilioning the dust of him who planned
This refuge for his memory, doth stand

Like flame transformed to marble; and beneath,
A field is spread, on which a newer band
Have pitched in Heaven's smile their camp of death,
Welcoming him we lose with scarce extinguished breath.

Here pause: these graves are all too young as yet
To have outgrown the sorrow which consigned
Its charge to each; and if the seal is set,
Here, on one fountain of a mourning mind,
Break it not thou! too surely shalt thou find
Thine own full well, if thou returnest home,
Of tears and gall. From the world's bitter wind
Seek shelter in the shadow of the tomb.
What Adonais is, why fear we to become?

The One remains, the many change and pass;
Heaven's light forever shines, Earth's shadows fly;
Life, like a dome of many-coloured glass,
Stains the white radiance of Eternity,
Until Death tramples it to fragments.—Die,
If thou wouldst be with that which thou dost seek!
Follow where all is fled!—Rome's azure sky,
Flowers, ruins, statues, music, words, are weak
The glory they transfuse with fitting truth to speak.

Why linger, why turn back, why shrink, my Heart?
Thy hopes are gone before: from all things here
They have departed; thou shouldst now depart!
A light is passed from the revolving year,
And man, and woman; and what still is dear
Attracts to crush, repels to make thee wither.
The soft sky smiles,—the low wind whispers near:
'Tis Adonais calls! oh, hasten thither,
No more let Life divide what Death can join together.

That Light whose smile kindles the Universe,
That Beauty in which all things work and move,
That Benediction which the eclipsing Curse
Of birth can quench not, that sustaining Love
Which through the web of being blindly wove
By man and beast and earth and air and sea,
Burns bright or dim, as each are mirrors of
The fire for which all thirst; now beams on me,
Consuming the last clouds of cold mortality.

The breath whose might I have invoked in song
Descends on me; my spirit's bark is driven,
Far from the shore, far from the trembling throng
Whose sails were never to the tempest given;
The massy earth, and spherèd skies are riven!
I am borne darkly, fearfully, afar;
Whilst, burning through the inmost veil of Heaven,
The soul of Adonais, like a star,
Beacons from the abode where the Eternal are.

SIR PHILIP SIDNEY (1554-1586)

Sleep
No More, My Dear
Fourth Song

It would be difficult to name an activity or adventure that Sir Philip Sidney did not crowd into the thirty-two years of his brilliant life, except the consummation of the love he celebrated in his famous sonnets to Stella.

Born of distinguished and immensely wealthy parents, Sidney resolved he would achieve fame by virtue of his own ability. He became a superb horseman and swordsman, a leader in tournaments and revels, a translator of Plato and the Psalms. He had the wit, social graces and intellect to make him a favorite courtier at the court of Queen Elizabeth, twice a member of Parliament, joint Master of the Queen's Ordnance, and at twenty-two he carried out a delicate diplomatic mission.

Although Sidney regarded diplomacy and war as his true vocations, writing was close to his heart, especially poetry. It was then the convention that a gentleman wrote not for publication but merely as a polite exercise done with casual effort.

However, this greatly gifted idealist's writing was no courtly affectation. He obeyed his own famous dictum: "Fool, saith my Muse to me, look in thy heart and write."

At first Sidney did follow the custom of selecting a lady to whom his poetry should be addressed in adoring terms but with no romantic intentions. He chose Penelope Deveraux whom he had known since childhood. The initial poems to her (called Stella in the poems) were fine enough, but they were not love poems.

However, a change soon took place in the sonnets that mirrored a change in Sidney. It happened in 1581, the year Penelope married a rich but loutish

lord. The gentle intellectual found himself in love with his friend of childhood and his sonnets reveal the intensity of his passion, the pangs of conscience suffered by a man of high principles who was tempting dishonor, and
the strife of unrequited love. The sonnets form the sequence titled *Astrophel
and Stella;* poems of love and longing, of remorse and reluctant renunciation.
But they have not the frank sensuality characteristic of most Elizabethan
poets.

Experts are not agreed as to the probable progress of the romance, except
that Penelope liked and perhaps loved Sidney, but apparently avoided an
illicit relationship. Some of the sonnets were deliberately placed out of proper
sequence to defeat conclusions as to precisely what took place on several occasions.

In any event, Sidney's passion waned after a year or so. He became engaged
to Frances Walsingham and a few years later was killed in battle while assist-
ing the Dutch defend their land against the Spaniards.

For all his many achievements, however, Sidney today is best remembered
for the more than one hundred sonnets he began almost idly but which
quickly rose to supreme expressions of his love for Penelope Deveraux.

> Come Sleep! O Sleep, the certain knot of peace,
> The baiting-place of wit, the balm of woe,
> The poor man's wealth, the prisoner's release,
> The indifferent judge between the high and low!
> With shield of proof, shield me from out the press
> Of those fierce darts Despair at me doth throw:
> O make in me those civil wars to cease!
> I will good tribute pay if thou do so.
> Take thou of me, smooth pillows, sweetest bed,
> A chamber deaf to noise and blind to light,
> A rosy garland, and a weary head:
> And if these things, as being thine in right,
>   Move not thy heavy grace, thou shalt in me,
>   Livelier than elsewhere, Stella's image see.

* * * * * *

> No more, my Dear, no more these counsels try;
> O give my passions leave to run their race!
> Let Fortune lay on me her worst disgrace;
> Let folk o'ercharged with brain, against me cry;
> Let clouds bedim my face, break in mine eye;
> Let me no steps but of lost labour trace;
> Let all the earth with scorn recount my case;
> But do not will me from my love to fly!
> I do not envy Aristotle's wit;

Nor do aspire to Caesar's bleeding fame;
Nor aught do care, though some above me sit;
Nor hope, nor wish another course to frame,
But that which once may win thy cruel heart:
Thou art my Wit, and thou my Virtue art.

The romance apparently reached its climax in the episode described by Sidney in the fourth of a number of *Songs* interspersed among the *Sonnets*. It probably occurred in the Spring of 1582, when Penelope was visiting her mother and where Sidney was also a guest. Obviously his passionate wooing of her under propitious circumstances was to no avail; Penelope was obdurate:

Only Joy, now here you are,
Fit to hear and ease my care,
Let my whispering voice obtain
Sweet reward for sharpest pain;
Take me to thee, and thee to me:
"No, no, no, no, my Dear, let be."

Night hath closed all in her cloak,
Twinkling stars love-thoughts provoke,
Danger hence, good care doth keep,
Jealousy himself doth sleep;
Take me to thee, and thee to me:
"No, no, no, no, my Dear, let be."

Better place no wit can find,
Cupid's knot to loose or bind;
These sweet flowers our fine bed too,
Us in their best language woo:
Take me to thee, and thee to me:
"No, no, no, no, my Dear, let be."

This small light the moon bestows,
Serves thy beams but to disclose;
So to raise my hap more hie,
Fear not else, none us can spy;
Take me to thee, and thee to me:
"No, no, no, no, my Dear, let be."

That you heard was but a mouse,
Dumb Sleep holdeth all the house:
Yet asleep me thinks they say,
Young fools take time while you may;

Take me to thee, and thee to me:
"No, no, no, no, my Dear, let be."

Niggard time threats, if we miss
This large offer of our bliss,
Long stay, ere he grant the same:
Sweet, then, while each thing doth frame,
Take me to thee, and thee to me:
"No, no, no, no, my Dear, let be."

Your fair mother is a-bed,
Candles out and curtains spread;
She thinks you do letters write;
Write, but first let me endite;
Take me to thee, and thee to me:
"No, no, no, no, my Dear, let be."

Sweet, alas, why strive you thus?
Concord better fitteth us;
Leave to Mars the force of hands,
Your power in your beauty stands;
Take thee to me, and me to thee:
"No, no, no, no, my Dear, let be."

Woe to me, and do you swear
Me to hate? but I forbear;
Cursed be my destinies all,
That brought me so high to fall;
Soon with my death I will please thee:
"No, no, no, no, my Dear, let be."

For a brief period after this Sidney's verse became angry and abusive:
Penelope was a tyrant and a devil. They met again and finally she persuaded
Sidney they must end the affair.

ROBERT LOUIS STEVENSON (1850-1894)

The Land of Story-Books
Requiem

One summer day in the Scottish Highlands Stevenson picked up Kate Greenaway's *Birthday Book for Children,* with verses by Mrs. Sale Barker, and began to read it. "These are rather nice rhymes," said the painfully frail and semi-invalided novelist to his mother. "I don't think it would be diffi-cult to do." Whereupon he put aside whatever adult work that was then engaging his attention, and wrote fourteen of the poems that appeared in his *A Child's Garden of Verse.* Shortly afterwards he added three more to the collection.

It was apparently as easy for Stevenson to write these verses as he antici-pated. It was relatively simple for him because he had almost total recall impressions of his childhood and drew on these memorable years to the delight of generations of children and their elders.

No doubt the nature of his childhood contributed to the clarity of his recol-lections when he began to write the poems. In addition to being an only child of prosperous parents, he was a delicate little boy tormented by "terribly long nights awake, praying for sleep and morning from the bottom of my shaken little body" and beset by bouts of fever. He wrote most touchingly of his nurse, Alison Cunningham, whose "unwearied sympathy and long-suffering displayed to me on a hundred such occasions . . . She was more patient than I can suppose of an angel; hours together she would help and console me." Stevenson never forgot this nurse; he wrote her often, sent her copies of all his books, and when he had a house he had her come for visits. *A Child's Garden of Verse* is dedicated "To Alison Cunningham, From Her Boy."

Two years after he wrote the first seventeen poems for *A Child's Garden of Verse,* Stevenson was living on the French Riviera, at the Chalet de Soli-tude. It had been a bad eight months; several lung hemorrhages and recur-ring prostrations had prevented him from continuous work on the several things that pressed his mind for execution. When he began to recover he turned to verse writing, his unfailing resource in illness and convalescence, and completed the poems of his vivid memories of childhood—some fifty-odd poems all told.

It is interesting to note that much of the raw material for *A Child's Garden of Verse* is found in Stevenson's *Memories and Portraits,* written when he was twenty-two. Here, for example, he tells about his frequent residence at Colinton Manse, his grandfather's home outside Edinburgh. "That was my golden age," he remarked, as he tells of the spacious sun-soaked lawn, his many cousin playmates and how "I have lain perdue, with a toy-gun in my hand, waiting for a herd of antelopes to defile past me down the carriage drive, and waiting (need I add?) in vain."

And in the house itself: "After dinner, when the lamp was brought in and shaded, and my aunt sat down to read in the rocking chair, there was a great open space behind the sofa left entirely in shadow. This was my especial domain—once round the corner of the sofa, I had left the lightsome, merry indoors, and was out in the cool, dark night. I could almost see the stars. I looked out the back window at the bushes outside. I lay in the darkest corner, rifle in hand, like a hunter in a lonely bivouac. I crawled about stealthily watching the people in the circle of the lamplight."

But of course, it's all told with so much more compression and charm in such memorable poems as:

> At evening when the lamp is lit,
> Around the fire my parents sit;
> They sit at home and talk and sing,
> And do not play at anything.
>
> Now, with my little gun, I crawl
> All in the dark along the wall,
> And follow round the forest track
> Away behind the sofa back.
>
> There, in the night, where none can spy,
> All in my hunter's camp I lie,
> And play at books that I have read
> Till it is time to go to bed.
>
> These are the hills, these are the woods,
> These are my starry solitudes;
> And there the river by whose brink
> The roaring lions come to drink.
>
> I see the others far away
> As if in firelit camp they lay,
> And I, like to an Indian scout,
> Around their party prowled about.
>
> So, when my nurse comes in for me,
> Home I return across the sea,
> And go to bed with backward looks
> At my dear land of Story-books.

In August, 1879, Robert Louis Stevenson left England for the United States, over the protests of his parents and friends, and with limited funds. He had previously met in France and become intimate with an American woman, Mrs. Frances (Fanny) Osbourne, separated from her husband. She had earlier returned to her home in California, presumably to obtain a divorce so she could marry Stevenson.

Stevenson's parents opposed this prospective marriage to an American divorcee who was eleven years older than he was. They refrained from supplying him with money for the trip, in the hope of discouraging the venture. Stevenson went directly to Monterey, California, then a ramshackle village of Mexicans, Italians, Chinese and miscellaneous characters. He arrived there on the verge of collapse. His condition was soon aggravated by his disappointment either at Fanny's difficulty in working out divorce arrangements with her husband, or her vacillating attitude toward divorce and remarriage to Stevenson. In addition to his health and heart distress, he was further burdened by unsuccessful attempts to support himself with his writing. In a letter at that time he said he had a "broken-heart."

In these circumstances the ill and distraught man decided to camp out in the nearby mountains to recover his strength. But there he broke down completely and lay two days beneath a tree in a stupor, until found by two goat ranchers who kept him in their home for several weeks, where he made some progress back toward health.

Stevenson had been near death, and he knew it. In fact, when he returned to Monterey and weeks later went to San Francisco, he said "I hear the breakers roar; I shall be steering headfirst for another rapid before many days. . . . I am going for thirty now; and unless I snatch a little rest before long, I have, I may tell you in confidence, no hope of seeing thirty-one . . . But death is no bad friend."

In one of these letters at that time he enclosed the first version of his famous "Requiem" and asked his friend Sidney Colvin to see that it was used for his epitaph. Fortunately, fifteen productive and mostly happy years were to pass before the lines were to be placed over his grave on a lonely hill in Samoa:

> Under the wide and starry sky,
> Dig the grave and let me lie.
> Glad did I live and gladly die,
>   And I laid me down with a will.

> This be the verse you grave for me:
> *Here he lies where he longed to be,*
> *Home is the sailor, home from the sea,*
>   *And the hunter home from the hill.*

ALGERNON CHARLES SWINBURNE (1837-1909)

From The Triumph of Time

Swinburne had but one romance in his life, but it left its mark on the strange looking man. In fact, his appearance may easily have been a handicap that his charm and wit—when he chose to employ them—could not overcome. He had a small body, with very thin wrists and tiny feet. A grotesquely long neck led to a disproportionately large head, which was crowned by unruly red hair. His voice was rich but his mouth weak and the chin receded. These liabilities were underlined by eccentricities, odd mannerisms, supersensitivity to slights, and a volatile temper that exploded with venomous attacks on real or imagined enemies.

But certainly Swinburne, highly intelligent and with a vast knowledge of great literature, had attractive traits. He was a welcome guest at the homes of aristocratic relatives and friends, and would spend many happy weeks riding and swimming at their estates.

Among these friends were Sir John Simon and his wife Jane, who regularly entertained a small but distinguished group, including Swinburne. The twenty-six-year-old poet became intimate with the family and in their home met a young kinswoman of the family. This vivacious girl stirred Swinburne's heart. Either she was a coquette or else he mistook her gracious friendliness to be encouragement of his tentative advances. In any case, this step-child of nature suddenly and with characteristic lack of reasonableness and tenderness declared his passionate love to her. The girl, perhaps from nervousness born of knowledge of the poet's violent temper, laughed in the pathetic little man's face. Crushed but not silenced, Swinburne rebuked her in terms that promptly ended all possibility of further friendship.

Sad and depressed, Swinburne went up to Northumberland to brood by the sea he loved as few Englishmen did. And there, as his anger waned, he told in beautiful lyric lines what was going through his mind where only pity and pain now remained. Here he reveals himself as in no other poem; no doubt because it was the only love of his life. He never married, and died a lonely eccentric at the age of seventy-two.

> I will go back to the great sweet mother,—
> Mother and lover of men, the Sea.
> I will go down to her, I and none other,
> Close with her, kiss her, and mix her with me;
> Cling to her, strive with her, hold her fast;
> O fair white mother, in days long past
> Born without sister, born without brother,
> Set free my soul as thy soul is free.

O fair green-girdled mother of mine,
    Sea, that art clothed with the sun and the rain,
Thy sweet hard kisses are strong like wine,
    Thy large embraces are keen like pain.
Save me and hide me with all thy waves,
Find me one grave of thy thousand graves,
Those pure cold populous graves of thine,
    Wrought without hand in a world without stain.

I shall sleep, and move with the moving ships,
    Change as the winds change, veer in the tide;
My lips will feast on the foam of thy lips,
    I shall rise with thy rising, with thee subside;
Sleep, and not know if she be, if she were,
Filled full with life to the eyes and hair;
As a rose is fulfilled to the rose-leaf tips
    With splendid summer and perfume and pride.

This woven raiment of nights and days,
    Were it once cast off and unwound from me,
Naked and glad would I walk in thy ways,
    Alive and aware of thy waves and thee;
Clear of the whole world, hidden at home,
Clothed with the green, and crowned with the foam,
A pulse of the life of thy straits and bays,
    A vein in the heart of the streams of the Sea.

Fair mother, fed with the lives of men,
    Thou art subtle and cruel of heart, men say;
Thou hast taken, and shalt not render again;
    Thou art full of thy dead, and cold as they.
But death is the worst that comes of thee;
Thou art fed with our dead, O Mother, O Sea,
But when hast thou fed on our hearts? or when
    Having given us love, hast thou taken away?

O tender-hearted, O perfect lover,
    Thy lips are bitter, and sweet thine heart.
The hopes that hurt and the dreams that hover,
    Shall they not vanish away and apart?
But thou, thou art sure, thou art older than earth;
Thou art strong for death and fruitful of birth;
Thy depths conceal and thy gulfs discover;
    From the first thou wert; in the end thou art.

ALFRED, LORD TENNYSON (1809-1892)

From In Memoriam
Crossing the Bar

In the Spring of 1828, nineteen-year-old Alfred Tennyson met and became friendly with one of the more extraordinary young men of his day, Arthur Hallam, son of a leading literary and historical scholar. Twenty-one-year-old Arthur had given early evidence of intellectual powers. He read Latin and Greek fluently at nine, at fifteen had written several tragedies in prose and verse, and was eloquent and skilled in debate. Hallam's gaiety, enthusiasm and singularly sweet nature drew Tennyson out of himself, gave him self-confidence and expanded his mental horizons. Their friendship was further strengthened when the brilliant youth became engaged to Tennyson's sister Emily.

But after four years this ideal relationship was ended by Hallam's death in Vienna from a stroke, in September, 1833. His body was returned to England from Trieste by boat. The poet was bereft not only of a dear friend, but of a powerful influence in his life.

Within a few weeks Tennyson began work on his famous "In Memoriam," a poem founded on his friendship with Hallam, though not an actual biography. But during the seventeen years Tennyson was writing this monument to his friend, the poem also became the history of a soul stricken by a great sorrow that ultimately emerges from the shadows, with faith that the God of Love gives purpose to life and a high destiny to the individual man.

Aubrey De Vere told of visiting the poet late one evening when he was writing "In Memoriam." The tears ran down Tennyson's cheeks as he read stanzas to his visitor. Here are some of the more notable passages from the long poem:

Strong Son of God, immortal Love,
  Whom we, that have not seen thy face,
  By faith, and faith alone, embrace,
Believing where we cannot prove;

Thine are these orbs of light and shade;
  Thou madest Life in man and brute;
  Thou madest Death; and lo, thy foot
Is on the skull which thou hast made.

Thou wilt not leave us in the dust:
  Thou madest man, he knows not why;
  He thinks he was not made to die;
And thou hast made him: thou art just.

Thou seemest human and divine,
   The highest, the holiest manhood, thou:
   Our wills are ours, we know not how;
Our wills are ours, to make them thine.

Our little systems have their day;
   They have their day and cease to be:
   They are but broken lights of thee,
And thou, O Lord, art more than they.

We have but faith: we cannot know;
   For knowledge is of things we see;
   And yet we trust it comes from thee,
A beam in darkness: let it grow.

Let knowledge grow from more to more,
   But more of reverence in us dwell;
   That mind and soul, according well,
May make one music as before,

But vaster. We are fools and slight;
   We mock thee when we do not fear;
   But help thy foolish ones to bear;
Help thy vain worlds to bear thy light.

Forgive what seem'd my sin in me;
   What seem'd my worth since I began;
   For merit lives from man to man,
And not from man, O Lord, to thee.

Forgive my grief for one removed,
   Thy creature, whom I found so fair.
   I trust he lives in thee, and there
I find him worthier to be loved.

Forgive these wild and wandering cries,
   Confusions of a wasted youth;
   Forgive them where they fail in truth,
And in thy wisdom make me wise.

     *   *   *   *

O yet we trust that somehow good
   Will be the final goal of ill,
   To pangs of nature, sins of will,
Defects of doubt, and taints of blood;

That nothing walks with aimless feet;
That no one life shall be destroy'd,
Or cast as rubbish to the void,
When God hath made the pile complete;

That not a worm is cloven in vain;
That not a moth with vain desire
Is shrivell'd in a fruitless fire,
Or but subserves another's gain.

Behold, we know not anything;
I can but trust that good shall fall
At last—far off—at last, to all,
And every winter change to spring.

So runs my dream: but what am I?
An infant crying in the night:
An infant crying for the light:
And with no language but a cry.

* * * *

Ring out, wild bells, to the wild sky,
The flying cloud, the frosty light;
The year is dying in the night;
Ring out, wild bells, and let him die.

Ring out the old, ring in the new,
Ring, happy bells, across the snow:
The year is going, let him go;
Ring out the false, ring in the true.

Ring out the grief that saps the mind,
For those that here we see no more;
Ring out the feud of rich and poor,
Ring in redress to all mankind.

Ring out a slowly dying cause,
And ancient forms of party strife;
Ring in the nobler modes of life,
With sweeter manners, purer laws.

Ring out the want, the care, the sin,
The faithless coldness of the times;
Ring out, ring out my mournful rhymes,
But ring the fuller minstrel in.

Ring out false pride in place and blood,
  The civic slander and the spite;
  Ring in the love of truth and right,
Ring in the common love of good.

Ring out old shapes of foul disease;
  Ring out the narrowing lust of gold;
  Ring out the thousands wars of old,
Ring in the thousand years of peace.

Ring in the valiant man and free,
  The larger heart, the kindlier hand;
  Ring out the darkness of the land,
Ring in the Christ that is to be.

       *   *   *   *

Thy voice is on the rolling air;
  I hear thee where the waters run;
  Thou standest in the rising sun,
And in the setting thou art fair.

What are thou then? I cannot guess;
  But though I seem in star and flower
  To feel thee some diffusive power,
I do not therefore love thee less.

My love involves the love before;
  My love is vaster passion now;
  Though mixed with God and nature thou,
I seem to love thee more and more.

Far off thou art, but ever nigh;
  I have thee still, and I rejoice;
  I prosper, circled with thy voice;
I shall not lose thee though I die.

In the Fall of 1888 Alfred, Lord Tennyson, eighty years old, was dangerously ill in his home at Farringford, nursed by Emma Durham, an alert, intelligent woman of humor and candor. Tennyson admired her sincerity, and
obeyed orders from her he ignored from others. When he began to recover
his strength he grumbled to his nurse about the doctor's restrictions. After
hearing this protest a number of times, Miss Durham rebuked England's Poet
Laureate with the suggestion that instead of complaining he might more ap-
propriately express gratitude for the remarkable recovery he was making by
writing a hymn—and recover he did.

Some weeks later the venerable poet, returning from Aldworth to Farringford, was enjoying the twenty-minute crossing to Yarmouth from Lymington. Distant bells heard over water always charmed Tennyson. Perhaps he heard some ringing, for suddenly during the crossing his most famous lines flashed into his consciousness. He quickly jotted them down, without comment to anyone.

That evening Nurse Durham went to the poet's study to light the candles. Tennyson was at his desk. He picked up a paper and said, "Will this do for you, old woman?" and read the poem to her.

Later in the evening Tennyson handed the lines to his son, Hallam, saying, "It came in a moment." A few days before his death at eighty-four, the poet instructed Hallam: "Mind you put 'Crossing the Bar' at the end of all editions of my poems." It has ever since found a responsive chord in the hearts of its readers.

> Sunset and evening star,
> And one clear call for me!
> And may there be no moaning of the bar,
> When I put out to sea,
>
> But such a tide as moving seems asleep,
> Too full for sound and foam,
> When that which drew me out the boundless deep
> Turns again home.
>
> Twilight and evening bell,
> And after that the dark!
> And may there be no sadness of farewell,
> When I embark;
>
> For tho' from out our bourne of Time and Place
> The flood may bear me far,
> I hope to see my Pilot face to face
> When I have crossed the bar.

DYLAN THOMAS (1914-1953)

Do Not Go Gentle Into That Good Night

When one recalls the last years of Dylan Thomas—years of incredible drinking and carousing, parties and receptions where he repelled with his frank and often lewd talk, and poetry readings to large and admiring audiences—then one is momentarily puzzled that he was reluctant to read to his father a poem he had written to him.

However, in spite of his uninhibited behavior and his total lack of self-discipline, the likeable burly Welsh poet apparently was unable to free himself of family traditions and break down the reticence of the father-son relationship characteristic of a puritanical home that had moved a little way from its very humble beginnings.

Caitlin Thomas, Dylan's wife, said that his father was the most unhappy man she ever met. He had lifted himself from farming to schoolmaster in a country and a period when such transitions were achieved only with great difficulty. But, she added, the elder Thomas ultimately found himself so looked up to by his neighbors in the little Welsh village that he was unable to enjoy himself without being stigmatized. Apparently, too, he was by nature dour and perhaps embittered for whatever unstated reasons.

Further insight is provided by John Brinnin's account of his visit to Dylan Thomas's home in Laugharne, Wales, the isolated fishing village in which the poet's parents also lived. While there Brinnin and the poet visited the parents' modest little home. The mother fussed over her son, but the thin, withdrawn and elegantly dressed father sat silently by the fire observing his son with "curiously dispassionate interest." There was mutual respect between father and son, yet a wariness and an indefinite unease. Conversation with David Thomas was limited to commonplace observations; there was no true communication between father and son. Obviously they had never had any spontaneous and relaxed conversation, although Dylan had a talent for human relations. This was the way things were, in spite of the fact that the father early in life had wanted to be a poet and could not fail to be proud of his son's accomplishments and fame.

Before Brinnin left Laugharne, Dylan read to him a poem he had recently written for his father, but which he said he had not the courage to read to the parent. It is not known that he ever read it to him. But it would seem improbable in view of the formal nature of their relationship and the fact that the father's health began to fail. There would have to have been a fairly lively rapport between them to make at all bearable the reading by the son to his ailing father the following now famous poem—a plea to his father to "rage against the dying of the light":

Do not go gentle into that good night,
Old age should burn and rave at close of day;
Rage, rage against the dying of the light.

Though wise men at their end know dark is right,
Because their words had forked no lightning they
Do not go gentle into that good night.

Good men, the last wave by, crying how bright
Their frail deeds might have danced in a green bay,
Rage, rage against the dying of the light.

Wild men who caught and sang the sun in flight,
And learn, too late, they grieved it on its way,
Do not go gentle into that good night.

Grave men, near death, who see with blinding sight
Blind eyes could blaze like meteors and be gay,
Rage, rage against the dying of the light.

And you, my father, there on the sad height,
Curse, bless, me now with your fierce tears, I pray.
Do not go gentle into that good night.
Rage, rage against the dying of the light.

FRANCIS THOMPSON (1859-1907)

The Hound of Heaven

If Francis Thompson had lived a normal, conventional life he perhaps would have written poetry, but certainly never his famous "The Hound of Heaven." This poem could have come only from a soul deeply troubled by self-inflicted suffering that finally discovered its problem and began to solve it.

Thompson never really grew up. Late in life he admitted "There is a sense in which I have all my life been and even now remain a child." He was a shy, timid boy who preferred to be alone, who read voraciously, wrote poetry, and avoided routine duties to live in his world of illusions. By ordinary standards he was indolent. His weakness of will led to his downfall; his undeviating religious faith, superior intellect and sensitivity ultimately led to his rehabilitation.

After being rejected for the priesthood Thompson, at eighteen, entered medical school. There he loafed and dreamed away six years, spending more time in museums and libraries than with his studies. But even worse, at this time he began to console himself with laudanum, an opium derivative. After he failed his final medical examinations he worked briefly at several jobs and then drifted to London.

Thompson was twenty-six when he arrived in London with few possessions. The thin, gentle and sad-eyed young man here began three years of desolate existence that never degraded him beyond his increasing addiction to opium and a personal unkemptness that discouraged proximity. Avoiding all relatives and friends, doing little or no writing and unaware of his fine talent, he held light-laboring jobs for a while and then became a bum without the bum's customary vices. He blacked shoes, carried baggage, held horses, slept in parks and doorways and lived only for opium. When he had touched bottom a London prostitute took him to her room, fed him and gave him chaste companionship.

This pure friendship revived hope in the desperate derelict. He submitted some poems for publication but they were rejected. He then wrote an essay and sent it with some poems to Alfred Meynell, editor of a Catholic magazine. Six months later Meynell wrote Thompson at the post office address given, but received no reply. Then, fourteen months after Thompson submitted the essay and poems, Meynell published one of the religious poems in the hope that he would hear from the poet.

Thompson finally got in touch with Meynell and after months of diffidence and reluctance on Thompson's part Meynell gradually succeeded in gaining the poet's confidence and put him on the slow and painful road of rejection of the opium that had become Thompson's chief interest.

The most important phase of the poet's return to the world of reality was the year he spent at a monastery in Storrington, Sussex, arrangements for which had been made by the great-hearted Meynell. Here Thompson had no chance to return to the drug; and here, too, he was able and encouraged to increase and enrich the religious faith to which he had tenaciously clung no matter how low he sunk.

Now free of the thrall of opium, Thompson's muse was liberated and the poetry streamed from him. Apparently he was under the spell of a religious experience that made him realize it was only through the love and goodness of God that he had been salvaged from degradation and a despairing death. In this spiritual awakening the poet began to reflect on his past and to put into poetry his discovery that what he had been fleeing all his life was really what he had always sought—God. In telling his story, he tells the story of many tormented souls that ultimately rise from the depths when they dis-

cover what they thought was darkness was really the shadow of God's hand
reaching out to caress them.

> I fled Him, down the nights and down the days;
> I fled Him down the arches of the years;
> I fled Him, down the labyrinthine ways
> 　　Of my own mind; and in the mist of tears
> I hid from Him, and under running laughter.
> 　　　　Up vistaed hopes I sped;
> 　　　　And shot, precipitated,
> Adown Titanic glooms of chasmèd fears,
> From those strong Feet that followed, followed after.
> 　　　　But with unhurrying chase,
> 　　　　And unperturbèd pace,
> 　　　Deliberate speed, majestic instancy,
> 　　　　They beat—and a Voice beat
> 　　　　More instant than the Feet—
> "All things betray thee, who betrayest Me."
>
> 　　　　I pleaded, outlaw-wise,
> By many a hearted casement, curtained red,
> 　　Trellised with intertwining charities;
> (For, though I knew His love Who followèd,
> 　　　　Yet was I sore adread
> Lest, having Him, I must have naught beside);
> But, if one little casement parted wide,
> 　　The gust of His approach would clash it to.
> Fear wist not to evade, as Love wist to pursue.
> Across the margent of the world I fled,
> 　　And troubled the gold gateways of the stars,
> 　　Smiting for shelter on their clanged bars;
> 　　　　Fretted to dulcet jars
> And silvern chatter the pale ports o' the moon.
> I said to Dawn, Be sudden; to Eve, Be soon;
> 　　With thy young skiey blossoms heap me over
> 　　　　From this tremendous Lover!
> Float thy vague veil about me, lest He see!
> 　　I tempted all His servitors, but to find
> My own betrayal in their constancy,
> In faith to Him their fickleness to me,
> 　　Their traitorous trueness, and their loyal deceit.
> To all swift things for swiftness did I sue;
> 　　Clung to the whistling mane of every wind.
> 　　　But whether they swept, smoothly fleet,
> 　　　The long savannahs of the blue;

Or whether, Thunder-driven,
They clanged his chariot 'thwart a heaven,
Plashy with flying lightnings round the spurn o' their feet:—
Fear wist not to evade as Love wist to pursue.
Still with unhurrying chase,
And unperturbèd pace,
Deliberate speed, majestic instancy,
Came on the following Feet,
And a Voice above their beat—
"Naught shelters thee, who wilt not shelter Me."

I sought no more that after which I strayed
In face of man or maid;
But still within the little children's eyes
Seems something, something that replies;
They at least are for me, surely for me!
I turned me to them very wistfully;
But, just as their young eyes grew sudden fair
With dawning answers there,
Their angel plucked them from me by the hair.
"Come then, ye other children, Nature's—share
With me" (said I) "your delicate fellowship;
Let me greet you lip to lip,
Let me twine you with caresses,
Wantoning
With our Lady-Mother's vagrant tresses,
Banqueting
With her in her wind-walled palace,
Underneath her azured daïs,
Quaffing, as your taintless way is,
From out a chalice
Lucent-weeping out of the dayspring."
So it was done:
I in their delicate fellowship was one—
Drew the bolt of Nature's secrecies.
I knew all the swift importings
On the wilful face of skies;
I knew how the clouds arise
Spumèd of the wild sea-snortings;
All that's born or dies
Rose and drooped with—made them shapers
Of mine own moods, or wailful or divine—
With they joyed and was bereaven.
I was heavy with the even,
When she lit her glimmering tapers

Round the day's dead sanctities.
I laughed in the morning's eyes.
I triumphed and I saddened with all weather,
    Heaven and I wept together,
And its sweet tears were salt with mortal mine;
Against the red throb of its sunset-heart
    I laid my own to beat,
    And share commingling heat;
But not by that, by that, was eased my human smart.
In vain my tears were wet on Heaven's grey cheek.
For ah! we know not what each other says,
    These things and I; in sound I speak—
Their sound is but their stir, they speak by silences.
Nature, poor stepdame, cannot slake my drouth;
    Let her, if she would owe me,
Drop yon blue bosom-veil of sky, and show me
    The breasts o' her tenderness:
Never did any milk of hers once bless
    My thirsting mouth.
    Nigh and nigh draws the chase,
    With unperturbèd pace,
  Deliberate speed, majestic instancy;
    And past those noisèd Feet
    A voice comes yet more fleet—
"Lo! naught contents thee, who content'st not Me."

Naked I wait Thy love's uplifted stroke!
My harness piece by piece Thou hast hewn from me,
    And smitten me to my knee;
    I am defenseless utterly.
    I slept, methinks, and woke,
And, slowly gazing, find me stripped in sleep.
In the rash lustihood of my young powers,
    I shook the pillaring hours
And pulled my life upon me; grimed with smears,
I stand amid the dust o' the mounded years—
My mangled youth lies dead beneath the heap.
My days have crackled and gone up in smoke,
Have puffed and burst as sun-starts on a stream.
    Yea, faileth now even dream
The dreamer, and the lute the lutanist;
Even the linked fantasies, in whose blossomy twist
I swung the earth a trinket at my wrist,
Are yielding; cords of all too weak account
For earth with heavy griefs so overplussed.

          Ah! is Thy love indeed
A weed, albeit an amaranthine weed,
Suffering no flowers except its own to mount?
          Ah! must—
          Designer infinite!—
Ah! must Thou char the wood ere Thou canst limn with it?
My freshness spent its wavering shower i' the dust;
And now my heart is as a broken fount,
Wherein tear-drippings stagnate, spilt down ever
          From the dank thoughts that shiver
Upon the sighful branches of my mind.
          Such is; what is to be?
The pulp so bitter, how shall taste the rind?
I dimly guess what Time in mists confounds;
Yet ever and anon a trumpet sounds
From the hid battlements of Eternity;
Those shaken mists a space unsettle, then
Round the half-glimpsèd turrets slowly wash again.
          But not ere him who summoneth
          I first have seen, enwound
With glooming robes purpureal, cypress—crowned;
His name I know, and what his trumpet saith.
Whether man's heart or life it be which yields
          Thee harvest, must Thy harvest fields
          Be dunged with rooten death?

          Now of that long pursuit
          Comes on at hand the bruit;
That Voice is round me like a bursting sea:
          "And is thy earth so marred,
          Shattered in shard on shard?
Lo, all things fly thee, for thou fliest Me!
Strange, piteous, futile thing,
Wherefore should any set thee love apart?
Seeing none but I makes much of naught?" (He said),
"And human love needs human meriting:
          How hast thou merited—
Of all man's clotted clay the dingiest clot?
          Alack, thou knowest not
How little worthy of any love thou art!
Whom wilt thou find to love ignoble thee
          Save Me, save only Me?
All which I took from thee I did but take,
          Not for thy harms,
But just that thou might'st seek it in My arms.

All which thy child's mistake
Fancies as lost, I have stored for thee at home:
Rise, clasp my hand, and come!"

Halts by me that footfall:
Is my gloom, after all,
Shade of His hand, outstretched caressingly?
"Ah, fondest, blindest, weakest,
I am He Whom thou seekest!
Thou dravest love from thee, who dravest Me."

FRANCIS ORR TICKNOR (1822-1874)

Little Giffen

Ticknor, a successful physician in Georgia when the Civil War began, devoted much of his time attending wounded soldiers in the hospitals. One of these improvised hospitals was The Banks Building in Columbus, Georgia. Mrs. Ticknor, a frequent visitor to the hospital, became interested in Isaac Newton Giffen, the sixteen-year-old son of a blacksmith in east Tennessee. The boy was so seriously wounded that his recovery depended upon better care than could be given him in the crowded and almost primitive hospital. She persuaded her doctor-husband to bring the youth to Torch Hill, their plantation home seven miles outside Columbus.

There, for seven months, the boy was slowly nursed back to health and left to return to the army, never to be heard from again by the Ticknors. After telling Little Giffen's story in verse the doctor read it to his wife and started to tear it up, saying it was too true to be good poetry. His wife prevailed upon him not to destroy it. The South has always loved the poem, the only one of the doctor's many that is still read:

Out of the focal and foremost fire,
    Out of the hospital walls as dire,
Smitten of grapeshot and gangrene,
Eighteenth battle and he sixteen—
Specter such as you seldom see,
Little Giffen of Tennessee.

"Take him and welcome," the surgeon said;
"Not the doctor can help the dead!"
So we took him and brought him where

The balm was sweet in our summer air;
And we laid him down on a wholesome bed;
Utter Lazarus, heel to head!

And we watched the war with abated breath,
Skeleton boy against skeleton death!
Months of torture, how many such!
Weary weeks of the stick and crutch—
And still a glint in the steel-blue eye
Told of a spirit that wouldn't die,

And didn't! Nay! More! in death's despite
The crippled skeleton learned to write—
"Dear mother!" at first, of course, and then
"Dear Captain!" inquiring about the men.
Captain's answer: "Of eighty and five,
Giffen and I are left alive."

"Johnston pressed at the front," they say;—
Little Giffen was up and away!
A tear, his first, as he bade good-by,
Dimmed the glint of his steel-blue eye.
"I'll write if spared!" There was news of fight,
But none of Giffen—he did not write!

I sometimes fancy that were I King
Of the courtly Knights of Arthur's ring,
With the voice of the minstrel in mine ear
And the tender legend that trembles here,
I'd give the best on his bended knee—
The whitest soul of my chivalry—
For Little Giffen of Tennessee.

HENRY VAUGHAN (1622-1695)

The World
Beyond the Veil

After a childhood and early youth spent among the abundant natural
beauty of the Welsh countryside, Henry Vaughan went to Oxford in 1638,
studied law in London for two years, lived in the electric atmosphere of the
period, and was happy by 1642 to turn his back on critical events and retire

to the home and rural scenes of his boyhood. He had seen mobs storm court-rooms, the Long Parliament impeached, altars defaced, images destroyed and within a few years the fanatical Puritans would execute the King and threaten both the Church and State that Vaughan, a fervid royalist, revered.

The more hopeless seemed the future of the things Vaughan believed in, the more his thoughts turned to the unseen spiritual world while he began to practice medicine in his native village of Trenewydd. The deeper and more intense his thinking, the more majestic became the poetry to which he dedicated himself, in the hope "a door may be opened to me in heaven." Many of his religious poems came out of the solitude and meditation he prac-ticed often during the night—in the midst of nature's riches. Stars, "fair, order'd lights" "without noise," particularly attracted him. Little wonder, then, that a man with his mystical nature and distaste for the world he lived in should write that he "saw eternity the other night" in his poem "The World":

> I saw Eternity the other night,
> Like a great Ring of pure and endless light,
> 　All calm, as it was bright;
> And round beneath it, Time, in hours, days, years,
> 　Driven by the spheres
> Like a vast shadow moved; in which the world
> 　And all her train were hurled.
>
> The doting lover in his quaintest strain
> 　Did there complain;
> Near him, his lute, his fancy, and his flights,
> 　Wit's sour delights,
> With gloves, and knots, the silly snares of pleasure,
> 　Yet his dear treasure,
> All scattered lay, while his eyes did pour
> 　Upon a flower.
>
> The darksome statesman, hung with weights and woe,
> Like a thick mid-night fog, moved there so slow,
> 　He did not stay, nor go;
> Condemning thoughts—like sad eclipses—scowl
> 　Upon his soul,
> And clouds of crying witnesses without
> 　Pursu'd him with one shout.
> Yet digg'd the mole, and lest his ways be found,
> 　Worked under ground,
> Where he did clutch his prey; (But One did see
> 　That policy);

Churches and altars fed him; perjuries
   Were gnats and flies;
It rained about him blood and tears; but he
   Drank them as free.

The fearful miser on a heap of rust
Sate pining all his life there, did scarce trust
   His own hands with the dust,
Yet would not place one piece above, but lives
   In fear of thieves.
Thousands there were as frantic as himself,
   And hugged each one his pelf;

The downright epicure placed heaven in sense,
   And scorn'd pretense,
While others, slipp'd into a wide excess,
   Said little less;
The weaker sort slight, trivial wares enslave,
   Who think them brave;
And poor, despised Truth sate counting by
   Their victory.

Yet some, who all this while did weep and sing,
And sing, and weep, soared up into the Ring;
   But most would use no wing.
O fools (said I) thus to prefer dark night
   Before true light!
To live in grots and caves, and hate the day
   Because it shows the way,
The way, which from this dead and dark abode
   Leads up to God,
A way where you might tread the sun, and be
   More bright than he.
But as I did their madness so discuss,
   One whisper'd thus,
This Ring the Bridegroom did for none provide
   But for his bride.

On several occasions Vaughan referred to his "youthful, sinful age," when
he "played with fire" and recalled that at "the height of this career I met
with a dead man." Whoever this may have been—some say his brother—it
had a profound effect on the retiring young poet who several times was
dangerously ill for lengthy periods. He gave increasing thought to the life
after death and to relatives and friends who had already been summoned to
eternity. Again, meditating out of doors in the evening, he is reminded of the

departed when he gazes at the glow after sunset: "those faint beams in which this hill is dressed." Thus was he inspired to write his famous "Beyond the Veil":

> They are all gone into the world of light,
>   And I alone sit lingering here;
> Their very memory is fair and bright,
>   And my sad thoughts doth clear.
>
> It glows and glitters in my cloudy breast,
>   Like stars upon some gloomy grove,
> Or those faint beams in which this hill is dressed
>   After the sun's remove.
>
> I see them walking in an air of glory,
>   Whose light doth trample on my days:
> My days, which are at best but dull and hoary,
>   Mere glimmerings and decays.
>
> O holy Hope, and high Humility,
>   High as the heavens above!
> These are your walks, and you have showed them me,
>   To kindle my cold love.
>
> Dear beauteous death! the jewel of the just,
>   Shining nowhere but in the dark;
> What mysteries do lie beyond thy dusk,
>   Could Man outlook that mark!
>
> He that hath found some fledg'd bird's nest, may know
>   At first sight, if the bird be flown;
> But what fair well or grove he sings in now,
>   That is to him unknown.
>
> And yet, as angels in some brighter dreams
>   Call to the soul when man doth sleep,
> So some strange thoughts transcend our wonted themes,
>   And into glory peep.
>
> If a star were confined into a tomb,
>   Her captive flames must needs burn there;
> But when the hand that locked her up, gives room,
>   She'll shine through all the sphere.

O Father of Eternal Life, and all
  Created glories under Thee!
Resume Thy spirit from this world of thrall
  Into true liberty.

Either disperse these mists, which blot and fill
  My perspective still, as they pass,
Or else remove me hence unto that hill,
  Where I shall need no glass.

WALT WHITMAN (1819-1892)

Out of the Cradle Endlessly Rocking

One day in 1858 big, bearded, easy-going Walt Whitman paid one of his frequent visits to the home of Mrs. Abby Price of Brooklyn, N. Y., a friend of long-standing who was sympathetic to the poet's then misunderstood and often derided *Leaves of Grass,* published a few years earlier.

The eccentrically dressed and white-haired bard of forty years chatted about various matters and then diffidently mentioned he had just written a new piece. It was about a mockingbird, based on a real incident, he replied in answer to inquiries by Mrs. Price and her two daughters. The sometime carpenter, editor, school-teacher, and seemingly indolent lounger about town and country, promised to bring the poem on another visit and read it. Several days later he arrived with the manuscript of "Out of the Cradle Endlessly Rocking"—first titled "A Word Out of the Sea"—and it was read aloud a number of times by those present. Several months later it was published in *The Saturday Press* under the title "A Child's Reminiscence."

This is all that is positively known about one of Whitman's best-loved and most perfectly fashioned chants. But readers, critics and biographers have not been content with the sheer poignant beauty of this elegy of a remembered love; it has a pulsing quality that seems to compel analysis of its message and speculation as to its origin in the poet's experience. Although Whitman consistently refused to explain the poem's history, the lines themselves are sufficiently revealing to permit reasonable deductions which may be related to equally reasonable speculations about hidden phases of Whitman's life. Granted, this is opinion rather than fact; but opinion that the poem itself persuades one to reach.

The ballad tells how a little boy left his farm-house one Spring night to watch and listen to a mockingbird as it sat on its nest by the sea and plaintively called for its mate that would never return. The boy had previously seen the bird and its mate, and observed them carefully on several earlier occasions. He repeated his nocturnal visit several times and came to understand the bird's cry and his memory treasured every note he heard. Pondering these events, the boy become man identifies himself with the bird and echoes its song in his own mournful cry for a lost love. Finally, when he seeks for some clue to the mystery of separation and destiny the sea answers with the "delicious word" "Death."

Obviously, the boy is the poet, who was born on Long Island within sound of the sea and spent much of his childhood and youth exploring the seashore and time and again returned to it for rest and solace when he reached manhood. The poem is of course initially a reminiscence of childhood, but the memory is made poignant and meaningful by the recent loss of a lover. It would seem difficult to come to any other conclusion when one experiences the poet's tenderness and the intensity of his images.

Whether the poet's loss is that of an actual or ideal love, we do not know. There are hints in his notebooks of frustrated passions, and there have been dark mutterings of Whitman's romantic attachments while in New Orleans years earlier, and he himself—sometimes ridiculously—boasted of his illicit affairs with women who bore his children. But there is also evidence that Whitman's excessive sexuality remained unrealized and was necessarily sublimated in the rhetorical fantasy of poetry.

Whatever the details in the poet's life that led to the poem, it is clear that Whitman was lonely from unsatisfied love, fearful of emotional and spiritual chaos, and searching for that which would transcend personal grief. When he realizes the answer is death, and understands its meaning, he becomes reconciled—even serene.

Out of the cradle endlessly rocking,
Out of the mocking-bird's throat, the musical shuttle,
Out of the Ninth-month midnight,
Over the sterile sands, and the fields beyond, where the child, leaving his
    bed, wander'd alone, bare-headed, barefoot,
Down from the shower'd halo,
Up from the mystic play of shadows, twining and twisting as if they were
    alive,
Out from the patches of briers and blackberries,
From the memories of the bird that chanted to me,
From your memories, sad brother—from the fitful risings and fallings I heard,
From under that yellow half-moon, late-risen, and swollen as if with tears,
From those beginning notes of sickness and love, there in the transparent
    mist,

From the thousand responses of my heart, never to cease,
From the myriad thence-arous'd words,
From the word stronger and more delicious than any,
From such, as now they start, the scene revisiting,
As a flock, twittering, rising, or overhead passing,
Borne hither—ere all eludes me, hurriedly,
A man—yet by these tears a little boy again,
Throwing myself on the sand, confronting the waves,
I, chanter of pains and joys, uniter of here and hereafter,
Taking all hints to use them—but swiftly leaping beyond them,
A reminiscence ring.

2

Once, Paumanok,
When the snows had melted—when the lilac-scent was in the air, and the
    Fifth-month grass was growing,
Up this sea-shore, in some briers,
Two guests from Alabama—two together,
And their nest, and four light-green eggs, spotted with brown,
And every day the he-bird, to and fro, near at hand,
And every day the she-bird, crouch'd on her nest, silent, with bright eyes,
And every day I, a curious boy, never too close, never disturbing them,
Cautiously peering, absorbing, translating.

3

Shine! shine! shine!
Pour down your warmth, great Sun!
While we bask—we two together.

Two together!
Winds blow South, or winds blow North,
Day come white, or night come black,
Home, or rivers and mountains from home,
Singing all time, minding no time,
While we two keep together.

4

Till of a sudden,
May-be kill'd, unknown to her mate,
One forenoon the she-bird crouch'd not on her nest,
Not return'd that afternoon, nor the next,
Nor ever appear'd again.

And thenceforward, all summer, in the sound of the sea,
And at night, under the full of the moon, in calmer weather,
Over the hoarse surging of the sea,
Or flitting from brier to brier by day,
I saw, I heard at intervals, the remaining one, the he-bird,
The solitary guest from Alabama.

5

Blow! blow! blow!
Blow up, sea-winds, along Paumanok's shore!
I wait and I wait, till you blow my mate to me.

6

Yes, when the stars glisten'd,
All night long, on the prong of a moss-scallop'd stake,
Down, almost amid the slapping waves,
Sat the lone singer, wonderful, causing tears.

He call'd on his mate;
He pour'd forth the meanings which I, of all men, know.

Yes, my brother, I know;
The rest might not—but I have treasur'd every note;
For once, and more than once, dimly, down to the beach gliding,
Silent, avoiding the moonbeams, blending myself with the shadows,
Recalling now the obscure shapes, the echoes, the sounds and sights after
    their sorts,
The white arms out in the breakers tirelessly tossing,
I, with bare feet, a child, the wind wafting my hair,
Listen'd long and long.

Listen'd, to keep, to sing—now translating the notes,
Following you, my brother.

7

Soothe! soothe! soothe!
Close on its wave soothes the wave behind,
And again another behind, embracing and lapping, every one close,
But my love soothes not me, not me.

Low hangs the moon—it rose late;
O it is lagging—O I think it is heavy with love, with love.

O madly the sea pushes, pushes upon the land,
With love—with love.

O night! do I not see my love fluttering out there among the breakers?
What is that little black thing I see there in the white?

Loud! loud! loud!
Loud I call to you, my love!

High and clear I shoot my voice over the waves;
Surely you must know who is here, is here;
You must know who I am, my love.

Low-hanging moon!
What is that dusky spot in your brown yellow?

O it is the shape, the shape of my mate!
O moon, do not keep her from me any longer.

Land! land! land!
Whichever way I turn, O I think you could give me my mate back again,
*   if you only would;*
For I am almost sure I see her dimly whichever way I look.
O rising stars!
Perhaps the one I want so much will rise, will rise with some of you.

O throat! O trembling throat!
Sound clearer through the atmosphere!
Pierce the woods, the earth;
Somewhere listening to catch you, must be the one I want.

Shake out, carols!
Solitary here—the night's carols!
Carols of lonesome love! Death's carols!
Carols under that lagging, yellow, waning moon!
O, under that moon, where she droops almost down into the sea!
O reckless, despairing carols.

But soft! sink low;
Soft! let me just murmur;
And do you wait a moment, you husky-voiced sea;
For somewhere I believe I heard my mate responding to me,
So faint—I must be still, be still to listen;
But not altogether still, for then she might not come immediately to me.

Hither, my love!
Here I am! Here!
With this just-sustain'd note I announce myself to you;
This gentle call is for you, my love, for you.

Do not be decoy'd elsewhere!
That is the whistle of the wind—it is not my voice;
That is the fluttering, the fluttering of the spray;
Those are the shadows of leaves.

O darkness! O in vain!
O I am very sick and sorrowful.
O brown halo in the sky, near the moon, dropping upon the sea!
O troubled reflection in the sea!
O throat! O throbbing heart!
O all—and I singing uselessly, uselessly all the night.

Yet I murmur, murmur on!
O murmurs—you yourselves make me continue to sing, I know not why.

O past! O life! O songs of joy!
In the air—in the woods—over fields;
Loved! loved! loved! loved! loved!
But my love no more, no more with me!
We two together no more.

8

The aria sinking,
All else continuing—the stars shining,
The winds blowing—the notes of the bird continuous echoing,
With angry moans the fierce old mother incessantly moaning,
On the sands of Paumanok's shore, gray and rustling;
The yellow half-moon enlarged, sagging down, drooping, the face of the sea
    almost touching;
The boy ecstatic—with his bare feet the waves, with his hair the atmosphere
    dallying,
The love in the heart long pent, now loose, now at last tumultuously bursting,
The aria's meaning, the ears, the Soul, swiftly depositing,
The strange tears down the cheeks coursing,
The colloquy there—the trio—each uttering,
The undertone—the savage old mother, incessantly crying,
To the boy's Soul's questions sullenly timing—some drown'd secret hissing,
To the outsetting bard of love.

9

Demon or bird! (said the boy's soul,)
Is it indeed toward your mate you sing? or is it mostly to me?
For I, that was a child, my tongue's use sleeping,
Now I have heard you,
Now in a moment I know what I am for—I awake,
And already a thousand singers—a thousand songs, clearer, louder and more
    sorrowful than yours,
A thousand warbling echoes have started to life within me, never to die.

O you singer, solitary, singing by yourself—projecting me;
O solitary me, listening—nevermore shall I cease perpetuating you;
Never more shall I escape, never more the reverberations,
Never more the cries of unsatisfied love be absent from me,
Never again leave me to be the peaceful child I was before what there, in the
    night,
By the sea, under the yellow and sagging moon,
The messenger there arous'd—the fire, the sweet hell within,
The unknown want, the destiny of me.

O give me the clew! (it lurks in the night here somewhere;)
O if I am to have so much, let me have more!
O a word! O what is my destination? (I fear it is henceforth chaos;)
O how joys, dreads, convolutions, human shapes, and all shapes, spring as
    from graves around me!
O phantoms! you cover all the land and all the sea!
O I cannot see in the dimness whether you smile or frown upon me;
O vapor, a look, a word! O well-beloved!
O you dear women's and men's phantoms!

A word then, (for I will conquer it,)
The word final, superior to all,
Subtle, sent up—what is it?—I listen;
Are you whispering it, and have been all the time, you sea-waves?
Is that it from your liquid rims and wet sands?

10

Whereto answering, the sea,
Dallying not, hurrying not,
Whisper'd me through the night, and very plainly before daybreak,
Lisp'd to me the low and delicious word DEATH;
And again Death—ever Death, Death, Death,
Hissing melodious, neither like the bird, nor like my arous'd child's heart,

But edging near, as privately for me, rustling at my feet,
Creeping thence steadily up to my ears, and laving me softly all over,
Death, Death, Death, Death, Death.

Which I do not forget,
But fuse the song of my dusky demon and brother,
That he sang to me in the moonlight on Paumanok's gray beach,
With the thousand responsive songs, at random,
My own songs, awaked from that hour;
And with them the key, the word up from the waves,
The word of the sweetest song, and all songs,
That strong and delicious word which, creeping to my feet,
The sea whisper'd me.

JOHN GREENLEAF WHITTIER (1807-1892)

Maud Muller
Barbara Frietchie

Whittier said "Maud Muller" had no real foundation in fact, but was suggested by an incident years before the poem was written. He and his sister had been traveling in Maine and stopped in the shade of an apple-tree to rest their horse and refresh him with water from a brook at the roadside. "A very beautiful young girl in scantest summer attire was at work in the hayfield, and as we talked with her we noticed that she strove to hide her bare feet by raking hay over them, blushing as she did so, through the tan on her cheek and neck."

No doubt this is all that Whittier could really tell about the poem's origin. But one of his biographers, Albert Mordell, convincingly argues that the poem is in effect a retrospective glance at the poet's own fruitless love affairs and their failures because wealth and social status were placed above love.

It is interesting to note how Whittier, at least subconsciously, had his own tragedy in mind when relating the story of Maud Muller who was spurned by the judge because she was a poor farm girl.

Whittier was a poor farm boy without social position. For years he had known Mary Emerson Smith, beginning from childhood when they had roamed the countryside together. As they grew up he would recite his early poems to her. At nineteen he was deeply in love with her. But she was capricious; encouraging him one time, rejecting him another. But finally she stated she would not marry him. He was too poor. She married a judge and went to Ohio to live. Whittier's varying emotions on this affair are found in poems of tenderness, reproach, farewell, anger, reconciliation and reminiscence. Eventually they resumed their friendship through correspondence and late in life, when Mary was widowed, the poet saw her often when she spent the summers in New England. She was the great and enduring love of Whittier's life—the coquette who spurned him because he was poor, and instead married a judge. But the poet referred to it only to a few friends and kept most of his love poems out of his collected poems.

Another girl rejected Whittier's proposal of marriage because of his poverty and lack of social standing. And her father was a judge.

Whittier never married. But he did write "I know something very sweet and beautiful has been missed." And surely he told something of his own story when he related the unhappy fate of Maud Muller:

> Maud Muller on a summer's day
> Raked the meadows sweet with hay.
>
> Beneath her torn hat glowed the wealth
> Of simple beauty and rustic health.
>
> Singing, she wrought, and her merry glee
> The mock-bird echoed from his tree.
>
> But when she glanced to the far-off town,
> White from its hill-slope looking down,
>
> The sweet song died, and a vague unrest
> And a nameless longing filled her breast,—
>
> A wish that she hardly dared to own,
> For something better than she had known.
>
> The Judge rode slowly down the lane,
> Smoothing his horse's chestnut mane.
>
> He drew his bridle in the shade
> Of the apple-trees, to greet the maid,
>
> And ask a draught from the spring that flowed
> Through the meadow across the road.
>
> She stooped where the cool spring bubbled up,
> And filled for him her small tin cup,

And blushed as she gave it, looking down
On her feet so bare, and her tattered gown.

"Thanks!" said the Judge, "a sweeter draught
From a fairer hand was never quaffed."

He spoke of the grass and flowers and trees,
Of the singing birds and humming bees;

Then talked of the haying, and wondered whether
The clouds in the west would bring foul weather.

And Maud forgot her brier-torn gown,
And her graceful ankles bare and brown;

And listened, while a pleased surprise
Looked from her long-lashed hazel eyes.

At last, like one who for delay
Seeks a vain excuse, he rode away.

Maud Muller looked and sighed: "Ah, me!
That I the Judge's bride might be!

"He would dress me up in silks so fine,
And praise and toast me at his wine.

"My father should wear a broadcloth coat,
My brother should sail a painted boat.

"I'd dress my mother so grand and gay,
And the baby should have a new toy each day.

"And I'd feed the hungry and clothe the poor,
And all should bless me who left our door."

The Judge looked back as he climbed the hill,
And saw Maud Muller standing still.

"A form more fair, a face more sweet,
Ne'er hath it been my lot to meet.

"And her modest answer and graceful air
Shows her wise and good as she is fair.

"Would she were mine, and I to-day,
Like her, a harvester of hay:

"No doubtful balance of rights and wrongs,
Nor weary lawyers with endless tongues,

"But low of cattle and song of birds,
And health and quiet and loving words."

But he thought of his sister, proud and cold,
And his mother, vain of her rank and gold.

So, closing his heart, the Judge rode on,
And Maud was left in the field alone.

But the lawyers smiled that afternoon,
When he hummed in court an old love tune;

And the young girl mused beside the well,
Till the rain on the unraked clover fell.

He wedded a wife of richest dower,
Who lived for fashion, as he for power.

Yet oft, in his marble hearth's bright glow,
He watched a picture come and go;

And sweet Maud Muller's hazel eyes
Looked out in their innocent surprise.

Oft, when the wine in his glass was red,
He longed for the wayside well instead;

And closed his eyes on his garnished rooms,
To dream of meadows and clover-blooms.

And the proud man sighed with a secret pain,
"Ah, that I were free again!"

"Free as when I rode that day
Where the barefoot maiden raked her hay."

She wedded a man unlearned and poor,
And many children played around her door.

But care and sorrow and child-birth pain,
Left their traces on heart and brain.

And oft, when the summer sun shone hot
On the new-mown hay in the meadow lot,

And she heard the little spring-brook fall
Over the roadside, through the wall,

In the shade of the apple-tree again
She saw a rider draw his rein;

And, gazing down with a timid grace,
She felt his pleased eyes read her face.

Sometimes her narrow kitchen walls
Stretched away into stately halls;

The weary wheel to a spinnet turned,
The tallow candle an astral burned,

And for him who sat by the chimney lug,
Dozing and grumbling o'er pipe and mug,

A manly form at her side she saw,
And joy was duty and love was law.

Then she took up her burden of life again,
Saying only, "It might have been."

Alas for maiden, alas for judge,
For rich repiner and household drudge!

God pity then both! and pity us all,
Who vainly the dreams of youth recall.

For of all sad words of tongue or pen,
The saddest are these: "It might have been!"

Ah, well! for us all some sweet hope lies
Deeply buried from human eyes;

And, in the hereafter, angels may
Roll the stone from its grave away!

Of all American poets John Greenleaf Whittier would be the least likely to falsify or distort the facts of history for the sake of producing a popular poem. But that is what this quiet, rigidly correct New England gentleman did unwittingly, to his subsequent distress.

It happened during the Civil War, a cause in which the poet's emotions were heavily involved. The novelist Emma D. E. N. Southworth, of Georgetown, D.C., had written Whittier, telling him the Barbara Frietchie story as she had heard it, and suggested it would make a fine poem. The poet responded with unwonted fervor and within two weeks completed the stanzas, which were published in the *Atlantic* for October, 1863. Northern papers widely reprinted the poem, it was published in leaflet form and became Whittier's best-known piece.

When the authenticity of the story was later challenged Whittier explained he had written it in good faith on the strength of sources he regarded as reliable; that the story had appeared in the press before he wrote the poem; that he was "still constrained to believe it had foundation in fact," and concluding with, "I have no pride of authorship to interfere with my allegiance to truth."

The poet did not fall back on the perfectly valid reminder that poetry is not necessarily or always based on precise facts.

As for Barbara Frietchie, some authorities say she was a Southern sympathizer, others insist her allegiance was to the North. In any event, she was ninety-six, bedridden and at the point of death at the time of the incident; hardly a mood or condition conducive to flag-waving. Moreover, the Southern troops entering Frederick on September 6, 1862, did not march past Barbara's house, and they were not led by General Jackson, who had been injured by a horse and did not rejoin his troops until four days later.

Nevertheless, there was another and younger Barbara Frietchie, named Mary Quantrill, and the story about her fully justifies the spirit of Whittier's poem. General Ambrose P. Hill led his soldiers past the Quantrill house, which was about four blocks from the dying Barbara's home, and Mrs. Quantrill did wave a Union flag at the Southern soldiers. General Hill apparently had not noticed the flag, but he did become aware of commotion at his rear. Hill learned that some of his soldiers had seized Mrs. Quantrill's flag, broken the staff, that Mrs. Quantrill had obtained another flag and the soldiers were struggling to take it from her. Hill ordered the soldiers to leave the woman and her flags alone, and to fall in. Just how poor old Mrs. Frietchie got into the fracas is one of those minor mysteries that trouble historians while they delight poets and public.

> Up from the meadows rich with corn,
> Clear in the cool September morn,

The clustered spires of Frederick stand
Green-walled by the hills of Maryland.

Round about them orchards sweep,
Apple and peach-tree fruited deep,

Fair as a garden of the Lord
To the eyes of the famished rebel horde,

On that pleasant morn of the early Fall
When Lee marched over the mountain wall;

Over the mountains winding down,
Horse and foot, into Frederick town.

Forty flags with their silver stars,
Forty flags with their crimson bars,

Flapped in the morning wind: the sun
Of noon looked down, and saw not one.

Up rose old Barbara Frietchie then,
Bowed with her fourscore years and ten:

Bravest of all in Frederick town,
She took up the flag the men hauled down;

In her attic window the staff she set,
To show that one heart was loyal yet.

Up the street came the rebel tread,
Stonewall Jackson riding ahead.

Under his slouched hat left and right
He glanced; the old flag met his sight.

"Halt!"—the dust-brown ranks stood fast.
"Fire!"—out blazed the rifle blast.

It shivered the window, pane and sash;
It rent the banner with seam and gash.

Quick, as it well, from the broken staff
Dame Barbara snatched the silken scarf.

She leaned far out on the window-sill,
And shook it forth with a royal will.

"Shoot, if you must, this old grey head,
But spare your country's flag," she said.

A shade of sadness, a blush of shame,
Over the face of the leader came;

The nobler nature within him stirred
To life at that woman's deed and word;

"Who touches a hair of yon grey head
Dies like a dog! March on!" he said.

All day long through Frederick street
Sounded the tread of marching feet:

All day long that free flag tost
Over the heads of the rebel host.

Ever its torn folds rose and fell
On the loyal winds that loved it well;

And through the hill-gaps sunset light
Shone over it with a warm good-night.

Barbara Frietchie's work is o'er,
And the rebel rides on his raids no more.

Honor to her! and let a tear
Fall, for her sake, on Stonewall's bier.

Over Barbara Frietchie's grave,
Flag of freedom and union, wave!

Peace and order, and beauty draw
Round thy symbol of light and law;

And ever the stars above look down
On thy stars below in Frederick town!

OSCAR WILDE (1856-1900)

The Ballad of Reading Gaol

Few famous men have so quickly fallen from fame to shame as did Oscar Wilde in 1895 when he was sentenced to two years at hard labor, following a sensational and sordid trial on a charge of flagrantly violating public morality with young Lord Alfred Douglas. The brilliant wit, who had shed discretion and flaunted his degeneracy, suddenly proved that he spoke more truly than intended when he said "One must always set one's heart upon the most tragic." He was mocked and jeered by crowds when, manacled and chained to other criminals, he was led away to prison. His children were taken from him legally, he was bankrupt, and only a few friends stood by him.

After six months he was transferred to little more than a cage in Reading Gaol. This was a penal hell, with the harshest regulations and severest punishments for their infraction. For example, for two hours every morning and every afternoon the prisoners walked single file, three paces apart to prevent conversation, in a stone-paved circle. Crushed, cowed, humiliated and suffering physically, the once haughty sensualist began to learn the nature of sorrow and the meaning of pity.

Among Wilde's fellow-prisoners was Charles Thomas Woolridge, a young British soldier who had murdered his wife in a jealous rage. For six weeks he daily tramped the paved circle with the other prisoners. He was the man who looked "With such a wistful eye" at the sky. He was the one of whom it was said "That fellow's got to swing" because "The man had killed the thing he loved." Then one morning in July the bells of St. Lawrence's church began to toll; Woolridge was hung in a crude little shed in the prison yard; a black flag was hoisted over the prison, and the inmates saw a small mound of mud and burning lime in the yard where the man had been hurriedly buried.

Woolridge and his terrible fate made a deep impression upon Wilde who, through suffering, had come to have compassion for his fellow-man. Perhaps in Reading Gaol he began to plan the great Ballad he would center around the unfortunate soldier, although the poet was not allowed to write while in prison.

When Wilde was released in May, 1897, he went that same day to France, hopeful of vindicating himself as man and writer. Several weeks later he began to put on paper his most humane, understanding and powerful writing, speaking to and reaching the hearts of men. But it was a peak from which, during the next three years, he quickly fell to the grossness, drunkenness and despair in which he died in November, 1900.

I

He did not wear his scarlet coat,
    For blood and wine are red,
And blood and wine were on his hands
    When they found him with the dead,
The poor dead woman whom he loved,
    And murdered in her bed.

He walked among the Trial Men
    In a suit of shabby grey;
A cricket cap was on his head,
    And his step seemed light and gay;
But I never saw a man who looked
    So wistfully at the day.

I never saw a man who looked
    With such a wistful eye
Upon that little tent of blue
    Which prisoners call the sky,
And at every drifting cloud that went
    With sails of silver by.

I walked with other souls in pain,
    Within another ring,
And was wondering if the man had done
    A great or little thing,
When a voice behind me whispered low,
    "That fellow's got to swing."

Dear Christ! the very prison walls
    Suddenly seemed to reel,
And the sky above my head became
    Like a casque of scorching steel;
And, though I was a soul in pain,
    My pain I could not feel.

I only knew what hunted thought
    Quickened his step, and why
He looked upon the garish day
    With such a wistful eye;

The man had killed the thing he loved,
   And so he had to die.

     *   *   *   *   *

Yet each man kills the thing he loves,
   By each let this be heard,
Some do it with a bitter look,
   Some with a flattering word,
The coward does it with a kiss,
   The brave man with a sword!

Some kill their love when they are young,
   And some when they are old;
Some strangle with the hands of Lust,
   Some with the hands of Gold:
The kindest use a knife, because
   The dead so soon grow cold.

Some love too little, some too long,
   Some sell, and others buy;
Some do the deed with many tears,
   And some without a sigh:
For each man kills the thing he loves,
   Yet each man does not die.

He does not die a death of shame,
   On a day of dark disgrace,
Nor have a noose about his neck,
   Nor a cloth upon his face,
Nor drop feet foremost through the floor
   Into an empty space.

     *   *   *   *   *

He does not sit with silent men
   Who watch him night and day;
Who watch him when he tries to weep,
   And when he tries to pray;
Who watch him lest himself should rob
   The prison of its prey.

He does not wake at dawn to see
   Dread figures throng his room,
The shivering Chaplain robed in white,
   The Sheriff stern with gloom,
And the Governor all in shiny black,
   With the yellow face of Doom.

He does not rise in piteous haste
  To put on convict-clothes,
While some coarse-mouthed Doctor gloats, and notes
  Each new and nerve-twitched pose,
Fingering a watch whose little ticks
  Are like horrible hammer-blows.

He does not know that sickening thirst
  That sands one's throat, before
The hangman with his gardener's gloves
  Slips through the padded door,
And binds one with three leathern thongs,
  That the throat may thirst no more.

He does not bend his head to hear
  The Burial Office read,
Nor, while the terror of his soul
  Tells him he is not dead,
Cross his own coffin, as he moves
  Into the hideous shed.

He does not stare upon the air
  Through a little roof of glass:
He does not pray with lips of clay
  For his agony to pass;
Nor feel upon his shuddering cheek
  The kiss of Caiaphas.

II

Six weeks our guardsman walked the yard,
  In the suit of shabby grey:
His cricket cap was on his head,
  And his step seemed light and gay,
But I never saw a man who looked
  So wistfully at day.

I never saw a man who looked
  With such a wistful eye
Upon that little tent of blue
  Which prisoners call the sky,
And at every wandering cloud that trailed
  Its ravelled fleeces by.

He did not wring his hands, as do
  Those witless men who dare

To try to rear the changeling Hope
   In the cave of black Despair:
He only looked upon the sun,
   And drank the morning air.

He did not wring his hands nor weep,
   Nor did he peek or pine,
But he drank the air as though it held
   Some healthful anodyne;
With open mouth he drank the sun
   As though it had been wine!

And I and all the souls in pain,
   Who tramped the other ring,
Forgot if we ourselves had done
   A great or little thing,
And watched with gaze of dull amaze
   The man who had to swing.

And strange it was to see him pass
   With a step so light and gay,
And strange it was to see him look
   So wistfully at the day,
And strange it was to think that he
   Had such a debt to pay.

             *   *   *   *   *

For oak and elm have pleasant leaves
   That in the spring-time shoot:
But grim to see is the gallows-tree,
   With its adder-bitten root,
And, green or dry, a man must die
   Before it bears its fruit!

The loftiest place is that seat of grace
   For which all worldings try:
But who would stand in hempen band
   Upon a scaffold high,
And through a murderer's collar take
   His last look at the sky?

It is sweet to dance to violins
   When Love and Life are fair:
To dance to flutes, to dance to lutes
   Is delicate and rare:

But it is not sweet with nimble feet
  To dance upon the air!

So with curious eyes and quick surmise
  We watched him day by day,
And wondered if each one of us
  Would end the self-same way,
For none can tell to what red Hell
  His sightless soul may stray.

At last the dead man walked no more
  Amongst the Trial Men,
And I knew that he was standing up
  In the black dock's dreadful pen,
And that never would I see his face
  In God's sweet world again.

Like two doomed ships that pass in storm
  We had crossed each other's way:
But we made no sign, we said no word,
  We had no word to say;
For we did not meet in the holy night,
  But in the shameful day.

A prison wall was round us both,
  Two outcast men we were:
The world had thrust us from its heart,
  And God from out His care:
And the iron gin that waits for Sin
  Had caught us in its snare.

III

In Debtors' Yard the stones are hard,
  And the dripping wall is high,
So it was he took the air
  Beneath the leaden sky,
And by each side a Warder walked,
  For fear the man might die.

Or else he sat with those who watched
  His anguish night and day;
Who watched him when he rose to weep,
  And when he crouched to pray;
Who watched him lest himself should rob
  Their scaffold of its prey.

The Governor was strong upon
   The Regulations Act:
The Doctor said that Death was but a scientific fact:
And twice a day the Chaplain called,
   And left a little tract.

And twice a day he smoked his pipe,
   And drank his quart of beer:
His soul was resolute, and held
   No hiding-place for fear;
He often said that he was glad
   The hangman's hands were near.

But why he said so strange a thing
   No warder dared to ask:
For he to whom a watcher's doom
   Is given as his task,
Must set a lock upon his lips,
   And make his face a mask.

Or else he might be moved, and try
   To comfort or console:
And what should Human Pity do
   Pent up in Murderers' Hole?
What word of grace in such a place
   Could help a brother's soul?
       *   *   *   *   *

With slouch and swing around the ring
   We trod the Fools' Parade!
We did not care: we knew we were
   The Devil's Own Brigade:
And shaven head and feet of lead
   Make a merry masquerade.

We tore the tarry rope to shreds
   With blunt and bleeding nails;
We rubbed the doors, and scrubbed the floors,
   And cleaned the shining rails:
And, rank by rank, we soaped the plank,
   And clattered with the pails.

We sewed the sacks, we broke the stones,
   We turned the dusty drill:
We banged the tins, and bawled the hymns,
   And sweated on the mill:

But in the heart of every man
  Terror was lying still.

So still it lay that every day
  Crawled like a weed-clogged wave:
And we forgot the bitter lot
  That waits for fool and knave,
Till once, as we trampled in from work,
  We passed an open grave.

With yawning mouth the yellow hole
  Gaped for a living thing;
The very mud cried out for blood
  To the thirsty asphalt ring:
And we knew that ere one dawn grew fair
  Some prisoner had to swing.

Right in we went, with soul intent
  On Death and Dread and Doom:
The hangman, with his little bag,
  Went shuffling through the gloom:
And each man trembled as he crept
  Into his numbered tomb.

                 *   *   *   *   *

That night the empty corridors
  Were full of forms of Fear,
And up and down the iron town
  Stole feet we could not hear,
And through the bar that hide the stars
  White faces seemed to peer.

He lay as one who lies and dreams
  In a pleasant meadow-land,
The watchers watched him as he slept,
  And could not understand
How one could sleep so sweet a sleep
  With a hangman close at hand.

But there is no sleep when men must weep
  Who never yet have wept:
So we—the fool, the fraud, the knave—
  That endless vigil kept,
And through each brain on hands of pain
  Another terror crept.

Alas! it is a fearful thing
  To feel another's guilt!
For, right within, the sword of Sin
  Pierced to its poisoned hilt,
And as molten lead were the tears we shed
  For the blood we had not spilt.

The Warders with their shoes of felt
  Crept by each padlocked door,
And peeped and saw, with eyes of awe,
  Grey figures on the floor,
And wondered why men knelt to pray
  Who never prayed before.

All through the night we knelt and prayed,
  Mad mourners of a corse!
The troubled plumes of midnight were
  The plumes upon a hearse:
And bitter wine upon a sponge
  Was the saviour of Remorse.

* * * * *

The grey cock crew, the red cock crew,
  But never came the day:
And crooked shapes of Terror crouched,
  In the corners where we lay:
And each evil sprite that walks by night
  Before us seemed to play.

They glided past, they glided fast,
  Like travellers through a mist:
They mocked the moon in a rigadoon
  Of delicate turn and twist,
And with formal pace and loathsome grace
  The phantoms kept their tryst.

With mop and mow, we saw them go,
  Slim shadows hand in hand:
About, about, in a ghostly rout
  They trod a saraband:
And the damned grotesques made arabesques,
  Like the wind upon the sand!

With the pirouettes of marionettes,
  They tripped on pointed tread:

But with flutes of Fear they filled the ear,
    As their grisly masque they led,
And loud they sang, and long they sang,
    For they sang to wake the dead.

"Oho!" they cried, "the world is wide,
    But fettered limbs go lame!
And once, or twice, to throw the dice
    Is a gentlemanly game,
But he does not win who plays with Sin
    In the secret House of Shame."

No thing of air these antics were,
    That frolicked with such glee:
To men whose lives were held in gyves,
    And whose feet might not go free,
Ah! wounds of Christ! they were living things,
    Most terrible to see.

Around, around, they waltzed and wound;
    Some wheeled in smirking pairs;
With the mincing step of a demirep
    Some sidled up the stairs:
And with subtle sneer, and fawning leer,
    Each helped us at our prayers.

The morning wind began to moan,
    But still the night went on:
Through its giant loom the web of gloom
    Crept till each thread was spun:
And, as we prayed, we grew afraid
    Of the Justice of the Sun.

The moaning wind went wandering round
    The weeping prison-wall:
Till like a wheel of turning steel
    We felt the minutes crawl:
O moaning wind! what had we done
    To have such a seneschal?

At last I saw the shadowed bars,
    Like a lattice wrought in lead,
Move right across the whitewashed wall
    That faced my three-plank bed,

And I knew that somewhere in the world
    God's dreadful dawn was red.

At six o'clock we cleaned our cells,
    At seven all was still,
But the sough and swing of a mighty wing
    The prison seemed to fill,
For the Lord of Death with icy breath
    Had entered in to kill.

He did not pass in purple pomp,
    Nor ride a moon-white steed.
Three yards of cord and a sliding board
    Are all the gallows' need:
So with the rope of shame the Herald came
    To do the secret deed.

We were as men who through a fen
    Of filthy darkness grope:
We did not dare to breathe a prayer,
    Or to give our anguish scope:
Something was dead in each of us,
    And what was dead was Hope.

For Man's grim Justice goes its way,
    And will not swerve aside:
It slays the weak, it slays the strong,
    It has a deadly stride:
With iron heel it slays the strong,
    The monstrous parricide!

We waited for the stroke of eight:
    Each tongue was thick with thirst:
For the stroke of eight is the stroke of Fate
    That makes a man accursed,
And Fate will use a running noose
    For the best man and the worse.

We had no other thing to do,
    Save to wait for the sign to come:
So, like things of stone in a valley lone,
    Quiet we sat and dumb:
But each man's heart beat thick and quick,
    Like a madman on a drum!

With sudden shock the prison-clock
  Smote on the shivering air,
And from all the gaol rose up a wail
  Of impotent despair,
Like the sound that frightened marshes hear
  From some leper in his lair.

And as one sees most fearful things
  In the crystal of a dream,
We saw the greast hempen rope
  Hooked to the blackened beam,
And heard the prayer the hangman's snare
  Strangled into a scream.

And all the woe that moved him so
  That he gave that bitter cry,
And the wild regrets, and the bloody sweats,
  None knew so well as I:
For he who lives more lives than one
  More deaths than one must die.

IV

There is no chapel on the day
  On which they hang a man:
The Chaplain's heart is far too sick,
  Or his face is far too wan,
Or there is that written in his eyes
  Which none should look upon.

So they us close till nigh on noon,
  And then they rang the bell,
And the Warders with their jingling keys
  Opened each listening cell,
And down the iron stairs we tramped,
  Each from his separate Hell.

Out into God's sweet air we went,
  But not in wonted way,
For this man's face was white with fear,
  And that man's face was grey,
And I never saw sad men who looked
  So wistfully at the day.

I never saw sad men who looked
  With such a wistful eye
Upon that little tent of blue
  We prisoners call the sky,
And at every careless cloud that passed
  In happy freedom by.

But there were those amongst us all
  Who walked with downcast head,
And knew that, had each got his due,
  They should have died instead:
He had but killed a thing that lived,
  Whilst they had killed the dead.

For he who sins a second time
  Wakes a dead soul to pain,
And draws it from its spotted shroud,
  And makes it bleed again,
And makes it bleed great gouts of blood,
  And makes it bleed in vain!
                    *   *   *   *   *
Like ape or clown, in monstrous garb
  With crooked arrows starred,
Silently we went round and round,
  The slippery asphalt yard;
Silently we went round and round
  And no man spoke a word.

Silently we went round and round
  And through each hollow mind
The Memory of dreadful things
  Rushed like a dreadful wind,
And Horror stalked before each man,
  And Terror crept behind.

The Warders strutted up and down,
  And kept their herd of brutes,
Their uniforms were spick and span,
  And they wore their Sunday suits,
But we knew the work they had been at,
  By the quicklime on their boots.

For where a grave had opened wide,
  There was no grave at all:
Only a stretch of mud and sand

By the hideous prison-wall,
And a little heap of burning lime,
That the man should have his pall.

For he has a pall, this wretched man,
Such as few men can claim:
Deep down below a prison-yard,
Naked for greater shame,
He lies, with fetters on each foot,
Wrapt in a sheet of flame!

And all the while the burning lime
Eats flesh and bone away,
It eats the brittle bone by night,
And the soft flesh by day,
It eats the flesh and bone by turns,
But it eats the heart alway.

      *   *   *   *   *

For three long years they will not sow
Or root or seedling there:
For three long years the unblessed spot
Will sterile be and bare,
And look upon the wondering sky
With unreproachful stare.

They think a murderer's heart would taint
Each simple seed they sow.
It is not true! God's kindly earth
Is kindlier than men know,
And the red rose would but blow more red,
The whiter rose whiter blow.

Out of his mouth a red, red rose!
Out of his heart a white!
For who can say by what strange way,
Christ brings His will to light,
Since the barren staff the pilgrim bore
Bloomed in the great Pope's sight?

But neither milk-white rose nor red
May bloom in prison air;
The shard, the pebble, and the flint,
Are what they give us there:
For flowers have been known to heal
A common man's despair.

So never will wine-red rose or white,
  Petal by petal, fall
On that stretch of mud and sand that lies
  By the hideous prison-wall,
To tell the men who tramp the yard
  That God's Son died for all.

*   *   *   *   *

Yet though the hideous prison-wall
  Still hems him round and round,
And a spirit may not walk by night
  That is with fetters bound,
And a spirit may but weep that lies
  In such unholy ground,

He is at peace—this wretched man—
  At peace, or will be soon:
There is no thing to make him mad,
  Nor does Terror walk at noon,
For the lampless Earth in which he lies
  Has neither Sun nor Moon.

They hanged him as a beast is hanged:
  They did not even toll
A requiem that might have brought
  Rest to his startled soul,
But hurriedly they took him out,
  And hid him in a hole.

They stripped him of his canvas clothes,
  And gave him to the flies:
They mocked the swollen purple throat,
  And the stark and staring eyes:
And with laughter loud they heaped the shroud
  In which their convict lies.

The Chaplain would not kneel to pray
  By his dishonoured grave:
Nor mark it with that Blessed Cross
  That Christ for sinners gave,
Because the man was one of those
  Whom Christ came down to save.

Yet all is well; he has but passed
  To life's appointed bourne:

And alien tears will fill for him
　Pity's long-broken urn,
For his mourners will be outcast men,
　And outcasts always mourn.

V

I know not whether Laws be right,
　Or whether Laws be wrong;
All that we know who lie in gaol
　Is that the wall is strong;
And that each day is like a year,
　A year whose days are long.

But this I know; that every Law
　That men have made for Man,
Since first Man took his brother's life,
　And the sad world began,
But straws the wheat and saves the chaff
　With a most evil fan.

This too I know—and wise it were
　If each could know the same—
That every prison that men build
　Is built with bricks of shame,
And bound with bars lest Christ should see
　How men their brothers maim.

With bars they blur the gracious moon,
　And blind the goodly sun:
And they do well to hide their Hell,
　For in it things are done
That Son of God nor son of Man
　Ever should look upon!
　　　　* * * * *
The vilest deeds like poison weeds,
　Bloom well in prison-air;
It is only what is good in Man
　That wastes and withers there:
Pale Anguish keeps the heavy gate,
　And the Warder is Despair.

For they starve the little frightened child
　Till it weeps both night and day:

And they scourge the weak, and flog the fool,
  And gibe the old and grey,
And some grow mad, and all grow bad,
  And none a word may say.

Each narrow cell in which we dwell
  Is a foul and dark latrine,
And the fetid breath of living Death
  Chokes up each grated screen,
And all, but Lust, is turned to dust
  In Humanity's machine.

The brackish water that we drink
  Creeps with a loathsome slime,
And the bitter bread they weigh in scales
  Is full of chalk and lime,
And Sleep will not lie down, but walks
  Wild-eyed, and cries to Time.

                  *   *   *   *   *

But though lean Hunger and green Thirst
  Like asp with adder fight,
We have little care of prison fare,
  For what chills and kills outright
Is that every stone one lifts by day
  Becomes one's heart by night.

With midnight always in one's heart,
  And twilight in one's cell,
We turn the crank, or tear the rope,
  Each in his separate Hell,
And the silence is more awful far
  Than the sound of a brazen bell.

And never a human voice comes near
  To speak a gentle word:
And the eye that watches through the door
  Is pitiless and hard:
And by all forgot, we rot and rot,
  With soul and body marred.

And thus we rust Life's iron chain,
  Degraded and alone:
And some men curse, and some men weep,
  And some men make no moan:

But God's eternal Laws are kind
  And break the heart of stone.

And every human heart that breaks,
  In prison-cell or yard,
Is as that broken box that gave
  Its treasure to the Lord,
And filled the unclean leper's house
  With the scent of costliest nard.

Ah! happy they whose hearts can break
  And peace of pardon win!
How else may man make straight his plan
  And cleanse his soul from Sin?
How else but through a broken heart
  May Lord Christ enter in?

And he of the swollen purple throat,
  And the stark and staring eyes
Waits for the holy hands that took
  The Thief to Paradise;
And a broken and a contrite heart
  The Lord will not despise.

The man in red who reads the Law
  Gave him three weeks of life,
Three little weeks in which to heal
  His soul of his soul's strife,
And cleanse from every blot of blood
  The hand that held the knife.

And with tears of blood he cleansed the hand,
  The hand that held the steel:
For only blood can wipe out blood,
  And only tears can heal:
And the crimson stain that was of Cain
  Became Christ's snow-white seal.

VI

In Reading gaol by Reading town
  There is a pit of shame,
And in it lies a wretched man
  Eaten by teeth of flame,

In a burning winding-sheet he lies,
    And his grave has got no name.

And there, till Christ call forth the dead,
    In silence let him lie:
No need to waste the foolish tear,
    Or heave the windy sigh:
The man had killed the thing he loved,
    And so he had to die.

And all men kill the thing they love,
    By all let this be heard,
Some do it with a bitter look,
    Some with a flattering word,
The coward does it with a kiss,
    The brave man with a sword!

RICHARD HENRY WILDE (1789-1846)

My Life is Like the Summer Rose

Wilde, a successful young Georgia lawyer, began this poem for the "amusement of the family," but tragedy changed it into grim reality.

The author related that his brother, James Wilde, was an officer in the U. S. Army who sometime prior to 1815 was included in an expedition sent to Florida to subdue the Seminole Indians, reported to be engaged in terror-tactics. When James returned to the family home in Augusta, Georgia, he gave fanciful accounts of the beauties and wonders of Florida—which in those days was relatively remote and unknown to people living even so nearby as the Wildes. His mother, sisters and brother were amused by what they believed to be, and may actually have been, exaggerated descriptions of the flora, fauna and life in the then mostly wild region of Florida.

Richard, who dabbled with poetry when not engaged with the law, laughingly promised his brother that he would immortalize his exploits in a poetic epic, for the family's entertainment.

But before he had written more than a few stanzas all his pleasure in the poem was destroyed when his brother was killed in a duel. Strangely enough, the few stanzas he had already written are sadly prophetic and appropriate to one whose life was snuffed out so early and so suddenly. The brother's death put an end to the poem, which apparently was allowed to

stand as originally written. It was set to music by **Sidney Lanier**. Wilde did
a great deal of other writing, but only this single lyric of his is read today:

My life is like the summer rose
That opens to the morning sky,
But ere the shades of evening close,
Is scattered on the ground—to die!
Yet on the rose's humble bed
The sweetest dews of night are shed,
As if she wept the waste to see,—
But none shall weep a tear for me!

My life is like the autumn leaf
That trembles in the moon's pale ray;
Its hold is frail,—its date is brief,
Restless,—and soon to pass away!
Yet, ere that leaf shall fall and fade,
The parent tree will mourn its shade,
The winds bewail the leafless tree,—
But none shall breathe a sigh for me!

My life is like the prints which feet
Have left on Tampa's desert strand;
Soon as the rising tide shall beat,
All trace will vanish from the sand;
Yet, as if grieving to efface
All vestige of the human race,
On that lone shore loud moans the sea,—
But none, alas! shall mourn for me!

CHARLES WOLFE (1791-1823)

The Burial of Sir John Moore After Corunna

Charles Wolfe, in spite of delicate health and marked intellectual talents,
dreamed of becoming a British soldier when he came of age. But the amiable
youth abandoned the idea when he learned such action would distress his
mother, who had high hopes for him as a scholar, and perhaps as a clergyman.

He did become a scholar, took orders in the Anglican Church and did
parish work in Ireland. But while still studying at Dublin University his
mind must often have dwelt upon the military career he had planned to

pursue. During his second year in college he wrote a long poem on the Battle of Busaco, when the French attacked Wellington in 1810.

Then several years later Wolfe added another poem to the few he wrote and did not destroy. He was inspired to it when he read Robert Southey's account of the death and burial of Sir John Moore. This was the kind of soldier Wolfe would have hoped to become, but for the disapproval of a doting mother.

Moore, who joined the Army at fifteen and rose rapidly, was a student of military science and highly regarded by the Army for his bravery and fairness. When England came to Spain's assistance against France in 1808, Moore was placed in charge of 35,000 men but was shot from his horse while protecting the retreat of his cavalry and artillery at the port of Corunna.

Wolfe's poem reveals how deeply he was affected by Southey's account of the valiant General's death and burial: how, with a shattered shoulder, he was carried in a blanket to his quarters in the town and died that night hoping England would recognize he had done his duty. Before the Army sailed from Corunna the next day it respected the fallen leader's request that he be buried where he fell. A grave was dug for him on the rampart of the Corunna citadel. No coffin was available. At 8:00 A.M. staff officers wrapped the General's body, dressed as it was, in a military cloak and blankets. Fearing Napoleon's army was preparing a new attack, Moore was quickly borne to the grave by his officers, a funeral service was read and the grave quickly covered with earth. Later, both the Spanish and British erected monuments at the grave site to Moore. But Wolfe, envisioning himself as one of the burial party, wrote a more enduring monument to Moore—to the kind of soldier he would like to have been:

> Not a drum was heard, not a funeral note,
>   As his corpse to the rampart we hurried;
> Not a soldier discharged his farewell shot
>   O'er the grave where our hero we buried.
>
> We buried him darkly at dead of night,
>   The sods with our bayonets turning;
> By the struggling moonbeam's misty light
>   And the lantern dimly burning.
>
> No useless coffin enclosed his breast,
>   Not in sheet nor in shroud we wound him;
> But he lay like a warrior taking his rest
>   With his martial cloak around him.
>
> Few and short were the prayers we said,
>   And we spoke not a word of sorrow;

But we steadfastly gazed on the face that was dead,
   And we bitterly thought of the morrow.

We thought, as we hollowed his narrow bed
   And smoothed down his lonely pillow,
That the foe and the stranger would tread o'er his head,
   And we far away on the billow!

Lightly they'll talk of the spirit that's gone,
   And o'er his cold ashes upbraid him,—
But little he'll reck, if they let him sleep on
   In the grave where a Briton has laid him.

But half of our heavy task was done
   When the clock struck the hour for retiring:
And we heard the distant and random gun
   That the foe was sullenly firing.

Slowly and sadly we laid him down,
   From the field of his fame fresh and gory;
We carved not a line, and we raised not a stone,
   But we left him alone with his glory.

WILLIAM WORDSWORTH (1770-1850)

We Are Seven
Lines Composed a Few Miles Above Tintern Abbey
"It is a Beauteous Evening, Calm and Free"
"She Was a Phantom of Delight"

One of the more popular but far from superior poems of Wordsworth arose out of an incident in 1793. The poet was on one of his almost interminable walking tours when he met the little girl heroine of "We Are Seven" in the area of Goodrich Castle. Although not particularly attracted to children, childhood and the mind of the child did interest Wordsworth. Consequently he was impressed when the little girl ignored the evidence of physical mortality and persistently clung to her belief in the survival of spirit over death.

Five years later Wordsworth and Coleridge decided to collaborate on a volume of poems on supernatural subjects taken from common life. Words-

worth thought of his meeting with the "simple child" and composed the poem
while walking in the grove at his Alfoxden home; composing the last stanza
first, beginning with the last line! When the volume was going through the
press a friend who saw it went to Wordsworth and pleaded with him to
remove "We Are Seven." "It will make you everlasting ridiculous" warned
the man. Forty-three years later the poet was again in the Goodrich Castle
area and regretted he did not know the name of the child of years earlier
so that he could call on her.

> —A Simple Child,
> That lightly draws its breath,
> And feels its life in every limb,
> What should it know of death?
>
> I met a little cottage Girl:
> She was eight years old, she said;
> Her hair was thick with many a curl
> That clustered round her head.
>
> She had a rustic, woodland air,
> And she was wildly clad:
> Her eyes were fair, and very fair;
> —Her beauty made me glad.
>
> "Sisters and brothers, little Maid,
> How many may you be?"
> "How many? Seven in all," she said,
> And wondering looked at me.
>
> "And where are they? I pray you tell."
> She answered: "Seven are we;
> And two of us at Conway dwell,
> And two are gone to sea.
>
> "Two of us in the church-yard lie,
> My sister and my brother;
> And, in the church-yard cottage, I
> Dwell near them with my mother."
>
> "You say that two at Conway dwell,
> And two are gone to sea,
> Yet ye are seven!—I pray you tell,
> Sweet Maid, how this may be."

Then did the little Maid reply,
"Seven boys and girls are we;
Two of us in the church-yard lie,
Beneath the church-yard tree."

"You run about, my little Maid,
Your limbs they are alive;
If two are in the church-yard laid,
Then ye are only five."

"Their graves are green, they may be seen,"
The little Maid replied,
"Twelve steps or more from my mother's door,
And they are side by side.

"My stockings there I often knit,
My kerchief there I hem;
And there upon the ground I sit,
And sing a song to them.

"And often after sunset, Sir,
When it is light and fair,
I take my little porringer,
And eat my supper there.

"The first that died that sister Jane;
In bed she moaning lay,
Till God released her of her pain;
And then she went away.

"So in the church-yard she was laid;
And, when the grass was dry,
Together round her grave we played,
My brother John and I.

"And when the ground was white with snow,
And I could run and slide,
My brother John was forced to go,
And he lies by her side."

"How many are you, then," said I,
"If they two are in heaven?"
Quick was the little Maid's reply,
"O Master! we are seven."

"But they are dead; those two are dead!
Their spirits are in heaven!"
'T was throwing words away; for still
The little Maid would have her will,
And said, "Nay, we are seven!"

Perhaps the secret behind no other great poem was for so long concealed as in the case of "Lines Written a Few Miles Above Tintern Abbey," which did not become public knowledge until 1925. Outwardly cold, painfully reticent, Wordsworth said only that the poem was composed under the most pleasant circumstances: while walking with his sister one summer day the ten miles from the ruins of Tintern Abbey to Bristol. Not a word was written down until he reached Bristol, and not a line was altered. That was all Wordsworth ever said about the poem.

But not even a free-wheeling extrovert, and one less jealous than Wordsworth was of his moral reputation, would be likely to reveal the chain of events that led to the state of mind the poet was in when he wrote the poem. Few people, in fact, would be able to stand off and take such an objective view of themselves. Certainly Wordsworth did not.

We must go back to 1791, seven years before Wordsworth wrote the poem. The gaunt, solemn-eyed and reserved Cambridge graduate went to France during the French Revolution, and sought cheap lodgings at Orleans to be "out of the way of my countrymen, that I might learn the language affluently." At Orleans he met Annette Vallon, the vivacious twenty-five-year-old daughter of a surgeon of Blois, who was staying at her brother Paul's home in Orleans. Wordsworth visited the Vallon home frequently, and found Annette a willing teacher of the language. They fell in love. Before many weeks had passed Annette realized she was going to have a child by the Englishman.

Wordsworth remained near Annette until about November 1, 1792, then went—or fled?—to Paris. Their child was born on December 15th and christened Anne Caroline Wordsworth, with the poet's permission. Annette wanted the dour poet to marry her. Why he avoided it is not known, but his pre-occupation with himself might be at least part of the explanation. Moreover, they were of different religions, he lacked money and position and when passion was spent they probably had little in common. On the other hand, Wordsworth was not a man who could blithely ignore his duty.

Wordsworth returned to England, January 1, 1793, without seeing his child. He explained to Annette that he was "dragged by a chain of harsh necessity." He may have been referring to the necessity for him to raise some money, or he may have become involved in revolutionary intrigues that forced him to flee France. Letters from Annette show that she was expecting her lover's early return.

But France declared war on England, February 1, 1793. This was a period of inner turmoil for the young poet: a fervent republican, sympathizer of France, and deeply in love with a French woman who bore him a child out of wedlock. There is much evidence that Wordsworth risked the dangers of war and the Terror to go to France in October, 1793, in the hope of seeing Annette and reaching an understanding that would hold until the war ended. Apparently the dangers were too great to effect a meeting between them.

The war between France and England lasted nine years. The first few of these years Wordsworth suffered the pains of separation and remorse—emotions not revealed in his inspired utterances of high calm. In fact, he was never the unfailingly serene man his poetry suggests. We know that at this period the poet went off on strange solitary jaunts, no doubt seeking to understand himself, building a hard shell around his emotions, resolving against any further surrender to passion, and seeking from nature the healing of his heart and mind. Although his conscience would not permit him to renounce Annette, nevertheless his ardor gradually waned and with it his sense of guilt.

Slowly over the years Wordsworth achieved the calm and ease of mind he sought. Nature—which had meant much to him as a boy and youth—now gave him joy and elevated his mind and spirit. In celebrating his communion with nature and its grandeur he suggests a pantheism under a cloak of orthodoxy.

Thus it was in 1798 a now peaceful Wordsworth, cleansed by nature of the passion that had lacerated body and soul, but still with memories and guilt too strong for time yet to have annulled, walked the beautiful English countryside with his beloved sister Dorothy, and in an unwonted burst of inspiration reached this height of his poetic genius. Henceforth little else but nature would seize his imagination and deeply charge his muse, except in a few notable instances.

> Five years have passed; five summers, with the length
> Of five long winters! and again I hear
> These waters, rolling from their mountain-springs
> With a soft inland murmur.—Once again
> Do I behold these steep and lofty cliffs,
> That on a wild secluded scene impress
> Thoughts of a more deep seclusion; and connect
> The landscape with the quiet of the sky.

The day is come when I again repose
Here, under this dark sycamore, and view
These plots of cottage-ground, these orchard-tufts,
Which at this season, with their unripe fruits,
Are clad in one green hue, and lose themselves
'Mid groves and copses. Once again I see
These hedge-rows, hardly hedge-rows, little lines
Of sportive wood run wild: these pastoral farms,
Green to the very door; and wreaths of smoke
Sent up, in silence, from among the trees!
With some uncertain notice, as might seem
Of vagrant dwellers in the houseless woods,
Or of some Hermit's cave, where by his fire
The Hermit sits alone.   These beauteous forms,
Through a long absence, have not been to me
As is a landscape to a blind man's eye:
But oft in lonely rooms, and 'mid the din
Of towns and cities, I have owed to them
In hours of weariness, sensations sweet,
Felt in the blood, and felt along the heart;
And passing even into my purer mind,
With tranquil restoration;—feelings too
Of unremembered pleasure: such, perhaps,
As have no slight or trivial influence
On that best portion of a good man's life,
His little, nameless, unremembered acts
Of kindness and of love. Nor less, I trust,
To them I may have owed another gift,
Of aspect more sublime; that blessèd mood,
In which the burthen of the mystery,
In which the heavy and the weary weight
Of all this unintelligible world,
Is lightened:—that serene and blessed mood,
In which the affections gently lead us on,—
Until, the breath of this corporeal frame
And even the motion of our human blood
Almost suspended, we are laid asleep
In body, and become a living soul:
While with an eye made quiet by the power
Of harmony, and the deep power of joy,
We see into the life of things.   If this
Be but a vain belief, yet, oh! how oft—
In darkness and amid the many shapes

Of joyless daylight; when the fretful stir
Unprofitable, and the fever of the world,
Have hung upon the beatings of my heart—
How oft, in spirit, have I turned to thee,
O sylvan Wye! thou wanderer thro' the woods,
How often has my spirit turned to thee!
   And now, with gleams of half-extinguished thought,
With many recognitions dim and faint,
And somewhat of a sad perplexity,
The picture of the mind revives again:
While here I stand, not only with the sense
Of present pleasure, but with pleasing thoughts
That in this moment there is life and food
For future years. And so I dare to hope,
Though changed, no doubt, from what I was when first
I came among these hills; when like a roe
I bounded o'er the mountains, by the sides
Of the deep rivers, and the lonely streams,
Wherever nature led: more like a man
Flying from something that he dreads, than one
Who sought the thing he loved. For nature then
(The coarser pleasures of my boyish days,
And their glad animal movements all gone by)
To me was all in all.—I cannot paint
What then I was. The sounding cataract
Haunted me like a passion; the tall rock,
The mountain, and the deep and gloomy wood,
Their colors and their forms, were then to me
An appetite; a feeling and a love,
That had no need of a remoter charm,
By thought supplied, nor any interest
Unborrowed from the eye.—That time is past,
And all its aching joys are now no more,
And all its dizzy raptures. Not for this
Faint I, nor mourn nor murmur; other gifts
Have followed; for such loss, I would believe,
Abundant recompense. For I have learned
To look on nature, not as in the hour
Of thoughtless youth; but hearing oftentimes
The still, sad music of humanity,
Nor harsh, nor grating, though of ample power
To chasten and subdue. And I have felt
A presence that disturbs me with the joy
Of elevated thoughts; a sense sublime
Of something far more deeply interfused,

Whose dwelling is the light of setting suns,
And the round ocean and the living air,
And the blue sky, and in the mind of man;
A motion and a spirit, that impels
All thinking things, all objects of all thought,
And rolls through all things. Therefore am I still
A lover of the meadows and the woods,
And mountains; and of all that we behold
From this green earth; of all the mighty world
Of eye, and ear,—both what they half create,
And what perceive; well pleased to recognize
In nature and the language of the sense,
The anchor of my purest thoughts, the nurse,
The guide, the guardian of my heart, and soul
Of all my moral being.
                              Nor perchance,
If I were not thus taught, should I the more
Suffer my genial spirits to decay:
For thou art with me here upon the banks
Of this fair river; thou my dearest Friend,
My dear, dear Friend; and in thy voice I catch
The language of my former heart, and read
My former pleasures in the shooting lights
Of thy wild eyes. Oh! yet a little while
May I behold in thee what I was once,
My dear, dear Sister! and this prayer I make,
Knowing that Nature never did betray
The heart that loved her; 't is her privilege,
Through all the years of this our life, to lead
From joy to joy: for she can so inform
The mind that is within us, so impress
With quietness and beauty, and so feed
With lofty thoughts, that neither evil tongues,
Rash judgments, nor the sneers of selfish men,
Nor greetings where no kindness is, nor all
The dreary intercourse of daily life,
Shall e'er prevail against us or disturb
Our cheerful faith, that all which we behold
Is full of blessings. Therefore let the moon
Shine on thee in thy solitary walk;
And let the misty mountain-winds be free
To blow against thee: and, in after years,
When these wild ecstasies shall be matured
Into a sober pleasure; when thy mind
Shall be a mansion for all lovely forms,

Thy memory be as a dwelling-place
For all sweet sounds and harmonies; oh! then,
If solitude, or fear, or pain, or grief,
Should be thy portion, with what healing thoughts
Of tender joy wilt thou remember me,
And these my exhortations! Nor, perchance—
If I should be where I no more can hear
Thy voice, nor catch from thy wild eyes these gleams
Of past existence—wilt thou then forget
That on the banks of this delightful stream
We stood together; and that I, so long
A worshipper of Nature, hither came
Unwearied in that service: rather say
With warmer love—oh! with far deeper zeal
Of holier love. Nor wilt thou then forget,
That after many wanderings, many years
Of absence, these steep woods and lofty cliffs,
And this green pastoral landscape, were to me
More dear, both for themselves and for thy sake!

Wordsworth's affair with Annette Vallon had an odd termination. In 1802 the poet and Mary Hutchinson, a friend since childhood, agreed to marry. He told her about his French mistress and before the marriage Wordsworth and his sister Dorothy went to Calais, France, to meet Annette and obtain her release. His peace of mind and dignity required such an agreement.

Exactly what happened at Calais is not known, and why they remained there a month can only be conjectured. Maybe Annette still wanted to marry him, at least for the sake of their child who was at Calais with her. Or perhaps the long stay was due to Wordsworth's ineptness in personal relations.

Eventually an understanding was reached. The tranquillity this settlement gave the poet is reflected in his lovely sonnet "It is a Beauteous Evening." The "Dear child" referred to in the poem is obviously his nine-year-old daughter Caroline, whom he was seeing for the first time.

In the years that followed Wordsworth grew callous about the affair. In 1820 he and his wife visited Paris, took lodgings in the same street where the now married Annette lived, and frequently visited her home with his wife. Annette died in 1841 in poor circumstances. The poet had since the Calais meeting provided Caroline with an annuity of thirty pounds, and in 1835 concluded the arrangement with a settlement of four hundred pounds.

It is a beauteous evening, calm and free,
The holy time is quiet as a Nun
Breathless with adoration; the broad sun

In sinking down in its tranquillity;
The gentleness of heaven broods o'er the Sea:
Listen! the mighty Being is awake,
And doth with his eternal motion make
A sound like thunder—everlastingly.
Dear Child! dear Girl! that walkest with me here,
If thou appear untouched by solemn thought,
Thy nature is not therefore less divine:
Thou liest in Abraham's bosom all the year;
And worship'st at the Temple's inner shrine,
God being with thee when we know it not.

Once Wordsworth thought of writing a love poem, but dismissed the idea because "I feared I might write it with a degree of warmth which could hardly have been approved by my principles, and which might be undesirable for the reader."

But it may also have been that when he married quiet, simple Mary Hutchinson he was seeking not raptures but a peaceful home, where he could seclude himself from the world and be ministered unto by a household centered around his poetic mission. Mary gave him this sweetness and devotion, believing him to be as great as he considered himself.

Five years after their marriage, Wordsworth wrote this lyric to the gentle, adoring woman he once admitted was "too good for him." Though devoid of passion, the lines breathe the comforting peace and selflessness of the gracious woman who shared the last forty-eight years of his life:

She was a Phantom of delight
When first she gleamed upon my sight;
A lovely Apparition, sent
To be a moment's ornament;
Her eyes as stars of Twilight fair;
Like Twilight's, too, her dusky hair;
But all things else about her drawn
From May-time and the cheerful Dawn;
A dancing Shape, an Image gay,
To haunt, to startle, and waylay.

I saw her upon nearer view,
A Spirit, yet a Woman too!
Her household motions light and free,
And steps of virgin-liberty;
A countenance in which did meet
Sweet records, promises as sweet;
A Creature not too bright or good

For human nature's daily food;
For transient sorrows, simple wiles,
Praise, blame, love, kisses, tears, and smiles.

And now I see with eye serene
The very pulse of the machine;
A Being breathing thoughtful breath,
A Traveller between life and death;
The reason firm, the temperate will,
Endurance, foresight, strength, and skill;
A perfect Woman, nobly planned,
To warn, to comfort, and command;
And yet a Spirit still, and bright
With something of angelic light.

SIR HENRY WOTTON (1568-1639)

The Character of a Happy Life

Although one of the most widely cultivated Englishmen of his time, Sir Henry Wotton's simple piety preserved his serenity when he fell from his monarch's good graces, and it caused him to put his musings into a famous poem. Odd as it may appear, a casually phrased quip produced the circumstances that led to the writing of the poem.

Despite a temperament that inclined him to scholarly pursuits, poetry, quiet days and a few intimate friends, nobly born Wotton early in life decided upon a diplomatic career. He set out to equip himself for it by studying history and statecraft in the course of extensive foreign travels, and serving the court of Queen Elizabeth in relatively minor capacities. When James I succeeded to the throne Wotton was appointed ambassador to the city-state of Venice.

On his way to Venice in 1604 a friend in Augsburg, Germany, asked Wotton to write a few lines in an album. The amiable ambassador wrote out a little jest in Latin, which in translation reads: "An ambassador is an honest man, sent to lie abroad for the good of his country." Harmless enough, though perhaps indiscreet coming from a diplomat.

Wotton was well-liked and successful at Venice, and with the support of Lord Salisbury, Secretary of State, and the Prince of Wales, was destined to be given higher positions by the King.

However, in 1611, an unscrupulous literary gladiator named Gaspar

Scioppius published a blistering attack on King James in which he quoted Wotton's quip about ambassadors and expatiated at length upon it to impeach the monarch's honor. The furious King refused to accept Wotton's explanation that the quotation was a mere piece of private fun. Moreover, just previously death had removed Salisbury and the Prince of Wales, the two people who could have stayed the King's anger and kept Wotton in position for promotion.

This was what Wotton called his "fatal year." But in his adversity he bore, not bitterness, but the philosophic-religious consolation of a scholarly gentleman who always thought of himself as "a plain Kentish man." At that time he wrote a friend "that we learn hereafter to plant ourselves better than upon the grace or breath of men." But more important, in this year of misfortunes the worldly-wise but essentially simple man spelled out his reflections in an immortal poem:

> How happy is he born and taught
> That serveth not another's will;
> Whose armor is his honest thought,
> And simple truth his utmost skill!
>
> Whose passions not his masters are;
>   Whose soul is still prepared for death,
> Not tied unto the world by care
>   Of public fame or private breath;
>
> Who envies none that chance doth raise,
>   Nor vice; who never understood
> How deepest wounds are given by praise;
>   Nor rules of state, but rules of good;
>
> Who hath his life from rumors freed;
>   Whose conscience is his strong retreat;
> Whose state can neither flatterers feed,
>   Nor ruin make oppressors great;
>
> Who God doth late and early pray
>   More of His grace than gifts to lend;
> And entertains the harmless day
>   With a well-chosen book or friend;
>
> —This man is freed from servile bands
>   Of hope to rise, or fear to fall:
> Lord of himself, though not of lands;
>   And having nothing, yet hath all.

WILLIAM BUTLER YEATS (1865-1939)

The Lake Isle of Innisfree

Sometime before his fifteenth year Yeats was inspired to the simple life when his father read to him passages from Thoreau's *Walden*. Years later he recalled "that having conquered bodily desires and the inclination of my mind towards women and love, I should live, as Thoreau lived, seeking wisdom." And since Sligo, Ireland, was always thought of as home by the Yeats children, what place could be more appropriate for the living of such a life? And where in Sligo but on the beautiful and legend-steeped island of Innisfree, in Lough Gill opposite Slish Wood? There, the dreamy youth decided, is where he would build his cottage and live as Thoreau lived.

Several years later the Yeats family moved to London. But Sligo was not forgotten: the poet painted a map of it and hung it on the wall of his room. And when Willie was urged by his father to write a story he wrote about a man in London who longed for Sligo whenever he was in distress.

The tall, darkly handsome young man was not happy in London: he rebelled against the hack literary work he was doing, sometimes imagined the streets of the metropolis as filled with "souls of the lost" and protested that the city was "dull and dirty." When Yeats vacationed briefly in Sligo he wrote that "it was more dear than any other place. . . . I should like to live here always."

But the poet had to return to London. Several months later, in December, 1888, he continued what he then called his "old day-dream," and told of it in his most quoted poem:

I will arise and go now, and go to Innisfree,
And a small cabin build there, of clay and wattles made:
Nine bean rows will I have there, a hive for the honey bee,
And live alone in the bee-loud glade.

And I shall have some peace there, for peace comes dropping slow,
Dropping from the veils of the morning to where the cricket sings;
There midnight's all a glimmer, and noon a purple glow,
And evening full of the linnet's wings.

I will arise and go now, for always night and day
I hear lake water lapping with low sounds by the shore;
While I stand on the roadway, or on the pavements gray,
I hear it in the deep heart's core.

Part II

THE SONGS

SARAH FLOWER ADAMS (1805-1848)

Nearer, My God, To Thee

Although we do not know the circumstances under which "Nearer, My God, To Thee" was written, the life of Sarah Flower Adams provides reasons enough for her to write these words of faith and spiritual yearning.

This English woman of singular beauty and high ideals was left motherless at an early age, saw her father, a Non-conformist newspaper proprietor, imprisoned for his attacks on the character of the bishop of Llandaff, and on her father's death she and her sister Eliza went to live in the home of Reverend Mr. Fox, a brilliant Liberal preacher, Member of Parliament and a man of some literary influence.

It is reasonable to suppose that the life of the two sisters in the Fox home was at least uncomfortable on occasion, especially to one of Sarah's delicate health and uncertain temperament. When the two sisters moved into the home, Mrs. Fox left with three of the children, leaving the other children to be cared for by Eliza Flower, who was placed in charge of the household. This meant the end of Eliza's musical career, in which her friend Robert Browning had such high hopes. It also terminated Browning's apparently romantic interest in Eliza, though he remained nominally friendly with the sisters and Mr. Fox. Incidentally, there is no suggestion that the friendship between Fox and Eliza was anything but intellectual. Nevertheless there was certain to have been gossip and unpleasant speculations by neighborhood busybodies, which would distress sensitive Sarah, as well as Eliza.

But Sarah Flower's greatest disappointment was her failure to achieve theatrical success, in spite of her feverish efforts. She wrote and studied hard for the stage, and repeatedly demonstrated her dramatic ability at private appointments with experts. Then just when she began to appear successfully in Shakespearean roles, deafness and a physical breakdown permanently removed her from the theatrical scene.

In 1834 Sarah married Brydes Adams, an engineer and occasional inventor. It was not a happy union.

If Harriet Martineau's acid characterization is to be accepted, Sarah Flower was well-meaning but impotent to perform, indecisive, socially blundering, unstable and fated to do wrong.

If Francis M. Sims is to be believed, Robert Browning wrote the famous hymn in a spirit of literary generosity for his friends, Sarah Flower allegedly being incapable of so lofty an effort, though a recognized poet.

And if careless popularizers are not to be read with discretion, we are to believe that Sarah wrote the words of the hymn on her deathbed.

Actually, the song was published in 1842 and apparently written two years earlier for a hymnal compiled by Eliza and Mr. Fox.

Sarah Flower Adams died eight years after the hymn was written. Surely her life of uncertainty, disappointment, unhappy marriage and persisting delicate health which eventually manifested itself as the tuberculosis of which she died—surely the total effect was enough to cause one of her temperament and ability to write this song of faith and hope. It is the prayer of a weary, disheartened soul, such as Sarah Flower Adams was in 1840.

> Nearer, my God, to Thee,
>   Nearer to Thee!
> E'en though it be a cross
>   That raiseth me;
> Still all my song shall be,
> Nearer, my God, to Thee,
>   Nearer to Thee!
>
> Though like the wanderer,
>   The sun gone down,
> Darkness be over me,
>   My rest a stone;
> Yet in my dreams I'd be
> Nearer, my God, to Thee,
>   Nearer to Thee!
>
> There let my way appear
>   Steps unto heaven;
> All that Thou sendest me
>   In mercy given;
> Angels to beckon me
> Nearer, my God, to Thee,
>   Nearer to Thee!
>
> Then with my waking thoughts
>   Bright with Thy praise,
> Out of my stony griefs,
>   Bethel I'll raise;
> So by my woes to be
> Nearer, my God, to Thee,
>   Nearer to Thee!
>
> Or, if on joyful wing,
>   Cleaving the sky,
> Sun, moon, and starts forgot,
>   Upward I fly,

Still all my song shall be
Nearer, my God, to Thee,
Nearer to Thee!

SABINE BARING-GOULD (1834-1924)

Onward, Christian Soldiers

The writing of "Onward, Christian Soldiers" was a slight event in the remarkable life and astonishing activities of Sabine Baring-Gould, country parson, archaeologist, folk-lorist, antiquarian, historian, poet and novelist. And yet this seeming minor achievement at the beginning of his long career is today the one piece of writing that has kept his name in the hall of fame.

A week after receiving Anglican orders Baring-Gould went to Harbury, England, as a curate. His pastor promptly put him to work establishing a mission chapel at Harbury Brig, a small boom-town within the parish. The young clergyman became popular with the tough canal boatmen and factory workers at the mission location and soon he had a robust choir and other religious activities underway.

On the Saturday before Whit Sunday of 1864 the versatile curate decided it would be interesting to have a new hymn for the children to march to when they paraded the next day from their mission chapel to the parish church in Harbury. Baring-Gould thereupon wrote the stirring lines for a tune arranged from the slow movement in Haydn's Symphony in D, number 15, and it was to this music that the children marched the next day behind a band. Neither the author, musicians or the hymn's first singers could possibly have realized they were introducing a song that would have few, if any, rivals in its sphere. Later the words were sung to Sir Arthur Sullivan's "St. Gertrude," the tune now always used.

Despite the universal popularity of the hymn, pacifists have objected it was militaristic, and a few have protested that the phrase "With the cross of Jesus" gave the hymn a Papal tinge. Nevertheless it continues to be the great song of militant Christianity:

Onward, Christian soldiers,
Marching as to war,
With the cross of Jesus
Going on before!
Christ, the royal Master,
Leads against the foe;

Forward into battle,
See his banners go.
Onward, Christian soldiers,
Marching as to war,
With the cross of Jesus
Going on before!

At the sign of triumph
Satan's host doth flee;
On, then, Christian soldiers,
On to victory!
Hell's foundations quiver
At the shout of praise;
Brothers, lift your voices,
Loud your anthems raise!

Like a mighty army
Moves the Church of God;
Brother, we are treading
Where the saints have trod;
We are not divided,
All one Body we,
One in body and doctrine,
One in charity.

Crowns and thrones may perish,
Kingdoms rise and wane,
But the Church of Jesus
Constant will remain;
Gates of hell can never
'Gainst that Church prevail;
We have Christ's own promise,
And that cannot fail.

Onward, then, ye people!
Join our happy throng!
Blend with ours your voices
In the triumph song!
Glory, laud, and honor,
Unto Christ the King;
This through countless ages
Men and angels sing.
Onward, Christian soldiers,
Marching as to war,
With the cross of Jesus
Going on before!

KATHARINE LEE BATES (1859-1929)

America the Beautiful

When Katharine Lee Bates returned to her native New England from Oxford University with a Master's Degree, she expressed her delight to be back among "the scenery that is most beautiful to me." America was a vision that shone as brightly within her on European trips as when she was teaching high school and later headed the English Department at Wellesley College. It was an ideal that flashed briefly in many of her poems, essays and stories. She thought of her native land as a "pioneer of brotherhood among nations," and a "pure, august, authentic commonweal." But she had yet to bring the vision to full flower in the poetry she began writing as a happy child in Falmouth, Massachusetts, on the Atlantic Ocean.

In 1893 Miss Bates was invited to lecture at the summer session of Colorado College. At Colorado Springs she met Woodrow Wilson, Hamlin Garland and other congenial colleagues and taught amid unsurpassed scenic splendors. One day she went with a party in a prairie-wagon to the summit of Pike's Peak, and later said "Our sojourn on the peak remains in memory hardly more than an ecstatic gaze. It was then and there, as I was looking out over the sea-like expanse of fertile country spreading away so far under those ample skies, that the opening lines of the hymn floated into my mind."

But her critical faculty failed her. She put the poem aside. It was not published until two years later, in *The Congregationalist,* a Boston journal, and quickly gained attention all over the nation. Oddly enough, a few people criticized her use of the word "Beautiful," an objection the poet firmly rejected because to her America was truly beautiful.

As the poem grew in popularity a competition for the best music to it was held in 1926. Nine hundred compositions were submitted, but none judged worthy. Today the words are sung to the music of Samuel A. Ward's "Materna." It is regarded by many as our second national anthem. Miss Bates believed its popularity "due to the fact that Americans are at heart idealists, with a fundamental faith in human brotherhood." Surely Americans are ennobled by it to celebrate the material splendor and spiritual qualities of the land and the people.

> O beautiful for spacious skies,
> For amber waves of grain,
> For purple mountain majesties
> Above the fruitful plain!
> America! America!
> God shed his grace on thee,

And crown thy good with brotherhood
From sea to shining sea!

O beautiful for pilgrim feet,
Whose stern, impassioned stress
A thoroughfare for freedom beat
Across the wilderness!
America! America!
God mend thine every flaw,
Confirm thy soul in self-control,
Thy liberty in law!

O beautiful for heroes proved
In liberating strife,
Who more than self their country loved,
And mercy more than life!
America! America!
May God thy gold refine
Till all success be nobleness
And every gain divine!

O beautiful for patriot dream
That sees beyond the years
Thine alabaster cities gleam
Undimmed by human tears!
America! America!
God shed His grace on thee
And crown thy good with brotherhood
From sea to shining sea!

STEPHEN FOSTER (1826-1864)

My Old Kentucky Home
Jeanie With the Light Brown Hair

In Bardstown, Kentucky, there is a stately old mansion named Federal Hill, originally the home of Judge and U. S. Senator John Rowan, a relative of Stephen Foster. Today it is owned and maintained by the State of Kentucky as a museum, and referred to as "My Old Kentucky Home." A plaque in the mansion claims that in 1852 Foster composed and wrote his song "My Old Kentucky Home" at Federal Hill. Visitors are shown the bed Foster slept in, and the piano he used in composing. Although the custodians of the building and local residents will not insist on the strict accuracy of these claims, they do state that Foster received his inspiration for the song while visiting the Rowan's home.

Evidence supporting Federal Hill as the song's inspiration has been marshaled by John Tasker Howard in his admirable biography of Foster, but Mr. Howard makes no unqualified claims.

For example, it has been said that Foster, on his honeymoon in August, 1850, visited Federal Hill. Howard states there is no documentary evidence of this, but that it has been proved that the Rowans were away from home at that time.

However, Foster and his wife did leave Pittsburgh in early March, 1852, on a New Orleans bound boat. They went to the Mardi Gras with a group of friends, the song-writer's first visit to the South his songs celebrated. Forty-eight years later one of those in the Foster party told a newspaper reporter that on this trip Foster visited and was captivated by Federal Hill, and upon his return to Pittsburgh wrote the song. Certainly the setting and traditions of Federal Hill were such as to evoke the genius of the gentle, dreamy, home-loving young man, and it seems quite likely Foster visited there at least once, and possibly several times in his youth while living for a short while in Cincinnati.

The probable truth of the song's origin is pleasant and logical enough to make unnecessary and inexcusable such legendary nonsense as that Foster, desperately in need of money, called on Judge Rowan with the manuscript of the song in the hope of selling it to him, but changed his mind and gave it to him. The absurdity of the yarn is patent because the Judge died nine years before the song was written.

However, when a song as appealing as this one becomes famous, legends are bound to gather about it.

> The sun shines bright in our old Kentucky home;
>   'Tis summer, the darkeys are gay;
> The corn top's ripe and the meadow's in the bloom,
>   While the birds make music all the day;
> The young folks roll on the little cabin floor,
>   All merry, all happy, and bright;
> By'm by hard times comes a knockin' at the door,—
>   Then, my old Kentucky home, good night!

> *Chorus:*
>   Weep no more, my lady; O, weep no more today!
>   We'll sing one song for my old Kentucky home,
>   For our old Kentucky home far away.

They hunt no more for the possum and the coon,
  On the meadow, the hill, and the shore;
They sing no more by the glimmer of the moon,
  On the bench by the old cabin door;
The day goes by, like a shadow o'er the heart,
  With sorrow where all was delight;
The time has come, when the darkeys have to part,
  Then, my old Kentucky home, good night!
Weep no more, my lady, &c.

The head must bow, and the back will have to bend,
  Wherever the darkey may go;
A few more days, and the troubles all will end,
  In the field where the sugar-canes grow;
A few more days to tote the weary load,
  No matter it will never be light;
A few more days till we totter on the road,
  Then, my old Kentucky home, good night!
Weep no more, my lady, &c.

"Jeanie With the Light Brown Hair" has generally been accepted as the auburn-haired beauty, Jane McDowell, whom Foster married in July, 1850, and separated from in 1854. It appears to have been one of those marriages where both parties loved one another, but not with ardor great enough to overcome the difficulties which arose during their brief life together.

Foster, though unfailingly kind and genial, was hardly the perfect husband for a woman of Jane's background and temperament. He was moody, she was buoyant and loved life. He was fond of drinking, associated with the theatre at a time when that was frowned upon by "respectable" people, and he was passionately devoted to music. Perhaps her husband's dreaminess and unpractical approach to life was more than Jane could take. Perhaps, too, she had faults that contributed to the marriage's failure. But the fact remained she had to earn her living when she realized how improvident her husband was.

They did not part in enmity. They saw each other from time to time, and they corresponded.

Foster used his wife's name in five of his songs, but only in "Jeanie With the Light Brown Hair" did he achieve a successful love song. And in it, written a year after their separation, he expressed the longing and tenderness of a man still in love.

Ten years later, when Foster died in a charity ward at Bellevue Hospital in New York City, thirty-eight cents were found in his pocket with a slip on which he had written "Dear Friends and Gentle Hearts." "Jeanie" accompanied Foster's brothers to New York when word came of the death.

I dream of Jeanie with the light brown hair,
Borne, like a vapor, on the summer air;
I see her tripping where the bright streams play,
Happy as the daisies that dance on her way.
Many were the wild notes her merry voice would pour,
Many were the blithe birds that warbled them o'er:
Oh! I dream of Jeanie with the light brown hair,
Floating like a vapor, on the summer air.

I long for Jeanie with the day-dawn smile,
Radiant in gladness, warm with winning guile;
I hear her melodies, like joys gone by,
Sighing round my heart o'er the fond hopes that die:—
Sighing like the wind and sobbing like the rain,—
Wailing for the lost one that comes not again:
Oh! I long for Jeanie and my heart bows low,
Never more to find her where the bright waters flow.

I sigh for Jeanie, but her light form strayed
Far from the fond hearts 'round her native glade;
Her smiles have vanished and her sweet songs flown,
Flitting like the dreams that have cheered us and gone.
Now the nodding wild flow'rs may wither on the shore
While her gentle fingers will cull them no more:
Oh! I sigh for Jeanie with the light brown hair,
Floating like a vapor, on the soft summer air.

JULIA WARD HOWE (1819-1910)

Battle Hymn of the Republic

In the Autumn of 1861 Dr. Samuel Gridley Howe and his charming wife arrived in Washington from their New England home. The adventurous and militantly humanitarian doctor, one of the pioneers of the semi-official U. S. Sanitary Commission, was a crusader in camps, hospitals and bureaus for better care of sick and wounded soldiers.

Mrs. Howe longed to make her contribution to the Union cause but could think of no way to help, except to make lint for bandaging. Her well-to-do and fashionable background had given her a facility in languages, a fine musical education, training of her excellent mezzo-soprano voice, and the opportunity to develop a talent for poetry. She was discouraged at her inability to discover a use for these polite accomplishments in behalf of the North.

Shortly after reaching the capital Mrs. Howe and some friends were returning in a carriage from a review of McClellan's troops outside the city. As they reached Washington's outskirts they were delayed by marching troops. To break the monotony she and her companions began to sing the war song of the day, "John Brown's Body," which the soldiers applauded and joined.

"Mrs. Howe," said one of the men in the party, "why don't you write some *good* words to that tune?"

"I have often wished to," replied Julia Ward Howe.

Before dawn the next morning Mrs. Howe awoke in her room at Willard's Hotel. Words, phrases and then sentences began swinging through her excited brain as it throbbed with the rhythm of marching feet. When the lines fell into their stanzas and began to march across her mind, Mrs. Howe arose in the half-light, groped for pencil and paper, hurriedly wrote out "The Battle Hymn of the Republic," and then went back to bed and sleep. When she awoke she had forgotten the words she had written down—but the nation has never forgotten them. They first appeared in the February, 1862, *Atlantic,* quickly spread to newspapers, broadsides, army song books, and became the words of the hour among Union soldiers. Today, one hundred years later, the verses hastily scrawled in the semi-dark on a scrap of paper still march on.

> Mine eyes have seen the glory of the coming of the Lord:
> He is trampling out the vintage where the grapes of wrath are stored;
> He hath loosed the fateful lightning of his terrible swift sword.
> > His truth is marching on.

> I have seen him in the watch-fires of a hundred circling camps;
> They have builded him an altar in the evening dews and damps;
> I can read his righteous sentence by the dim and flaring lamps.
> > His day is marching on.

> I have read a fiery gospel, writ in burnished rows of steel:
> "As ye deal with my contemners, so with you my grace shall deal;
> Let the Hero, born of woman, crush the serpent with his heel,
> > Since God is marching on."

> He has sounded forth the trumpet that shall never call retreat;
> He is sifting out the hearts of men before his judgment-seat:
> O, be swift, my soul to answer Him! be jubilant my feet!
> > Our God is marching on.

In the beauty of the lilies Christ was born across the sea,
With a glory in his bosom that transfigures you and me;
As he died to make men holy, let us die to make men free,
    While God is marching on.

FRANCIS SCOTT KEY (1779-1843)

The Star-Spangled Banner

Americans owe their national anthem to the friendship of Francis Scott Key, a young lawyer of Baltimore, for Dr. William Beanes of Upper Marlboro, Maryland. During the War of 1812 the British seized Beanes for suspected spying and put him aboard one of their war vessels in Chesapeake Bay. Key determined to visit British Admiral Cockburn and plead for the doctor's release before a trial and possible execution took place.

Armed only with credentials from President Monroe and evidence of Beanes' innocence, Key sailed out into Chesapeake Bay on a flag-of-truce boat used for the exchange of prisoners of war. It was a critical period for the young nation. The national Capitol and White House had been burned by the British, the shores of Chesapeake Bay raked by gunfire from British ships, and the southern coast invaded and villages and plantations pillaged. At the moment only Fort McHenry stood between the British and the capture of Baltimore and Annapolis, and a new march on Washington.

When Key's little boat drew alongside the Admiral's flagship he was told Dr. Beanes had been put in the custody of Vice Admiral Cochrane. The Vice Admiral courteously listened to Key and agreed to release the doctor, but refused to allow the American to return to shore before the British fleet had reduced Fort McHenry, an action then being prepared. Cochrane knew the prisoner and his rescuer had seen the fleet readying for the attack and did not want them to alert the Americans.

Key and his party were first detained on board the *Surprise* and later placed under guard on their flag-of-truce vessel after the battle began the morning of September 14, 1814. The young attorney's distress was great as he watched the attack on the fort, defended by a small force, including volunteers under the command of his brother-in-law, Judge Joseph Hopper Nicholson. He realized that as a volunteer in the artillery he belonged at the fort. All he could do was to keep his eyes on the fort's flag, until darkness enfolded it.

The British launched simultaneous land and sea attacks on Fort Mc-

Henry. While British vessels bombarded from two and one-half miles off shore—beyond range of the fort's smaller guns—a British land force moved against the small brick and earth fortification.

During that agonizing night the Americans on their little boat in the Bay knew only that the flag still flew over the fort when they glimpsed it by the light of exploding bomb shells. They became apprehensive a little after midnight when the British ships ceased firing. Did it mean that the fort had surrendered? An hour later the ships moved in closer and resumed their bombardment, indicating the fort was still holding out. Key did not know that the land force had been repulsed and that the capture of the fort was now solely up to the sixteen British frigates.

Just before dawn all firing ceased. Again the desperate apprehension. Had the fort surrendered or been captured? The young American attorney paced the deck of his little vessel, futilely peering with binoculars through the dawn-vapors rising off the water for a sign of the flag over the fort. At last, as the mist cleared and the sun began to peep over the horizon, Key saw that the British had failed and "the flag was still there."

At that inspiring moment Key began to jot down on the back of a letter words that will always thrill Americans. As the boat moved up the Bay to Baltimore, Key continued writing and that same day showed his immortal stanzas to Judge Nicholson, second in command at the fort. Nicholson immediately had the lines printed and distributed as a handbill titled "Bombardment of Fort McHenry," with the suggestion it be sung to the air "To Anacreon in Heaven," a tune then well-known. One hundred and seventeen years later Congress got around to designating it as the nation's national anthem—which in fact it had been accepted as for years.

> Oh, say, can you see, by the dawn's early light,
> What so proudly we hail'd at the twilight's last gleaming?
> Whose broad stripes and bright stars, through the perilous fight,
> O'er the ramparts we watched were so gallantly streaming,
> And the rockets' red glare, the bombs bursting in air,
> Gave proof through the night that our flag was still there;
> Oh, say, does that star-spangled banner yet wave,
> O'er the land of the free and the home of the brave?
>
> On the shore dimly seen, through the mists of the deep,
> Where the foe's haughty host in dread silence reposes,
> What is that which the breeze, o'er the towering steep,
> As it fitfully blows, half conceals, half discloses?
> Now it catches the gleam of the morning's first beam,
> In full glory reflected, now shines on the stream;
> 'Tis the star-spangled banner; Oh long way it wave
> O'er the land of the free and the home of the brave.

Oh, thus be it ever when freemen shall stand,
Between their lov'd homes and the war's desolation;
Blest with vict'ry and peace, may the heav'n-rescued land
Praise the Power that hath made and preserved us a nation.
Then conquer we must, when our cause it is just,
And this be our motto:—"In God is our trust";
And the star-spangled banner in triumph shall wave
O'er the land of the free, and the home of the brave.

HENRY FRANCIS LYTE (1793-1847)

Abide With Me

Henry Francis Lyte often needed the spiritual comfort given to so many by the famous hymn he wrote, and which in fact was composed primarily to assuage his own feelings at a critical period of his life.

Poverty plagued the youth of this English-born but Irish-educated clergyman of the Church of England. He took holy orders at the age of twenty-one and began his ministry in a remote parish in Ireland. But religious doubts soon troubled the always delicate young man, and he began to worry for fear he had made a grave mistake in choosing the Church instead of a medical career.

This gnawing indecision ended when a desperately ill brother-minister asked Lyte to call on him and give spiritual counsel that would sweep away the dying man's doubts. In the course of his long discussions with the mortally ill man, the younger minister not only guided his friend into the comforting channels of faith, but the force of the currents he activated turned him in the same direction.

Henry Lyte was at the bedside when his dying friend kept praying "Abide with me." When the end came the frail young man was greatly moved, and immediately wrote the hymn "Abide With Me."

Twenty-four years later—many of them troubled and a few of them stormy —Lyte was fifty-four and seriously ill of tuberculosis. He was clearing away papers preparatory to leaving the next day for Italy in search of better health, when he came upon the words of the hymn he had written. He recalled the occasion that inspired them and thought how appropriate to his present circumstances. Early that Sunday evening of September 4, 1847, the tired-out man worked over the poem and composed music for it. The next day he left for the Continent, stopped at Menton, France, then became too ill to go on to Italy. He died on November 20th, but his song lives on:

Abide with me: fast falls the eventide;
The darkness deepens; Lord with me abide:
When other helpers fail, and comforts flee,
Help of the helpless, oh, abide with me!

Swift to its close ebbs our life's little day;
Earth's joys grow dim, its glories pass away;
Change and decay in all around I see:
O Thou Who changeth not, abide with me!

Not a brief glance, I beg, a passing word,
But, as Thou dwell'st with Thy disciples, Lord,
Familiar, condescending, patient, free,—
Come, not to sojourn, but abide with me!

Come not in terrors, as the King of kings;
But kind and good, with healing in Thy wings:
Tears for all woes, a heart for every plea;
Come, Friend of sinners, and abide with me!

Thou on my head in early youth didst smile,
And, though rebellious and perverse meanwhile,
Thou hast not left me, oft as I left Thee;
On 'to the close, O Lord, abide with me!

I need Thy presence every passing hour:
What but Thy grace can foil the tempter's power:
Who like Thyself my guide and stay can be?
Through cloud and sunshine, oh, abide with me!

I fear no foe with Thee at hand to bless;
Ills have no weights, and tears no bitterness;
Where is death's sting? where, grave, thy victory?
I triumph still, if Thou abide with me.

Hold then Thy cross before my closing eyes;
Shine through the gloom, and point me to the skies;
Heaven's morning breaks, and earth's vain shadows flee—
In life and death, O Lord, abide with me!

JOSEPH MOHR (1792-1848)

Silent Night

Father Joseph Mohr sat alone working on the sermon he would deliver at St. Nicholas Church in Oberndorf in the Austrian Alps on Christmas Eve, 1818. He was refreshing his mind with the first Christmas story: "And this shall be a sign unto you: you shall find the babe—" There was a knock and a woman asked him to come and bless the mother and just-born child of a poor charcoal-maker high up in the mountains.

The village priest felt a strange exaltation when he arrived at the poor couple's crude hut and found the happy young mother proudly holding her sleeping child. He recalled with a start the words he had been reading when summoned to this primitive bed-side: "Ye shall find the babe."

When midnight Mass was over and the last parishioner had called out a cheerful "Gut Nacht!" the priest was still struck with wonder by the charming coincidence of his summons to the bedside in the mountain shack and the Bethlehem mystery celebrated a few hours later. He began to put his thoughts down on paper, and the words became verse. By dawn he had a poem which he took to Franz Xavier Gruber, nearby Arnsdorf music teacher, who on Christmas day composed music for "Silent Night," which soon became popular in Austria and Germany as "Song from Heaven."

> Silent Night! Holy Night!
> All is calm, all is bright.
> Round yon virgin mother and child!
> Holy Infant so tender and mild,
> Sleep in heavenly peace, sleep in heavenly peace.
>
> Silent Night! Holy Night!
> Shepherds quake at the sight!
> Glories stream from heaven afar,
> Heaven'ly hosts sing Alleluia,
> Christ the Saviour, is born! Christ the Saviour, is born!
>
> Silent Night! Holy Night!
> Son of God, love's pure light;
> Radiant beams from Thy holy face,
> With the dawn of redeeming grace,
> Jesus Lord, at Thy birth, Jesus Lord, at Thy birth.

JOHN HENRY, CARDINAL NEWMAN (1801-1890)

Lead, Kindly Light

At year's end in 1827 a nervous breakdown and the death of a dearly-loved younger sister caused John Henry Newman, Anglican churchman, Oxford don and author, to "awaken from his dream" of preferring the intellectual to the moral. His deeply spiritual nature now become more sensitive, he began a long study of the early Fathers of the Church.

In 1832, when social and political forces were threatening the integrity of the Church of England, Newman went on a Mediterranean trip which, he revealed in letters, gave him a feeling of solitude and as of a power drawing him nearer the God who was so much in his thoughts. Perhaps he experienced, as on other occasions, an intuitive consciousness of a relationship between his dimly emerging beliefs and the guiding hand of God.

Rome's grandeur and beauty moved him; he was spellbound by the ancient city's many reminders of the Apostles and the memorials of the Church Fathers he had been studying. But, vaguely uneasy in Rome, the thirty-one-year-old bachelor left for Sicily—and the great crisis of his life.

Physically, the Sicilian expedition was disastrous. An epidemic was raging, Newman contracted it, was delirious for days and dangerously ill for weeks. In one of his letters he mentions that repeatedly during the illness he kept saying to himself, "I have not sinned against the light."

In late May he was able to reach Palermo for the return to England. After a three-week wait he embarked upon a sailing ship. And on this vessel, while it was becalmed for seven days in the Straits of Bonifacio, the future Cardinal of the Roman Catholic Church reached the end of his first spiritual ordeal when he wrote, with a prophetic hint, lines that have often been sung in both Protestant and Catholic churches. Thirteen years after that he became a Catholic.

> Lead, kindly Light, amid the encircling gloom,
>   Lead Thou me on!
> The night is dark, and I am far from home—
>   Lead Thou me on!
> Keep Thou my feet; I do not ask to see
> The distant scene; one step enough for me.
>
> I was not ever thus, nor pray'd that Thou
>   Shouldst lead me on;
> I loved to choose and see my path; but now
>   Lead Thou me on!

I loved the garish day, and, spite of fears,
Pride ruled my will: remember not past years.

So long Thy power hath blest me, sure it still
   Will lead me on,
O'er moor and fen, o'er crag and torrent, till
   The night is gone;
And with the morn those Angels faces smile
Which I have loved long since, and lost awhile.

JOHN HOWARD PAYNE (1791-1852)

Home, Sweet Home

It is fitting that so hauntingly sad a song as "Home, Sweet Home" should
have been written in Paris by a lonely, jaded bachelor of thirty-two who had
not enjoyed a real home since his mother's death when he was thirteen, and
who had been away from his native land for ten years.

Shortly after John Howard Payne's birth in New York City the parents
and their six children moved to an old Dutch homestead in East Hampton,
Long Island. Although the family moved back to the city after five years,
this house is popularly, but improbably, supposed to be the place Payne had
in mind when he wrote his song.

However Payne was not merely writing about a house, but about *home*
as defined by Robert Frost: "Home is the place where, when you have to go
there, They have to take you in."

The song was written at a time in the author's life most likely to result
in a work wrought from the heart. At age eighteen he had been a juvenile
sensation on the American stage, his acting skill, handsome face and graceful
presence earning him an astonishing $10,000 in 1809, his first year in the
theater. After three more successful years in America he went to England
but within another few years found the stage was no longer favoring him. He
thereupon became successful in writing or adapting for the English stage
some fifty plays.

Then the manager of London's Covent Garden sent Payne to Paris to keep
an eye out for theatrical successes that he could adapt for England's theater.
It was at this time—1822-23—that Payne, who had roamed Europe and lived
in a succession of drab and dreary rooms, and in more sumptuous quarters
when the improvident man's finances permitted,—it was at this time he wrote

his brother: "I feel the want of some of you—part of myself—in this strange world . . . I long for a home *about* me."

This mood was upon Payne while he adapted the ballet "Clari, the Maid of Milan," which he made into an opera. He has Clari, the heroine, elope with a duke but then flee from him and return home when she hears a group of strolling players sing a tender song loved by her people. It was, of course, Payne's "Home, Sweet Home," music by Henry Rawley Bishop. Whether the song was written for the play, or the plot of the play devised to accommodate the song, has never been determined. But no one questions that it came from the heart of a homesick man.

The first night audience in London, in May, 1823, hailed the song, and it became an instantaneous hit. The song's publisher made a fortune; Payne received only his initial $250 for both it and the play.

The balance of Payne's life was anti-climax. Ten years later he returned to the United States broke, was widely acclaimed on occasion and helped by friends, became an eccentric wanderer and holder of various jobs, then was appointed U.S. Consul at Tunis in remote North Africa. He died there in 1852 at sixty-one, still lonely and homeless. Shortly before he died he wrote a friend that it was strange that he caused so many people "to boast of the delights of home when I never had a home of my own and never expect to have one now." Yes, perhaps strange, but it was his yearning and dreaming that gave the song its heart-tugging tenderness:

> Mid pleasures and palaces though we may roam,
> Be it ever so humble, there's no place like home;
> A charm from the sky seems to hallow us there,
> Which, seek through the world, is ne'er met with elsewhere.
> Home, home, sweet, sweet home!
> There's no place like home, oh, there's no place like home!
>
> An exile from home, splendor dazzles in vain;
> Oh, give me my lowly thatched cottage again!
> The birds singing gayly, that came at my call—
> Give me them—and the peace of mind, dearer than all!
> Home, home, sweet, sweet home!
> There's no place like home, oh, there's no place like home!
>
> I gaze on the moon as I tread the drear wild,
> And feel that my mother now thinks of her child,
> As she looks on that moon from our own cottage door
> Thro' the woodbine, whose fragrance shall cheer me no more.
> Home, home, sweet, sweet home!
> There's no place, oh, there's no place like home!

How sweet 'tis to sit 'neath a fond father's smile,
And the cares of a mother to soothe and beguile!
Let others delight mid new pleasures to roam,
But give me, oh, give me, the pleasures of home,
Home, home, sweet, sweet home!
There's no place like home, oh, there's no place like home!

To thee I'll return, overburdened with care;
The heart's dearest solace will smile on me there;
No more from that cottage again will I roam;
Be it ever so humble, there's no place like home;
Home, home, sweet, sweet home!
There's no place like home, oh, there's no place like home!

For Further Reading

Among the hundreds of volumes consulted in preparing this book, the following have been found the most helpful:

ARNOLD, MATTHEW *Matthew Arnold*, J. D. Jump (1955)

BROOKE, RUPERT *The Red Wine of Youth*, Arthur Stringer (1948)

BRONTE, EMILY *The Brontës, Charlotte and Emily*, Laura L. Hinkley (1945)
Very good.
> *Three Virgins of Haworth* (*The Brontë Sisters*), Emile and Georges Romieu (1930)

BROWNING, ELIZABETH BARRETT *Life of Elizabeth Barrett Browning*, Gardner B. Taplin (1958)
Scholarly but never dull.

BROWNING, ROBERT *Robert Browning*, Betty Miller (1952)
> *The Brownings: Their Life and Art*, Lillian Whitney (1911)
> *Robert Browning, the Poet and Man*, L. M. Sim (1923)

BRYANT, WILLIAM CULLEN *Gotham Yankee*, Harry Houston Peckham (1951)
Straight biography, a minimum of critical comment.

BURNS, ROBERT *Robert Burns: How to Know Him*, William A. Neilson (1917)

BYRON, LORD *Byron: A Biography*, Leslie A. Marchant, 3 vols. (1957)
A magnificent work.
> *Byron*, André Maurois (1930)
> A fine one-volume biography.

CARROLL, LEWIS *Victoria Through the Looking-Glass, Life of Lewis Carroll*, Florence Becker Lennon (1945)
Factually exhaustive and much psychological interpretation.

CLARE, JOHN *John Clare*, J. W. and A. Tibble (1932)
Comprehensive, sympathetic and readable.

COLERIDGE, SAMUEL TAYLOR *The Road to Xandu* (*A Study in the Ways of the Imagination*), John Livingston Lowes (1927)
Exciting proof that great scholarship can also be fine reading. This is a massive study of the sources of "The Rime of the Ancient Mariner."

COWPER, WILLIAM *William Cowper*, Gilbert Thomas (1935)
Informed with a sympathetic understanding, yet blinks at no facts.

DICKINSON, EMILY *This Was a Poet*, George F. Whicher (1939)
Avoids the fanciful and unfounded speculations about her private life found in other books about her, and it has an authoritative ring.

DONNE, JOHN *Life and Letters of John Donne*, Edmund Gosse, 2 vols. (1899)

DOWSON, ERNEST *Ernest Dowson*, Mark Longaker (1944)

DRAYTON, MICHAEL *Michael Drayton*, Oliver Elton (1905)
> *Elizabethans*, A. H. Bullen (1924)

EMERSON, RALPH WALDO *Life of Ralph Waldo Emerson*, R. L. Rusk (1949)
A standard biography.

FITZGERALD, EDWARD *Life of Edward Fitzgerald*, Alfred McK. Terheen (1947)
> *Edward Fitzgerald*, A. C. Benson (1905)

FOSTER, STEPHEN *Stephen Foster: America's Troubadour*, John Tasker Howard (1934)

FROST, ROBERT *Robert Frost: The Trial by Existence*, Elizabeth Shepley Sergeant (1960)
Complete and authoritative, much of it based on conversations with Frost.
> *The Dimensions of Robert Frost*, Reginald L. Cooke (1958)

Entertaining critical study, stemming from friendship with Frost.
Fire and Ice: The Art and Thought of Robert Frost, Lawrance Thompson (1942)
A critical biography.

GRAY, THOMAS *Thomas Gray,* R. W. Ketton-Cremer (1955)
Comprehensive and scholarly.

HALLECK, FITZ-GREENE *Fitz-Greene Halleck,* Nelson Frederick Adkins (1930)

HARDY, THOMAS *The Life of Thomas Hardy,* Ernest Brennecke, Jr. (1925)
A critical study of the man as a writer.

HENLEY, WILLIAM ERNEST *William Ernest Henley,* John Connell (1949)

HERBERT, GEORGE *Two Gentlemen* (Herbert and Herrick), Marchette Chute (1960)

HERRICK, ROBERT *Two Gentlemen* (Herbert and Herrick), Marchette Chute (1960)
A biographer of exceptional skill and grace, writing of a period in which she is expert.
Youth Immortal: A Life of Robert Herrick, Emily Easton (1934)

HOLMES, DR. OLIVER WENDELL *Holmes of the Breakfast Table,* M. A. De Wolfe Howe (1939)

KEATS, JOHN *Adonais: A Life of John Keats,* Dorothy Hewlett (1938)
John Keats, Amy Lowell, 2 vols. (1925)
Recognized as outstanding; a standard biography.

KIPLING, RUDYARD *The Life of Rudyard Kipling,* C. E. Carrington (1956)

LANIER, SIDNEY *Sidney Lanier,* Aubrey Harrison Starke (1933)
Admiring, massive and authoritative.

LANDOR, WALTER SAVAGE *Savage Landor,* Malcolm Elwin (1941)
Comprehensive and otherwise excellent.

LAZARUS, EMMA *The World of Emma Lazarus,* H. E. Jacob (1949)

LINDSAY, VACHEL *The West-Going Heart: A Life of Vachel Lindsay,* Eleanore Ruggles (1959)
Deserves to become a standard source.

LONGFELLOW, HENRY WADSWORTH *Henry Wadsworth Longfellow,* Edward Wagenknecht (1955)
Reliable, sympathetic and not overburdened with critical commentary.

LOVELACE, RICHARD *The Cavalier Spirit and Its Influence on the Life and Work of Richard Lovelace,* Cyril Hughes Hartmann (1925)

LOWELL, JAMES RUSSELL *Victorian Knight-Errant,* Leon Howard (1952)
An excellent interpretation of Lowell's early adult years.

MEREDITH, GEORGE *The Ordeal of George Meredith,* Lionel Stevenson (1953)
Meredith, Siegfried Sassoon (1948)
Both are valuable; Stevenson's more comprehensive, Sassoon's more interpretative.

MILLER, JOAQUIN *Splendid Poseur,* M. M. Marberry (1953)

MILTON, JOHN *Milton,* Rose Macaulay (1934)
An excellent short biography.

MOODY, WILLIAM VAUGHAN *William Vaughan Moody,* David D. Henry (1934)

MOORE, THOMAS *The Harp That Once,* Howard Mumford Jones (1937)
Minstrel Boy—A Portrait of Tom Moore, L. A. G. Strong (1937)
Both equally good and sympathetic biographies.

NEWMAN, JOHN HENRY CARDINAL *Newman: His Life and Spirituality,* Louis Bouyer (1958)

OWEN, WILFRED *Wilfred Owen's Poems,* Ed. E. Blunden (1931)
Contains valuable biographical material.

PATMORE, COVENTRY *Life and Times of Coventry Patmore,* Derek Patmore (1949)
Detailed, sympathetic but not lacking in objectivity.

POE, EDGAR ALLAN   *Israfel*, Hervey Allen, 2 vols. in 1 (1934)
    Exhaustive exploration of every facet of Poe's life; fascinating reading.
ROSSETTI, CHRISTINA   *Christina Rossetti*, Marya Zaturenska (1949)
    Comprehensive, scholarly, and good reading.
RALEIGH, SIR WALTER   *Sir Walter Raleigh*, Milton Waldman (1928)
    By a lawyer, with a lawyer's emphasis on Raleigh's trials.
ROBINSON, EDWIN ARLINGTON   *Edwin Arlington Robinson*, Emery Neff
    (1948)
    Emphasis is critical.
    Edwin Arlington Robinson: A Biography, Herman Hagedorn (1938)
    Thus far the most complete biography of Robinson, and always readable.
SHELLEY, PERCY BYSSHE   *Shelley*, Newman Ivey White, 2 vols. (1940)
    A great achievement; outstanding among biographies of poets.
SIDNEY, SIR PHILIP   *Astrophel: The Life of Sir Philip Sidney*, Alfred H. Bill
    (1937)
    Scholarly and readable, with much about the period.
STEVENSON, ROBERT LOUIS   *Voyage to Windward: The Life of Robert Louis
    Stevenson*, J. C. Furnas (1951)
    Comprehensive and lively.
    Life of Robert Louis Stevenson, Graham Balfour (1911)
SWINBURNE, ALGERNON CHARLES   *The Life of Algernon Charles Swinburne*,
    Edmund Gosse, 2 vols. (1899)
TENNYSON, ALFRED LORD   *Alfred Tennyson*, Charles Tennyson (his grandson),
    (1949)
    Alfred Lord Tennyson: A Memoir by His Son, 2 vols. (1897)
    Both of the above are important, but by no means the final word.
THOMAS, DYLAN   *Dylan Thomas in America*, John Malcolm Brinnin (1955)
    A painfully revealing account of the poet's last hectic years.
THOMPSON, FRANCIS   *Francis Thompson*, J. C. Reid (1959)
    An objective study; some might think it an unfriendly one.
VAUGHAN, HENRY   *Henry Vaughan*, F. E. Hutchinson (1947)
WHITMAN, WALT   *The Solitary Singer, A Critical Biography*, Gay Wilson Allan
    (1955)
    A recent, detailed and worthy addition to the many Whitman biographies.
    Whitman: An Interpretation in Narrative, Emory Holloway (1926)
    The author is a Whitman authority.
    Walt Whitman, Henry Seidel Canby (1943)
    Comprehensive, searching and readable.
WHITTIER, JOHN GREENLEAF   *John Greenleaf Whittier: Friend of Man*, John
    A. Pollard (1949)
    Emphasizes Whittier's political activities.
    Quaker Militant: Whittier, Albert Mordell (1933)
    A probing and penetrating study.
WILDE, OSCAR   *Wilde and the Yellow Nineties*, Frances Winwar (1940)
WORDSWORTH, WILLIAM   *Farewell to the Banner—"Three Persons in One
    Soul"* (S. T. Coleridge, Wm. Wordsworth and Dorothy Wordsworth), Fran-
    ces Winwar (1938)
    Emphasis is on their personal lives.
    Wordsworth—How to Know Him, C. T. Winchester (1916)
    Wordsworth, Herbert Read (1930)
    Acute critical probing.
    The Early Life of William Wordsworth (1770-1798), Emile Legouis (1897)
    William Wordsworth of Rydal Mount, Frederika Beatty (1939)
    Confined to the last decade of poet's life.

WOTTON, SIR HENRY   *Life and Letters of Sir Henry Wotton*, 2 vols., Logan Pearsall Smith (1898)
YEATS, WILLIAM BUTLER   *William Butler Yeats*, Joseph Hone (1943)

COLLECTIVE BIOGRAPHIES

Ten Modern Poets, Rica Brenner (1930)
Twelve American Poets Before 1900, Rica Brenner (1933)
Elizabethans, A. H. Bullen (1924)
       Bullen is an authority on Elizabethan literature.
Victorian Poets, E. C. Stedman (1875)

ON POETS AND POETRY IN GENERAL

Poems in Process, Phyliss Brooks Bartlett (1951)
How Does a Poem Mean, John Ciardi (1960)
Poetry: A Modern Guide to its Understanding and Enjoyment, Elizabeth Drew (1959)
A History of American Poetry 1900-1940, H. Gregory and M. Zaturenska (1946)
On English Poetry, Robert Graves (1922)
The Way of the Makers, Marguerite Wilkinson (1925)
The Inspiration of Poetry, George Edward Woodberry (1911)
The Lives of the English Poets (3 volumes), Samuel Johnson (1779-1781)

INDEX OF TITLES

Index of Titles

325

SONGS

INDEX OF FIRST LINES

Index of First Lines

SONGS

THE AUTHOR AND HIS BOOK

RALPH L. WOODS *was born in St. Louis, Missouri in 1904. For many years he worked for the Sinclair Oil Company, then left to write full-time. In 1948 he joined the N.A.M. as staff writer. After five years he returned to full-time, free-lance writing and anthologizing, interrupted by several periods as a consulting editor for the* Catholic Digest. *He has written numerous articles for* The Saturday Review, The Critic, Catholic Digest, The Sign, American Legion Magazine, The Freeman *and others. He is the author of* America Reborn: A Plan for Decentralization of Industry *(Longmans Green, 1939),* Pilgrim Places in North America *(Longmans Green, 1939),* A Treasury of the Familiar *(Macmillan, 1942),* Behold the Man *(Macmillan, 1944),* The World of Dreams *(Random, 1947),* A Second Treasury of the Familiar *(Macmillan, 1950),* A Treasury of Inspiration *(Crowell, 1951),* The Businessman's Book of Quotations *(McGraw-Hill, 1953),* A Treasury of Catholic Thinking *(Crowell, 1953),* The Consolations of Catholicism *(Appleton Century, 1954),* The Catholic Companion to the Bible *(Lippincott, 1956),* A Treasury of the Dog *(Putnam, 1956),* A Treasury of Friendship *(McKay, 1957),* The Catholic Concept of Love and Marriage *(Lippincott, 1958), and* The Family Reader of American Masterpieces *(Crowell, 1959). Mr. Woods lives with his wife, Lillias, in Ramsey, New Jersey.*

FAMOUS POEMS AND THE LITTLE-KNOWN STORIES BEHIND THEM *(Hawthorn, 1961), was set in type by Pyramid Composition Co., Inc., New York, N.Y. The body type is Fairfield, which was designed for the Linotype by Rudolph Ruzicka in 1939. The book was printed and bound by American Book-Stratford Press, Inc., New York, N.Y.*

A HAWTHORN BOOK